HOME OF SPRINGS

Trengwainton

Published by awen productions CIC, 2018
www.trengwaintonheritage.co.uk
www.awen.org.uk

A Glimpse of some of the Pictures at Trengwainton;
John Opie, John Wolcot and the Prices
© Viv Hendra 2018

Price and Related Portraits by John Opie, RA
and a Miniature
© Viv Hendra and Michael Burrell 2018

Paintings and Portraits at Trengwainton,
and other Price and Badcock Portraits
© Michael Burrell and Viv Hendra 2018

Copyright © awen productions CIC, 2018

ISBN 978-1-9164082-0-3

Designed by Nick Harpley
www.satzooma.co.uk

Printed and bound in Great Britain
by Print2Demand
FSC accredited paper

HOME OF SPRINGS

Trengwainton

Produced by Barbara Santi

awen productions CIC

ACKNOWLEDGEMENTS

Home of Springs, Trengwainton has been collaboratively written by a number of contributors.

All photographs have obtained appropriate copyright to the best of our abilities. References, bibliography and copyright information of photographs are found at the end of this book.

Contemporary oral histories transcribed for this book form part of the long-form documentary, *Home of Springs, Trengwainton* which, along with other interviews, is available to view at www.awen.org.uk or www.trengwaintonheritage.co.uk

PARTNERS

Cornwall Archæological Unit

Cornwall Records Office

National Trust

COMMUNITY GROUPS

Age Concern

Hearing Voices Network

Shallal Dance Theatre

SCHOOLS

Heamoor Junior School

St Maddern's Junior School

Mount's Bay Secondary School

Newlyn Junior School

St Mary's Church of England Junior School

Trythall Junior School

WORKSHOP ARTISTS

Dr Jane Bailey, Barbara Santi, Dominica Williamson

VOLUNTEERS AND CONTRIBUTORS

Cedric Appleby, Llyn Aubrey, Marieanne Ball, Billy Barr, Jeannie Bates, Selina Bates, Roy Blewitt, Edward Bolitho, Elizabeth Bolitho, Lou Brett, Florence Browne, Billy Burman, Michael Burrell, David Bushrod, Nancy Carter, Linda Collins, Ben Cooper, Roger Curtis, Betty Davy, Ann Foreman, Diana Goss, Annette Gibbons, Phil Griffiths, Rev Tim Hawkins, Viv Hendra, Diana Heyer, Ginnie Hignett, Tom Holway, David Holyoake, Pauline Hope, Peter Horder, Sally Keen, Tamar Kendal, Robin Knight, Sue Knight, Anna Lawson-Jones, Sophie Lewis, Ian Marsh, Ian McGoldrick, David McIntosh, Kathy McPhee, Esme-Rianna Merrick, Vicky Merrick, Jacky Meyers, Milli Morgan, Rowan Musser, Mat Nixon, Jacky Nowakowski, Pauline Ryan, Nicola Osborne, Claire Ozdolek, Carol Partridge, Claire Penlerick, Charlotte Price, Ros Prigg, Beth Rose, Timothy Rose Price, Marina Rule, Tony Russell, Rosie Schneider, Cat Saunders, Peter and Sally Scrase, Claire Shaw, Pauline Sheppard, Ros Smith (Duchy College), Keith Spurgin, Violet Stevens, John Thomas, Oliver Tooley, Margaret Tremeer, Tommy Tucker, Craig Weatherhill, Ian Willsdon, Gareth Wearne, Paul Witte, Ian Wright

FUNDERS

      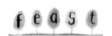 

CONTENTS

GARDENERS THEN AND NOW

TRENGWAINTON GARDENERS 1947–48

Left to Right: Mr Thomas (Head Gardener), Jennifer Thomas, Sydney Guy, Tom Pollard, Ross, unknown, unknown, Billy Barr, Leonard Simmonds, Clifford Pollard.

Trengwainton Gardeners and National Trust Team 2018

Left to right Back row: Gareth Wearne (gardener), Phil Griffiths (Head Gardener), Matt Nixon (gardener)

Front row: Catrina Saunders (Garden Projects Manager), Marine Rule (Visitor Engagement Officer), Beth Rose (Visitor Services & Enterprises Manager), Ian McGoldrick (volunteer gardener), Baz (the dog).

The Drive c1890

WELCOME to *Home of Springs, Trengwainton,* a three-year heritage project that discovered and explored the stories and legacy of Trengwainton Garden, Madron near Penzance in Cornwall.

The project has taken us on a journey through dusty archive records and research libraries, ancient maps and contemporary interviews.

This book, *Home of Springs, Trengwainton,* brings together oral histories, research, images, stories and articles. It has been created collaboratively with volunteers and specialists in their field delving deep into different aspects of Trengwainton's past and present.

In *Home of Springs, Trengwainton,* you will get to know various people through time. Take a peek into the lives of the owners and gardeners who have lived and worked side by side at Trengwainton and see how their past has left an imprint on the place and the wider Penwith landscape.

Alongside the story of the people and place, our book celebrates nature, the unique plants at Trengwainton and the cyclical seasons of the year. Explore the legacy of the flora that has been introduced into this fascinating garden over the centuries and from across continents.

The story of the educational programme we delivered over the course of the three years (2015 – 2018) is also presented. Workshops engaging with local community groups, volunteers and schools have reached new audiences using Trengwainton as an outdoor learning space. The experience has provided a different perspective with which to reinterpret our surroundings.

We also had an exhibition at The Exchange Gallery's Engine Room, Penzance (8 June 2018 – 28 July 2018) and created an interactive documentary film that can be viewed at www.awen.org.uk.

It's been an honour to observe the garden and the gardeners that tend it, over such an extended period of time.

We would like to thank all the staff and team at Trengwainton, detective Phil Griffiths, Head Gardener and his ever so knowledgeable right hand man Gareth Wearne, the wonderful Marina Rule, National Trust, the Bolitho family, Lear Associates (for the initial comprehensive research materials), our partners, funders and to all the people we have interviewed and who have contributed to the project.

We hope you enjoy what we have discovered.

Barbara Santi, awen productions CIC
Project Director/Filmmaker

Trengwainton Archway

left Snow at Trengwainton

INTRODUCTION

Barbara Santi, Project Director

Trengwainton Garden is part of a wider estate that includes a Grade II listed house, a home farm and tenanted farms, tenants' cottages, laundry house, Western Hunt kennels and hunting, shooting and fishing grounds. The influence of its past owners can be seen further afield including the naming of 'Jamaica Place' in Heamoor, Madron's Landithy Hall and cottages, the clock in the church tower bought by T.R. Bolitho to celebrate Queen Victoria's diamond jubilee and the Bolitho Bank in Penzance. Little is known about the gardeners and staff over the centuries who have lived and worked at Trengwainton – this book aims to redress the balance.

The name Trengwainton has been spelt in various ways over the centuries. It is believed that Trengwainton is Cornish for 'farm/settlement of endless spring,' as in the season. However, others have suggested an alternative including 'farmstead/house by the spring'[1] or 'farmstead/house of the spring'[2] due to the many water springs found on the grounds. Either meaning is very fitting as not only can you find wells, springs and ponds as you wander around the grounds, early spring blooms such as magnolias, camellias, azeleas and the spectacular creamy yellow flowered *Rhododendron macabeanum* can be marvelled at year on year. Our project name *Home of Springs, Trengwainton* is a creative interpretation bringing together different elements of the possible meaning.

There has been a house on the site at Trengwainton since at least the 16th century. Today, Trengwainton House is the private dwelling of Col Edward Bolitho and his family.[4] Over the years the house has

left
Tithe Map Madron
1840

right
Trengwainton House
c1950s

TRENGWAINTON (settlement, SW 445 315)

<**Tredhigwenton**> (Trengwainton Farm)

<**Plas Tredhigwenton**> (Trengwainton House)

<**Lowarthow Tredhigwenton**>
(Trengwainton Garden)

<**Carn Tredhigwenton**> (Trengwainton Carn)

Tredygwaenton 1302; Tregwaynton 1317; Trethigwaynton 1319; Trenygwaynton 1324; Trewygwaynton 1325; Trenguenton 1371; Trengwaynton 1565; Tringwenton 1659; Trengwanton c. 1660; Trengwainton 1808.

tre, 'farm, settlement' + **gwenton**, 'springtime.' The latter was preceded by the intensive prefix **di-** (lenited to **dhi-**), often meaning 'double' but can also imply some other form of intensification. A likely translation would be 'farm of endless spring,' which can be easily understood from its sheltered position and prolific gardens. [3]

Craig Weatherhill

been remodelled and altered along with significant changes to the surrounding grounds. Our research has centred on the garden and the gardeners but without the house and its owners the garden would not exist. Trengwainton Garden can be said to have been created over three main periods of history by two key influential families: The early 1800s when it was in the ownership of Sir Rose Price (1814 – 1834) and the late Victorian era and early 20th century when the Bolitho family, in particular Thomas Robins Bolitho (1887 – 1925) and later Lt Col Edward H.W. Bolitho (1924 – 1969), were so influential.

Sales Catalogue 1866

opp Mr and Mrs T. S. Bolitho 1890

Frontispiece from Sales Catalogue 1866

The *London Chronicle* reported in October 17-19 1758 that Trengwainton was to be sold by William Arundell Esq. and was proudly described as a:

…handsome well built House fit for a gentleman to live in, with a Good Stable, Coach House &c. and a large walled-garden stored with the best Fruit-trees, and from the House there is a pleasant extensive Prospect both by Sea and Land.

In 1814 William Praed…sold Trengwainton to Rose, afterwards Sir Rose, Price who [re] built the [present] mansion in 1817. Sir Rose Price who had been created a baronet in 1814, the year of his shrievalty, died in 1834, and in the following year his trustees conveyed Trengwainton with other lands to Henry Lewis Stephens, from whom it was purchased in 1835 [1867] by Thomas Simon Bolitho for £33,000. Thomas Robins Bolitho succeeded at his father's death in 1887, and has made Trengwainton his chief place of residence.

THE OWNERS

Sir Rose Price bought Trengwainton in 1814 and transformed the house and grounds with the help of his designer George Brown who developed the foundations and the structure of the garden. Their layout of the pleasure grounds, the landscape park and the walled garden is what we see at Trengwainton today. [5]

Prior to Rose Price's purchase Trengwainton was a 'barton' [6] with various owners including the Cowling family (c 1549 – 1668), the Arundell family (1668 – 1761) and the Praed family (1761 – 1814). One of the most significant changes that occurred, sometime between 1809 and 1840, was the planting of a shelter-belt on the land. An 1809 map (prior to Price's purchase) shows the access to Trengwainton House having a tree-lined drive. [7] Brown and Price continued to develop the shelterbelt by planting beech, ash and sycamore. [8] Today we can enjoy the many unusual specimens from all over the world as a result of this shelterbelt.

The protection from the harsh south-westerly weather creates a micro-climate in the garden where tender and exotic plants flourish, and the unique walled garden enables a large variety of fruit and vegetables to grow. In Rose Price's time the surrounding land, along with Trengwainton Carn and Hill, was Upland Rough Ground. [9]

When Henry Lewis Stephens bought the estate for £28,500, the Journal of the Statistical Society of London describes the Trengwainton estate as follows:

The total number of statute acres was 773; it therefore averaged only 37L per acres: but 519 of these acres have never been cultivated, being used as a rabbit-warren and for pasturing sheep; and of the remaining 254 there are 71 plantation, leaving only 183 of arable land.

Journal of the Statistical Society of London vol 2, 1839, p. 208

Ornamental Land

Ornamental Land is land that has been manipulated to form parklands and gardens surrounding large country houses. Ornamental Landscapes are normally of 18th and 19th century date, although some extend into the very early 20th century.

In Cornwall many of these parks and gardens were created by people made wealthy by local copper and tin mines. 18th century parkland was designed with the great house as its focus. Designed parklands contain carefully positioned clumps of trees and open vistas uninterrupted by hedges – often through the construction of sunken ha-has and carefully produced 'natural' aspects.

Many Ornamental Landscapes included walled gardens, fruit and flower houses and carriage drives. By the 19th century there was a shift towards the planting of specimen trees and shrubs, camellias, rhododendrons and other more delicate exotics. These gardens were often smaller, more intricately designed, and often included planted shelterbelts, carefully created ponds and pools, gazebos with carefully positioned urns etc.

Trengwainton Carn and Hill still form highly visible landmarks within the surrounding landscape, and as such attracted the attention of Trengwainton's park designers, who transformed what was an Upland Rough Ground landscape in to an Ornamental Landscape.

The 1840 Tithe map depicts a long north to south running swathe of planted trees, referred to in the accompanying apportionment lists as 'plantation' and 'fir plantation'. They represent part of Sir Rose Price's c1815 landscaping and plantation establishment.

Anna Lawson-Jones, Cornwall Archæology Unit

However, Price and his designer George Brown converted these inhospitable surroundings into pleasant ornamental land. The location of the house, up on high ground, commanded spectacular views. To the east and southeast of Trengwainton House, Price and Brown planted trees on both sides of the farmland which over the years framed the views across Penzance to Mount's Bay and St Michael's Mount.[10]

Throughout its history Trengwainton has been a place of experimentation and innovation. In addition to modernising the house and designing the garden and shelterbelt, Price constructed three ponds and built the first and most southerly icehouse in Cornwall (believed to utilise the ice from the ponds).

Price also made bricks near the site to construct the walled garden with its sloping beds (laying the bricks in Flemish bond style – the most expensive way of building – which involves the highest use of bricks per square metre). He diverted water from surrounding land down to the site and developing town of Penzance and created a woodland walk to enjoy the new pleasure grounds. Price's wealth, made from his family's Jamaican sugar plantation, enabled him to access all the latest innovations of the time.

Today, in the private area of the stable yard at Trengwainton House a gas house is still visible and old design maps locate gas lamps around the building. Was Trengwainton House the first home in West Cornwall to have gaslight and central heating? We may never know.

The next occupant, Lewis Stephens, 'had no intention of occupying or maintaining Trengwainton as a grand country-house, partially demolishing and letting the mansion, and subdividing the estate for commercial purposes.'[11] So when Thomas Simon Bolitho bought Trengwainton in 1867 he and his son Thomas Robins Bolitho (T.R. Bolitho) set about renovating and extending the house and grounds for generations to come.

In 1877 The Old Carriage Drive became the main drive to the house from the Doric entrance lodge. Today there are two lodges at the entrance to Trengwainton. The lodge on the left was built in 1992/3 and is now the National Trust reception and shop. The lodge on the right is the original building.

left
Looking into the Park
c1890

opp
The Drive 1957

THE GARDEN

In 1895 T.R. Bolitho laid out the broad driveway and in 1898 Ernest Povey was appointed as Head Gardener. T.R. Bolitho's nephew Lt Col Edward H.W. Bolitho was the next person to leave his mark on Trengwainton when he inherited the estate in 1924. Influenced by his horticultural cousins Canon A.T. Boscawen of Ludgvan and J.C. and P.D. Williams (who designed the gardens at Caerhays and Lanarth),[12] planting started in earnest. Trengwainton has often been called 'a plantsman's paradise'.[13]

In 1926 G.H. Johnstone of Trewithen and Lawrence Johnstone of Hidcote offered Col Bolitho a share in the 1927/8 expedition of English botanist and plant hunter Frank Kingdon-Ward. The seeds and plants Kingdon-Ward returned with from north-east of Assam and the Mishmi Hills of Burma became many of the rhododendrons we see at Trengwainton today. In a letter, Col Bolitho wrote about this plant hunting expedition: 'In fact, the whole garden is founded on this one sending.'[14] Combined with the gardening skill of Head Gardener Alfred Creek (c1906 – 1934), this unique collection thrived and includes the magnificent

left
Miss Bolitho at Trengwainton entrance and Doric lodge 1890

right
The Gas House, Trengwainton

Rhododendron macabeanum which was awarded a Royal Horticultural Society Award of Merit in 1937 and the RHS First Class Certificate in 1938.[15] Additionally, *Rhododendron elliottii, Rhododendron taggianum* and *Rhododendron concatenans* all first flowered at Trengwainton and can be traced back to this expedition.

In 2012 *Rhododendron macabeanum* was affected by *Phytophthora ramorum* (sudden oak death), a fungus disease that has destroyed many plants all over the world. However, thanks to the National Trust Plant Conservation scheme *Rhododendron macabeanum* was saved from extinction by using an innovative micropropogation procedure.

Following the immense contribution of Head Gardener Alfred Creek, G.W. Thomas (Head Gardener 1934–1948) followed in his green-fingered footsteps by making a number of significant rhododendron crosses including *Rhododendron* 'Morvah', *Rhododendron* 'Fusilier', *Rhododendron* 'Golden horn' and *Rhododendron* 'Miss Pink' which are all unique to Trengwainton.

According to the diary of Alfred Creek (Head Gardener c1906–1934), G.W. Thomas (Head Gardener 1934–1948) sent word to Creek that *Rhododendron macabeanum* first flowered at Trengwainton in 1937.

In 1948 G. Hulbert was appointed as the new Head Gardener and planted up the stream garden which had been partly opened in 1926 from an underground culvert. Today it is still a key feature at Trengwainton and enjoyed by many visitors.

above
Ice House, Trengwainton

right
Rhododendron macabeanum sinogrande
Rhododendron elliottii
The Stream

THE NATIONAL TRUST AND BEYOND

In 1961 Trengwainton was gifted to the National Trust. On March 10th 1962 the *Gardeners' Chronicle* reported that:

An important addition, just announced by the National Trust, are the gardens at Trengwainton, near Penzance, which are now open from March 1 to September 30, on Thursdays, Fridays, Saturdays and Bank Holidays, between 11am and 5pm.

Standing 400ft above the sea, with fine views over Mount's Bay, Trengwainton has been a garden since the 17th century, and it is interesting to note that about 150 years ago, the then owner, Sir Rose Price, built an ice-house to conserve ice taken from the ponds; today frosts are practically unknown in the district.

Over the years the garden has had quiet periods as well as great revivals as it has been enjoyed from generation to generation. There is no doubt that the work and dedication of the Head Gardeners that followed and their teams of workers, whether staff or volunteers, has enabled Trengwainton to continue to exist and flourish. It has overcome wars, social change and environmental challenges. In this book you will hear about these stories and memories of the people who have left their mark on this inimitable landscape.

Front view of the Head Gardener's Cottage, c1935

Rhododendron 'Fusilier'

TRENGWAINTON'S LONG HUMAN PAST

Jacqueline A Nowakowski fsa, Principal Archæologist, Cornwall Archæological Unit

In the last 10 years, the eradication and clearance of the diseased *Phytopthera* rhododendron, once a marvellous annual flourish of deep vibrant colour and a key signature of Trengwainton Carn and Hill, provided a fortuitous opportunity for an archæological survey of this distinctive part of the Bolitho estate. The work was carried out by the Cornwall Archæological Unit, Cornwall Council. This new survey revealed not only how the Carn became absorbed and domesticated into the wider historical landscape estate at Trengwainton as a whole, but also how this area has a long history of human engagement that goes right back – several thousand years even – into deep prehistory.

New insights into the long legacy of activity underlying the grand ornamental and designed landscapes of this rural estate were captured, and by mapping the character, small shapes and patterns of the ancient and historic field walls, it has become possible to see how the nineteenth century estate landscape was carved out of, and imposed upon, a more ancient place.

On the fringes of the Penwith moors, Trengwainton Carn would have been a prominent landmark overlooking the essential open character of the land which provided good grazing and attracted pastoralists since early prehistory – signs of their presence discovered in a handful of flint tools, including the beautifully crafted Trengwainton dagger, now recorded from the general area. We know that across the expansive Penwith moors were important places for ceremony and ritual marked by burial places (the barrows and cairns), standing stones, and gathering places such as the stone circles, and of course, the natural tors and prominent outcrops would also have had a special role to play in navigating around these open spaces: the small flints tools were lost in and around these landmarks. The Trengwainton dagger, made not of local stone but flint from the chalk lands of southern Britain, show how networks were cast far and wide between different communities as the object was

18

likely traded through gift exchange and was probably more symbolic than functional. But the continuing importance of the pasture land offered by essentially rough ground, and increasing importance of metal minerals such as tin and copper, and how ownership and control and pressure of these resources became critical particularly during the Bronze Age through to the Iron Age and Romano-British period (over 4,000 years ago), was marked by enclosure and taking in the land.

Piecemeal enclosure through the creation of long broad sinuous sturdy stone boundaries, with a channelling trackway (defined by orthostats, book-shaped granite stones, set upright) which linked settlement on the upper and lower lands, were mapped (previously hidden under thick vegetation cover) at Trengwainton.

On the eastern part of the Carn stretches of relict stone walls and banks which mark ancient fields, stone cairns which indicate moorland clearance and ground improvement, together with the vestigial footings of stone roundhouses – the dwelling houses of now lost small farms – were also discovered for the first time.

left
Madron Carn

in box
Bronze Age Dagger

All these archæological ruins (while fragmentary today) are likely to have witnessed long histories and reuse into the Roman and even medieval times, influencing patterns of later fields and pathways showing a strong attachment to place, and are a constant reminder of the special uniqueness of the time-depth grounded in ancient landscapes across the Land's End district.

The human story underlying the grandiose estate parkland of Trengwainton with its straight rectangular fields, formal stiles and gateways has a long legacy and is a major contribution to the wider story of people and land in Penwith.

BRONZE AGE FLINT DAGGER (2500 BC TO 801 BC) FOUND NEAR TRENGWAINTON HOUSE

A flint dagger was found in 1990 during the removal of storm damaged trees at Trengwainton House. The flint fell from earth around the roots of a tree after it had been dragged from its original position, so the exact find spot is unknown. The flint measures 15.9 CM by 5. CM and is of opaque light grey colour with some slightly darker areas. It is dated to the early bronze age and the lozenge shape suggests that it may have been made in Brittany. It is one of the finest types of flint implement and may have been used as a tool before being buried. It has patches of gloss on the surface which indicate that it was hafted and placed in a leather sheath.

With thanks to Royal Cornwall Museum and Anna Tyacke.
Extract from www.heritagegateway.org.uk

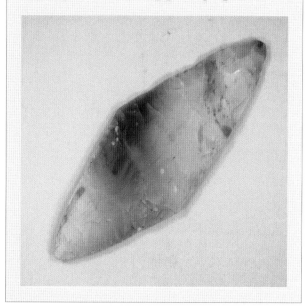

PLANTS
AGAPANTHUS

Marina Rule, Visitor Engagement Officer

The sea views from Trengwainton's Terrace are special at any time of year, but in July they're complimented by the white, blue and purple hues of the agapanthus border.

Running the full length of the sun-drenched Terrace, the agapanthus in bloom is a sure sign that summer is upon us as they thrive in sunny positions.

All agapanthus originate from the Cape of Good Hope in South Africa, with the first reaching Europe via Dutch settlers in 1652. They've now spread to many parts of the world and in some places, such as New Zealand, they're even considered an invasive weed.

Agapanthus is used in many traditional rituals and remedies in southern Africa; Xhosa women make a necklace from the roots of the plant to ensure healthy, strong babies and the Zulu use the plant to treat heart disease and paralysis. It's also said to revive the tired and swollen feet of hikers who wrap their feet in the leaves for half an hour. All of these remedies are despite the fact that it's considered poisonous to humans.

Their name comes from the Greek words 'agape' and 'anthus,' meaning 'love flower' but they're also known as the Lily of the Nile and the African Lily, even though they're not a lily. They're part of the amaryllis family and some can grow up to 2 metres (6.6 feet) in height.

Do you have agapanthus that refuse to flower? If so try moving them to a sunnier spot and making sure they're not lacking water. Like the rest of us, they'll feel much better for the addition of some warm sunshine, a cooling drink and some long summer days.

left
Magnolia campbellii

right
Trengwainton
Terrace and
agapanthus

TRENGWAINTON'S FLOWERS AND FERNS – THE WILD SIDE

Keith Spurgin FLS, MRes, Hon Member, Eden Florilegium, Recorder Emeritus, Botanical Society of Britain and Ireland, Ecological Genetics Researcher in collaboration with Edge Hill University

In 1879 Mrs M.L. Bolitho observed Yellowed-flowered Strawberry near Trengwainton, the first field record of this plant for Cornwall and – so far as we know – the British Isles. It is, botanically, an 'alien', one of the introduced species that are mapped alongside our native flowering plants and ferns. Over the years well over 200 species have been found in the grounds and nearby. Four years after H.L. Stephens bought the property from Sir Rose Price, early plant records made at Trengwainton were by Richard Edmonds Jnr., who in 1839 listed Oak, Ash and Elm 'with a few Beech and Sycamore trees'.[16] In West Cornwall woodland was frequently planted for timber, fuel and coppice, and unless the Elm was *Ulmus procera*, all those listed can regenerate from seed.

At the other end of the scale, in 1844 Helston bookseller William Curnow recorded Tunbridge Filmy-fern, a tiny plant scarcely bigger than a moss.

By the mid 1870s the eccentric John Ralfs had become the local expert on wild plants in Penzance and the Penwith area. He was often seen hunting for specimens, apparently oblivious to the fact that his clothes were soaked and covered with mud. That he enjoyed wading through bogs and across streams was clear from some of the plants he recorded: Cornish Moneywort, Ivyleaved Bellflower and Marsh Violet – all at home in watery habitats. Above Trengwainton Ponds he found Three-lobed Crowfoot, scarce in the British Isles and

now vulnerable and on the Red Data List. However Montgomery's claim to have discovered its cousin Round-leaved Crowfoot at Trengwainton has never been confirmed, the one and only colony in Cornwall having been, allegedly, destroyed when swans were introduced; more likely it was never there, the white-flowered 'Water-buttercups' being notoriously difficult to name. c20th wild plant records for Trengwainton became scarce until the 1960s, when several visitors began to report their finds. Male-ferns, Primroses, and Foxgloves are common enough in Cornwall but the

Royal fern by pond

Dog-violet, Herb Robert, Lesser Celandine and White Clover to name a few. G. Halliday recorded (among others) the hybrid between Common Ragwort and its close relation Marsh Ragwort.

In 2007 Dr Colin French, the Recorder for West Cornwall, found Chamomile on one of the Trengwainton lawns, another plant to be under threat in the British Isles. As wild species come under increasing pressure, estates like Trengwainton continue to play their part in protecting both the species and the habitats that support them.

As for Yellow-flowered Strawberry, it can still be seen in the walled gardens, along with its more familiar relatives Barren Strawberry, Wild Strawberry (both common wild flowers of Cornwall) and of course the cultivated Strawberry. The gardens are there for all to enjoy, those trees, shrubs and flowers so carefully tended by the gardeners and their colleagues, and their wild counterparts, both contributing their beauty and interest to the flora of Trengwainton.

data were beginning to show that many rarities were becoming even more scarce. Meanwhile specialists were identifying additions to the flora: J.R. Palmer's discovery that New Zealand Pheasant's-tail grass was self-seeding in one of the beds was a first record for Cornwall, and R.W. Gould listed half a dozen wild bramble names. In recent years detailed surveys by M. Atkinson, C. French and P.J. Worth have discovered or re-found a growing tally of familiar and to some of us much-loved wild flowers: Bird's-foot Trefoil, Common

MAGNOLIA CAMPBELLII SUBSP. MOLLICOMATA 'LANARTH'

Milli Morgan, Project Volunteer

I shall always remember my first sight of a group of these magnificent magnolias in full flower! I got within a mile of them, from which distance the masses of pink blossoms showed up distinctly, but surrounded, as the trees were, by heavy snowdrifts ten to twelve feet in depth, fully a week passed before I could secure specimens, by which time the flowers were almost gone. G. Forrest in Treseder (1978).

The *Magnolia campbellii* subsp. *mollicomata* 'Lanarth' was discovered by George Forrest in 1924, whilst collecting specimen samples in the Yunnan Province, making some 1200 new plant species discoveries. The *mollicomata* he found on the Salween-Kiu Chiang Divide, in the North-Western area of the Province.

Forrest, born in Falkirk, Scotland in 1873, led a life governed by his thirst for adventure. After returning to England from his pursuit of the Australian gold rush of 1891, Forrest was sponsored by A. K. Bulley to undertake the first of many expeditions into the Yunnan Region in China, arriving in Talifu in 1904.

In 1905 a mission to a largely unexplored region of the Yunnan near the Tibetan border saw disaster strike.

The Qing Dynasty government had let missionaries into Tibetan Buddhist areas, sparking outrage and anger among many Tibetan Buddhist Lamas. Primarily the Buddhist Gelug, or 'Yellow' Sect, resented the conversion of locals by Christian missionaries.

Tibetan lamas eventually militarized, massacring Chinese officials, as well as any foreigners or locals believed to be aiding such foreigners.

Magnolia 'Lanarth'

Forrest and his team of seventeen were attacked in Tzekou with only one making it out of the attack alive. Forrest hid by a river for eight days, until the threat of starvation led him to a nearby village, where inhabitants gave him food and shelter and by disguising him as a Tibetan, orchestrated his escape across the mountains at great risk to themselves and their village.

The *mollicomata* 'Lanarth' does not reproduce true from seed and there will always be variation from the parent plant if grown from seed. The 'Lanarth' variation of the *mollicomata* was particularly revered for its flower color, a vibrant, deep cyclamen purple. In order to retain this eye-catching magenta shade, the tree must be propagated by layering, budding or grafting, which means that every single magnolia given the name 'Lanarth' is genetically identical to the original tree grown from the *mollicomata* seed Forrest brought home from his adventures in the Yunnan Region in 1924.

The *Magnolia mollicomata* 'Lanarth' can be found in the old pumpkin patch in the Kitchen Walled Garden, one at the top of the drive behind the pond and a couple more scattered through the garden.[17]

MAGNOLIAS

Marina Rule

Of all the hundreds of different plants from around the world at Trengwainton Garden, surely the most spectacular when it flowers is the magnolia.

Imagine big waxy petals in shades of pink, white and magenta – with no leaves to dilute the colours – set against bright blue skies. Magical!

They were first introduced to this country due to the extraordinary efforts of the plant hunters in the early part of the 20th century. They went out to Southern China and Tibet, enduring months in the high mountainous regions, looking for exotic species to bring back with them to Britain.

Magnolias looking up

The first time some of those exotic species flowered in this country was at Trengwainton Garden in Madron.

Magnolias are ancient plants and have existed on the planet for at least 95 million years. Their flowers contain both male and female reproductive organs and have a sweet aroma. Bees are their main pollinators, but the flowers don't produce nectar; instead, they have pollen enriched with proteins which the bees use as food.

Their kidney-shaped seeds can be red, orange or pink in colour and are a favorite food for many birds.

Patience is needed when growing magnolias as the first flowers take seven years to develop. They can live to be more than 100 years old and Trengwainton's magnificent *Magnolia campbellii* is the grand old age of 97. As this isn't its native environment we wait to see how long it can last in Cornwall's mild climate.

Many species of magnolia are used in both Eastern and Western herbalism. In Chinese herbalism magnolia bark is associated with healing the stomach, spleen and large intestine, while the flower is associated with the lungs.

At one time magnolia root was used to treat rheumatism and was thought to be superior to quinine in treating chills and fever, but is not much used today.

Russian herbalists use oil extracted from the flowers and young leaves to treat hair loss and as an antiseptic on skin wounds. For us, it's more a case of their exotic beauty being medicine for the soul!

To see their colours after winter months consisting of dull browns and greys is something that really lifts the spirit. Their flowering season is brief (late February to early April) and vulnerable to any late frosts, so catch them while you can.

THE MAGNOLIAS AT TRENGWAINTON

Phil Griffiths, Head Gardener

In the Kitchen Walled Garden where the pumpkin patch is you will find *Magnolia campbellii* subsp. *mollicomata* and *Magnolia campbellii* subsp. *mollicomata* 'Lanarth'. *Magnolia campbellii* 'Darjeeling' is on the lower drive and in the magnolia garden behind Trengwainton House (not open to the public) is *Magnolia sargentiana* var. *robusta* which is believed to be Edward Bolitho's favourite plant in the garden.

Reeds Nursery collected some material from it in the early 1980s and have marketed it as *Magnolia sargentiana* var. *robusta* 'Trengwainton Glory'. In the Campbellii Garden Edward Bolitho's wife, Ali Bolitho, thinks the *Magnolia campbellii* has *Barum,* T.R. Bolitho's horse seen in the famous Alfred Munnings painting, buried beneath it. It was planted as a 5-year old tree in 1926, purchased for 10/- 6d from the Veitch Nursery, Exeter.

The *Rhododendron macabeanum* at Trengwainton won the Royal Horticultural Society medal in 1937. The extract below is from *Trees and Shrubs Hardy in the British Isles*, W. J. Bean:

At Trengwainton, where Sir Edward Bolitho raised many plants from KW 7724, some are deep yellow and among the finest in the country. But the trusses shown by him in 1937 and 1938 were of pale yellow flowers, though still fine enough for the species to receive the Award of Merit on the first occasion and a First Class Certificate on the second. The famous plant at Trewithen, Cornwall, was a gift from Sir Edward Bolitho to George Johnstone and is one of the original seedlings.

Rhododendron 'Morvah' first flowered in 1956 and was awarded RHS Award of Merit 1956 and First Class Certificate 1957.

RHODODENDRONS

Marina Rule

April is the month when the garden comes alive with the colours of Trengwainton's historic collection of rhododendrons – some of which flowered in this country for the first time here at Trengwainton.

The name rhododendron comes from the ancient Greek words rhódon and déndron meaning 'rose tree.' The colours range from the pale lemon of *Rhododendron macabeanum,* through to the deep blood red of *Rhododendron arboreum* 'Cornish Red.' *Rhododendron* 'Loderi King George' starts off with deep pink buds, but they open to become pure white flowers which have a rich fragrance on warm spring days.

It was from seed gathered by the great plant hunter Frank Kingdon-Ward that the rhododendron collection at Trengwainton was largely established. In 1938 Trengwainton was by far the most successful exhibitor at the RHS rhododendron show in London and those rhododendron are still winning prizes when entered in completions such as the West Cornwall Spring Show.

The rhododendron is the national flower of Nepal and is consumed there in the form of pickled flowers and juice, but honey produced from *Rhododendron ponticum* (often seen growing wild on Cornish hillsides) has hallucinogenic effects. Pollen and nectar from some species of rhododendron also contain a toxic substance that can induce poisoning in humans and animals and horses are especially sensitive to it.

On the other hand however, medical studies have shown that other extracts from rhododendrons have anti-inflammatory properties and can also act beneficially on the function of the liver.

Rhododendron 'Fusilier' Grex

Rhododendron macabeanum sinogrande

Rhododendron crassum

In recent years, these beautiful flowers at Trengwainton have become endangered by the plant disease *Phytophthora ramorum*, which causes them to weaken and die. Samples of some of Trengwainton's most important specimens have been sent to the micropropagation unit at Duchy College to save their DNA, in the hope that future generations can continue to enjoy their extraordinary beauty for many years to come.

27

OSMUNDA REGALIS (ROYAL FERN)

Milli Morgan

The royal fern is thought to have evolved on the supercontinent Gondwana (which is believed to have resided in the southern hemisphere and includes the modern day continents of Antarctica, India, Australia, South America and Africa), [18] sometime during the late Paleozoic Era (544 to 245 million years ago). The royal fern survived largely unchanged for millions of years and through numerous threats, including ice ages and mass extinctions.[19]

Ferns do not reproduce using seeds or flowers as one may think, but instead do so using single living cells, called spores (which have the appearance of a fine dust after they have been released). Unlike most other ferns, the royal fern grows its spores on modified leaves.

The royal fern is *so named for its 'crown' of sporeholding fronds, which develop on the tips of the fern fronds, making it appear as though they wear crowns.* Within the sori of a fern *hundreds of thousands of spores are developed in little packets known as sporangia, and released when mature.*[20] The sori will remain a green colour until they ripen, an eventual rustlike, paler colour indicating that the spores have been dispersed.[21]

The fibrous roots of the *Osmunda* have often been used as a growing medium for orchids, more frequently in the past, as the fern has been largely over-harvested for this purpose, meaning that orchid-growers have had to seek out alternatives, such as fir bark, Sphagnum moss or German peat.[22]

In Slavic mythology, the fern, which never flowers, is said to bloom once a year on Midsummer's Eve, offering those brave enough to seek out the flower's mystical powers such as the ability to make things invisible and to understand the language of animals.[23]

Royal fern in the Kitchen Garden June 2017

BLUEBELLS

Marina Rule

For anyone who loves flowers, the bluebell season is one of those joys we all look forward to, and the annual display at Trengwainton is something we eagerly anticipate.

Trengwainton's winding, wooded paths make for ideal conditions for seeing the bluebells that grow beneath the trees. Their early flowering means they can take advantage of the dappled sunlight that reaches the woodland floor before the trees are in full leaf.

Nearly half the world's population of bluebells are here in the UK and you'll find them in broadleaved woodland, along hedgerows and in fields.

Care needs to be taken with them though, because mythology has it that bluebells are used by fairies to trap passers-by! It's also said that wearing a wreath made of bluebell flowers compels the wearer to speak only the truth.

Historically, bluebells once had many uses; their bulbs produce a very sticky substance which was used to stick pages into books and feathers onto arrows. Elizabethans used crushed bluebell bulbs to provide starch for the ruffs of their collars and sleeves.

Britain's native bluebells though are under threat from a Spanish invader. You can tell the difference between them because the stem of a native bluebell droops to one side and nearly all the flowers are on one side.

The Spanish ones are more upright, with flowers all around the stem. Cross-fertilisation of the two is creating a fertile hybrid which dilutes the characteristics of the native bluebell.

The romantic poets of the 19th century, such as Keats and Tennyson, believed that bluebells symbolised solitude and regret. These days, you'd be hard-pressed to imagine a more uplifting sight than a carpet of bluebells bathed in the light of the warm May sunshine.

'HANDKERCHIEF' TREE, *DAVIDIA INVOLUCRATA*

Milli Morgan

It seemed as though the branches had been draped in thousands of ghostly, white handkerchiefs. Henry's diary, relayed through 'In the Footsteps of Augustine Henry'.

The *Davidia involucrata*, also known as the handkerchief, dove or ghost tree, for its flowing white bracts that can grow to be as long as 30cm, is native to central and southern China.

It was first discovered by a Westerner in 1868, a French priest, Father Armand David, for whom this tree's genus 'Davidia' is named after, and of which the Handkerchief Tree is the sole member. The tree was not brought to England in seed form until 1901, after a lengthy and tumultuous quest, by young Veitch Nursery commissioned botanist, Ernest Wilson.

Upon embarking on his journey to find the dove tree in 1899, Wilson did not speak any Chinese and was armed only with a botanical illustration of the tree, found in Franchet's *Plantæ Davidianæ*, a book featuring an organised collection of Father David Armand's specimens.

It was not until Wilson reached Simao in Yunan Province that a lead for the location of the tree could be found. Here he met already famed botanist Augustine Henry, who provided him with a sketched map for the location of the dove tree. After discovering the felling of this particular tree for lumber-use, Wilson continued his search, eventually finding the tree on May 19th 1901, describing it in his journal as 'the most interesting and beautiful of all trees of the north-temperate flora'.

After settling in the mountains to collect and record detailed descriptions of samples and try to work out a means of not only transporting the *Davidia* seeds from China to Britain, but also keeping them alive for the journey, Wilson eventually returns home in 1902, to finally introduce the sought-after Chinese dove tree to England. Yet when the seeds are planted, initially none of them sprout.

Unlike the beechnuts and acorns of beech and oak trees, which lose their protective layer relatively quickly so as to minimize the risk of being eaten by herbivores, like bird cherry trees, *Davidias* have a thick protective casing that takes several years to rot away.

This has a clear advantage: if the environment is particularly detrimental for plant growth one year, for example a particularly dry spell or reduced rainfall, it could quickly kill off a whole generation of oaks or beeches which germinate during the same year.

However, it would only kill the few *Davidia* seedlings that had already sloughed away their casing, leaving other seedlings to attempt germination the next year, or even the year after. This increases the chances of a new generation of *Davidia involucrata* surviving and producing seedlings of their own.

Effective as this evolutionary process seems, the dove tree is nonetheless marked as endangered in the China Red Plant Book and is a relict species or 'living fossil', meaning that its close relatives, in this case the *Tsukada davidiifolia*, have become extinct, making it the sole surviver and representative of a once much bigger group.[24]

SUNFLOWERS
Marina Rule

The botanical name for sunflowers is *Helianthus*, which comes from *Helia* for sun and *Anthus* for flower. They're well named of course, with their resemblance to images of the sun, but they're also renowned for tracking it across the sky by the movement of their flowering heads. This process of heliotropism is more obvious in younger flowers, while mature flowers usually remain facing east.

Sunflowers originate from the Americas and were used extensively by Native American Indians for food, as oil, in bread, medical ointments, dyes and body paints. The sunflower is the state flower of Kansas and they're also the national flower of Ukraine. Sunflower cultivation started in Europe in the 1600s and now 60% of the world's sunflowers are grown in Europe and Russia.

Sunflowers are a magnet for pollinating insects and their seeds help to feed birds as well. Their heads are actually made up of many tiny flowers called florets and after pollination every little flower or floret produces a seed. Sunflower seeds are an excellent source of calcium, iron, manganese, zinc, magnesium, selenium, and copper. There are two kinds of seeds; sunflower oil is made from the black seeds and those used as snacks are made from the striped ones. In Germany, sunflower

Cyanotypes drying at
the Head Gardener's
Cottage

seeds are mixed with rye flour to make a type of bread (Sonnenblumenkernbrot).

Sunflowers are very fast growing and, according to the Guinness World Records, the tallest one ever grown measured 30ft 1in (9.17m) in Karst, Germany, by Hans-Peter Schiffer in August 2014.

In 2015 in celebration of Year of the Sunflower, we planted a bed of these cheerful plants in the walled Kitchen Garden at Trengwainton. Six varieties of differing sizes created a striking display throughout the month of August.

They ranged from the giant *Kong* which can grow up to 15ft (450cm) and has lots of branches, to the dwarf *Teddy Bear* at just 6in (15cm) with its big, fluffy, double golden-yellow blooms.

If you thought sunflowers only come in varying shades of yellow, then the sunflower *Prado Red* will come as a surprise to you, with its rich, dark, mahogany-red flowers and bright golden halo around its centre.

TRENGWAINTON PLANTS CYANOTYPES

Barbara Santi

Inspired by the beautifully atmospheric cyanotypes of Anna Atkins, an English botanist and photographer (1799 – 1871), hand-made prints of plant specimens found at Trengwainton were created using the same techniques developed over 150 years ago. Anna Atkins is considered as the first female photographer[25] and her passion for plants led her to create what is known as the first illustrated book, *Photographs of British Algae: Cyanotype Impressions* (1843), which can be seen at The British Library.[26] This important ground-

breaking technique was as a result of knowing the pioneer of early photography William Henry Fox Talbot and Sir John Herschel who first devised the cyanotype process.[27]

The method of 'sun printing' uses ferric ammonium citrate and potassium ferricyanide on paper. The specimen is then laid on the paper and pressed down with a glass plate which is exposed in the sun. It is then washed in water and dried. The detailed imprint of the plant is left on the paper while the uncovered parts becomes dark blue when exposed to light.

Working with botanist Keith Spurgin and writer Selina Bates, filmmaker and project director Barbara Santi retraced Atkins' steps and produced ten 'impressions' on the grounds at Trengwainton.

TRENGWAINTON FLOWERING PLANTS

1 September 2017

Keith Spurgin

Wild Strawberry — *Fragaria vesca*

A frequent and familiar wild flower in Cornwall, it was an Elizabethan favourite before 1600 when its larger relative began to be imported from South America. Our native plant was found in the walled garden at Trengwainton, happily growing in shade with another introduced relative, Yellow-flowered Strawberry *Duchesnea indica*.

Phacelia — *Phacelia tanacetifolia*

Known as a garden plant since the early c19[th], this bee-friendly annual was first recorded for Cornwall by D. Lewis in 1981 at Porthgwarra, as an escape from (or relic of) cultivation. It has pretty spirals of bluish flowers and fern-like leaves, and has been grown as green manure. Other names include 'Fiddleneck', 'Scorpionweed' and 'Blue Tansy'.

Mexican Fleabane — *Erigeron karvinskiarnis*

This well-travelled member of the Daisy and Dandelion family thrives in open, frost-free situations such as cliffs and quarries, where it can form large masses. In mainland Britain it was first recorded in the wild in 1875 and the first Cornish records began to be made in 1950.

Germander Speedwell — *Veronica chamædrys*

Easily the most common Speedwell in Cornwall, this is also the easiest to recognise. Apart from the bright blue 'bird's-eye' flower it has two distinctive lines of hairs along the stems, alternating with the smooth sides at each pair of leaves. Gardeners know this plant well as it often grows in large patches; as Shakespeare wrote 'sweet flowers are slow and weeds make haste'.

Dill — *Anethum graveolens*

Prized for its mild aniseed flavour, Dill has been called 'Fennel light', resembling that herb but much shorter and rarely seen in a wild situation. Thought to have originated in Asia and to have spread westwards via Mediterranean cultures, it has been grown in English gardens for more than a millennium.

Dill is used to flavour fish and soup, in pickles, and is used by garden foragers as a salad leaf.

Yorkshire-fog — *Holcus lanatus*

Despite its name this is one of Cornwall's most common grasses. The reference to fog seems to be a poetic allusion to the sight of a multitude of small reddish flowers formed by the often large colonies it produces. The Latin name *Holcus* used by botanists is said to have been derived from the Roman naturalist Pliny the Elder (23-79 CE), who used it in the sense of 'grain'.

Ginkgo — *Ginkgo biloba*

The tall and handsome Ginkgos at Trengwainton are examples of so-called 'living fossils.' No evidence of its close relations having survived beyond the Pleistocene Era, more than 2.5 million years ago. It lived on as an apparently scarce plant in China and Japan, was brought to Europe in the early c18[th] and is now an extremely popular ornamental in many countries.

Also known as 'Maidenhair-tree' (its leaves being shaped like those of the fern of the same name), it is known and used as a medicinal plant.

Ribwort Plantain — *Plantage lanceolata*

There are four common species of Plantain in Cornwall, and this one is found most frequently. It has 'lanceolate' leaves (long and narrow), which children still break and pull apart to reveal the 'ribs' inside the veins, looking like violin strings. There is also a way of looping the stem round the flower spike and firing it, which is not recommended. Our two specimens look like rockets and the living plant has an attractive appearance when the stigmas and stamens protrude at flowering time.

Enchanter's Nightshade — *Circæa lutetiana*

Named after the ancient Greek enchantress Circe, this perennial plant has small but attractive white flowers that turn into seeds covered with tiny hooks. These are ideal for lodging in the fur of pets and wild visitors, even on the gardener's clothing, so that the plant will germinate and extend its persistent white roots almost anywhere suitably shady. It has apparently been used medicinally in some cultures.

Grapevine — *Vitis vinifera*

The fruit of the vine is well-known but its leaves less so, despite their use in medicine and nutrition. Dolmades are vine leaves stuffed with various fillings, rice, vegetables or meat, in countries as diverse as Russia and Morocco.

The leaves are variable in shape and texture, this specimen from Trengwainton being cordate with serrate margins. More interestingly, they are 'stuffed' too with vitamins and beneficial elements, earning them the title of 'superfood' in some quarters.

Cyanotypes:
Strawberry

Fern

HEAD GARDENERS

Trengwainton: A Great Cornish Gem

Under the auspices of three exceptional head gardeners, a few of the new introductions first flowered in Britain at Trengwainton – in particular, the yellow **Rhododendron macabeanum** *and the brilliant red* **R. elliottii**. *From seed sown in 1927, Mr A. Creek raised many plants which his successor, Mr G. Thomas, brought to maturity and also produced a number of fine hybrids. In his turn, Mr G. Hulbert successfully tended his charges and in 1961 handed over to Mr D. G. Austin, who had had some experience of tender plants in the mildest garden in Great Britain, Tresco in the Scilly Isles.*

**Gardeners' Chronicle
Gardening Illustrated
July 14 1962, p. 31**

PHIL GRIFFITHS, HEAD GARDENER

Taken from filmed interview, 2017

"I've worked here for 15 years as of January 1st, have been Head Gardener for six years and employed by the Trust for 17 years. I came in through the National Trust apprenticeship scheme, so I did three years training at a garden called Antony House and I've never worked for anybody else apart from the National Trust. I still can't imagine myself working for anybody else.

I'd never been to Trengwainton before. I'm from East Cornwall originally, so I moved from one end of the county to the other and a completely different garden to the one I was in before. Antony's very formal, whereas Trengwainton is primarily a woodland garden but what is especially exciting is the plant collection.

We currently have a team of myself, Gareth, Matt, and Katharine who looks after the Kitchen Garden three days a week. We're lucky then on top of that to have a team of about 18 garden volunteers.

The way I describe **The Garden** when we're doing guided tours is we've got plants from all four corners of the globe. So we've got plants from South America primarily Chile, Bolivia, from the foot of the mountainous regions over there, right over to the other side of Asia; sub-Himalayan plants, from a collection by Frank Kingdon-Ward in the 1920s. We have plants from right down the West coast of Asia, down to Australasia, across to South Africa, and then your usual European plants.

We've got rhododendrons, magnolias, camellias and fuchsias from South America, we have the tree ferns and plants from Australia and New Zealand, and then plants from the mountainous regions of South Africa.

When we're clearing an area because of plant disease we could expose a plant we didn't even know was in the collection, and it might have some fantastic herbal use in its native country, so it's the stories behind the plants as well as just appreciating them for their flowers or their leaves or the way they grow.

We are in the unique position that historically the Price and Bolitho families have invested in the surroundings. The Prices planted out the woods to provide shelter, not just for the garden and the estate but as some historians put it, 'to stop people looking in', so those woodlands have created a little microclimate.

The Prices built walled gardens which provide a sheltered environment for some of the more temperate plants to grow and because they're made of brick they act like a night storage heater; so they warm up during the day and release their heat at night. Some of the plants we have here you'd struggle to grow outside in other parts of the UK.

The Bolithos invested heavily at the end of the Victorian period in very large glasshouses. We think there were probably seven or eight of these really elaborate glasshouses here. The head gardener at the time, Alfred Creek, was head-hunted for his hybridisation skills. So the Bolithos were sent shares of the plants in Kingdon-Ward's expedition to grow them on, and then they were able to keep a certain number of that collection. Through this collection, Alfred Creek and Sir Edward Bolitho hybridised primarily the red rhododendrons.

Tour Around the Garden

Starting up around **The Bothy**, we have the glasshouses – made by a company in Loughborough called

Phil Griffiths and his
dog Meg outside
The Bothy

Messenger. We've tried to get the original documents but unfortunately there was a fire or a flood and there's an area of history where they don't know what came to Trengwainton, but they were very innovative as they had curved glass at the bottom. They were sent down on the train flat-packed and we're not quite sure whether Messenger sent their own carpenters or if the carpenters on the estate then built them.

Then we have **The Bee House** which is quite unusual. You have bee bowls in quite a lot of walled gardens but this is a brick-built structure with a slate roof; they do have some similar bee houses in Europe however. Primarily they started off as carts similar to a garden shed, which would have been towed around from village to village or district to district as an orchard was coming into flower or a vineyard. They would follow the seasons throughout Europe, so maybe this is something Sir Rose Price picked up on the grand tour, but it's very unusual.

Then we come down into **The Walled Garden** with its massive brick walls. They're 300 cubits long by 50 cubits wide, if you go by the Noah's Ark measurement (which is about 100 metres long).

There are various disputes: some people say Sir Rose Price brought the clay down and fired it on site, some other people say that they were fired at their point of origin, but there are very small bits of granite and quartz in there. I like to think they were mixed with some local material here because we know when the Bolithos bought the estate in the 1860s (Thomas Simon Bolitho bought Trengwainton for £33,000, 852 acres in 1867) there was still a brick kiln just down the road at the bottom of the garden at Polteggan.

There are lots of theories, but some people say if you look where the reservoir is opposite the garden, some of those fields have been scraped flat. Maybe that was part of building the reservoir, but it might have been that the material dug out of the reservoir site was used to make the bricks.

We're not sure exactly when they were fired, but it's not around before Sir Rose Price owned the estate, and it definitely appears in some of the maps later on.

We think that when Sir Rose Price built the walled garden, he built two long sections; one section being to the dimensions of Noah's Ark, which is now used as the **Kitchen Garden**, and the lower section. All of those areas would have been to provide food for the house. It was a bit of posturing and a bit of showing off too; he built the garden out of red brick, which was very rare in West Cornwall, and then at some point after that the sloping beds were put in.

We don't really know why the sloping beds were put in. They face west, so some thoughts are it's to allow brassicas and other vegetables to warm up so they don't get the sun on them too early. There was lots of rain in and around the time when Sir Rose Price was building the estate, so they also allow drainage. They're difficult to cultivate, so as soon as you start to turn the soil over all the earth washes down to the bottom, so you can see when you look at them after almost 200 years, there's quite a lot of soil erosion on them.

Along the south-facing wall, throughout the walled gardens, originally there would have been espaliered trees or fan-trained trees. This is to save space, but it's also showing off. To get the most out of a crop you would want that tree to be grown in the middle of an orchard or the middle of a fruit growing area, but to train it against a wall all of the buds have to be facing one way which is quite labour-intensive. Sir Rose Price paid for his baronetcy, so it's all about 'keeping up with the Joneses'.

We know that there was a brick-built structure here at some point and it's been the **Head Gardener's Cottage** since at least the early 1900s. Originally it was three cottages so if you look from the outside, there are various windows that have been bricked up and doorways where you can still see the lintels outside. The first person I know that lived here was Alfred Creek and you can see where his children have scratched their initials into the windows of the downstairs room. Head gardeners living in the middle of the orchard, in the middle of the estate, meant they could keep an eye on all the produce.

Then some time around the early 1900s, **the lower section of the walled gardens**, the lower five sections, that's where the exotic plants started to be put in. The upper section was kept as a Kitchen Garden where there were fruit cages and produce for the house. Then as the train came to Penzance and food became easier to get, slowly, as with a lot of estates, walled gardens went into decline and the real death knell came after the Second World War.

In around about 2004 / 2005, we reinstated the Kitchen Garden. When I first came here as a gardener, once a month we would go in there and spray all the perennial weeds to try and make it look a bit more maintained, but after 30 / 40 years of the soil being baked and continually sprayed, there was no life in it whatsoever; no worms, no beetles, no bugs, nothing. So we did three or four seasons of adding soil, adding green manures and adding farm manure. Then we grassed it over for a few years just to let the soil below really come back to life, and when we employed Katherine our Kitchen Gardener, she's slowly brought those areas back up to a really good standard of horticulture again.

The **lower section** we just keep on the same vein that the Bolithos had. Starting from the west we have the foliage garden, with lush, tender exotic plants. There should be very little flowering there, the main focus is the leaves; so very different textures, different leaf shapes, really lush and vibrant when you go in. From things that don't look like they should be in there like the *Pseudopanax*, they look like something out of a science-fiction movie, to bananas and the begonias.

Then we go into the **Fuchsia Garden**, which has lost its way for a while. Really it should be South American species fuchsias from Chile and Bolivia, so our project in a couple of years will be to really re-invigorate that garden. There are two trees in there that are on their last legs and once we take those down, that'll really add a lot more air and light into that garden so we can grow sub-tropical fuchsias again.

The **middle walled garden** was full of normal woody plants; maybe they weren't sure when they were first planted how they would grow here in the UK. Lots of fragrant rhododendrons, cianthus and I remember a really nice scented *Magnolia cylindrica*, that died a few years ago. Slowly through plant diseases we've sadly lost more and more.

Over the last two to three years we've done lots of soil improvement; again dug in farmyard manure, composts and really enriched the soil, because if you think these plants have been in there for almost 100 years and the soil they've been living in has very little nutrients left in it.

Then the next garden, we call it the **Campbellii Garden**, and that's because of the *Magnolia campbellii* in there. We've tried to start putting a lot more salvias back in there, the tender ones again.

The garden after that we call the **Veitchii Garden** after the largest magnolia that's in that garden, but that's sometimes called 'Colonel's corner' as well. It would have been planted up by Sir Edward Bolitho we believe before he became 'Sir'.

The Dig for Victory Garden – we're really lucky, we've got a gardener onsite who's very passionate about the First and Second World War, and in 2010 it was the 70th anniversary of the Dig for Victory campaign. A local volunteer had suggested this project to my general manager. He was going to put it somewhere else, but when he heard about Gareth's passion he suggested we put it here at Trengwainton.

It was originally going to be just a 5 year project but we just keep extending it. We're still not sure how long it's going to last but it's a great thing for people to come to now, and we've had some emotive stories come out of it. As people come in they'll see the Anderson shelter, they'll see the tape on the shed windows, or they'll recognise maybe some of the names of the crops. People have dropped in memorabilia for Gareth to put in the shed, or have sent over certificates from their parents when they were land army girls, local wardens or in the home guards, so it's been a great way of interacting with the public. It still has a relationship to Trengwainton because lots of the land here, the terrace and the lawn in front of the house and probably the orchard, was dug up for the war effort. We know they grew potatoes primarily. Also in the glasshouses we know they grew a lot of cucumbers and tomatoes to send off to market.

Mid-way up the drive there's an area we call **The Meadow** where some of the trees were planted to commemorate various royal events. So there's an Oak that was planted to commemorate Queen Victoria's Diamond Jubilee, and then various coronations of kings and queens up until Elizabeth II. Edward Bolitho is the Lord Lieutenant so whenever there is a royal visit he likes to plant a tree to commemorate that visit. The most recent was the Queen Mother in the 1960s, and then Princess Anne planted a tree in 2010.

As you come down through the garden, we have the **Upper Garden** and the **Upper Pond**. There's an area we call Asian Alley and the camellias up there are donations.

There's the **Azalea Garden** that leads down on to that. There's the **Old Nursery Area** where there's lots of plants that were originally heeled in which have been left alone and they've continued to grow on up.

Then we come down through the **Long Walk** which is primarily now planted up with hydrangeas. Up until the late 80s, they were still sent off to Covent Garden and the markets every week as a way of providing some income for the estate.

Having **The Drive** splits up the garden. It's really unusual to have a garden that is bisected by such a large, man-made feature. You might have a stream running down through, which we do have, but this is a particularly unusual set up.

As you go up the drive you will notice how it snakes and meanders. If you were to look at it on a map or from the air you will see that this is a much longer distance than if you were to take a gun barrel straight line from the entrance lodge up to the house, which would be more normal.

Perhaps they were following a historical track or maybe purposely taking in more of the garden for visitors to splendour at as they approached, we just don't know. The approach to the main house is from the side but the reason for this is that the front of the house looks down across the bay and the valleys. Perhaps before all of the trees grew up, the house would have dominated the landscape."

Horse Chestnut

ERNEST POVEY

Rev Tim Hawkins talking about his great-grandfather who was Head Gardener (1898 - 1906)

From filmed interview, 2016

"My name is Reverend Tim Hawkins and I've been the Vicar of Madron since November 2005. When I came here I realised a slight connection with the family. Two doors down the road, or at least two doors down before new houses were built up in Madron, my great-grandfather and his new wife Alice lived in the left of two cottages on the road by the National Trust car park. Ernest Povey was the then Head Gardener of Trengwainton. So he was here from around the turn of the century. He's mentioned in the local paper as providing a floral arrangement at an event in Madron Church in 1902. And then he married his wife Alice Povey, who I think was from southeast London, and they were married in 1905. They had a daughter, my grandmother, Vera Mabel Povey who became later on Vera Mabel Hawkins, which brings it into connection

with me and my dad specifically. She was baptised at Madron Church in 1907.

I believe sometime just before the First World War Ernest left the employ of the Bolithos, and I believe it was perhaps through a clash of vision should we say, about what could be done with the future of the garden.

I don't think it was a violent clash, I think it was simply a question that he thought it might be wise to find employment elsewhere. But a happy time apparently for them all. I don't know exactly what he was responsible for while he was there but I've got a photo of a large lake at Trengwainton, and I was told by my aunts that apparently that was one significant contribution he'd made while he was there. This is purely from, as it were, 'oral history' passed through the family.

I have a picture of him and Alice side by side in the left of the two cottages, which are on the hill. Jiglass Hill as we call it. From speaking to my grandmother and my aunt, we believe it was taken on their honeymoon. And they were married as I say at Madron Church, and yes a fascinating link with the present because I have been in that house talking to the tenants of it.

A few years ago I prepared their child for baptism, not knowing when I sat on their sofa that that would have been where my great-grandfather and great-grandmother would have sat on their sofa all those years ago."

My aunt was really the historian in the family and she was a regular visitor to my great-grandmother Alice who lived on till she was a hundred and one, and so was very much a part of my world as I grew up. She always regarded living in Cornwall as the best and happiest time of her life. She was full of anecdotes about buying pilchards for a penny down at Newlyn and what it used to be like and so forth, and also about Ernest singing in the choir. I believe he was an alto, I may have got that wrong, but that was unusual for a man. So that was just one of the things that came up in conversation.

ALFRED CREEK

Head Gardener 1906 – 1934

1863

Alfred Creek was born in 1863, the youngest son of the gardener at Springfield Lyons, Chelmsford, Essex. Family tradition says he wanted to become a teacher, but after the death of his father he had to start work as a boy in Springfield Lyons gardens.

c1880–1888

As was usual at that period, he moved from garden to garden, gaining experience, skill and promotion – from Albury, near Much Hadham, Herts to Birkfield, Ipswich to Sudbourne Hall, Wickham Market, Suffolk.

1888

He joined the garden staff at The Chantry, Ipswich, probably as foreman. When in 1892 the sight of the Head Gardener failed and he was unable to work, Alfred Creek became Head Gardener there – and the following year married his predecessor's daughter Alice.

Here they had three children, Hugh, Mabel and William. Alfred had many contacts with other Head Gardeners, and was on the committee of The Ipswich and District Gardeners' and Amateurs' Mutual Improvement Association when it was founded in 1900.

For the Ipswich Horticultural Shows a pantechnicon was hired to take displays of produce etc. from The Chantry – his employer, Sir Cecil Domville, used to give Alfred the prize money that was won.

In 1905 Sir Cecil died, and Alfred, apparently not liking the new lady owner and her family, looked for another job.

1906

Alfred Creek moved to Trengwainton as Head Gardener, and was paid 30/- a week, coal, oil, and a house together with vegetables. Besides maintaining the kitchen and pleasure gardens, he was involved in the planting of the 'new' long drive, and bred a strain of anemones with long stems which became a commercial success. When his employer, Mr Bolitho, died in 1925, he left £500 – a large sum in those days – to 'my good gardener.'

1918

When the WI arrived in Madron village in 1918, Creek was part of the entertainment: *Mr Creek to be asked to sing, recitations, lantern slides, Cornish stories.* (from *West Cornwall in the Twentieth Century: Life in Penwith* by Susan Hoyle).

1925

The gardens at Trengwainton were developed further by the new owner, Colonel Bolitho, and Alfred Creek's skill in propagation was fully used in raising seedlings from, in particular, Kingdon-Ward's plant hunting expedition in 1927-8. When Colonel Bolitho's rhododendrons won particular acclaim in a Royal Horticultural Show in London he made sure his gardeners' skills were acknowledged. He wrote the following letter, probably to *The Times*:

Sir, – Following your very kind notice of the above Show in which you mention my name, I write this letter as it does seem to me that the people who made it possible for me to show such beautiful blooms should have the credit. Practically every plant from which the blooms were cut was raised from seed or propagated by Mr A. Creek, now at Madron, who retired two years ago after serving for thirty years as head gardener

at *"Trengwainton"*. Mr Creek was succeeded by Mr G.W. Thomas, as head gardener, and it is to his care and maintenance of the plants, and to the skilled packing required to transport the flowers to London, that the successes were achieved.

Yours faithfully, E.H.W. Bolitho

"Trengwainton," Heamoor, S O. 1st. May, 1936.

1934

In December of that year Alfred Creek, then 70, retired with his wife to one of the Landithy Cottages, Madron, where he continued to be active in village and church affairs. Colonel Bolitho continued to be very supportive of his valued gardener, and the new Head Gardener at Trengwainton became a good friend.

His elder son Hugh, who had fought in Mesopotamia (now Iraq) in the 1914-18 war, was the headmaster of a village school in Suffolk; his daughter Mabel was a dresser, or lady's maid, to Queen Mary, and his younger son William worked in various gardens and fought in North Africa and Italy in the 1939-45 war.

1951

Alfred Creek, after increasing ill-health, died on Jan 4th 1951. *The Western Morning News* reported:

Mr A. J. Creek

Madron Resident was horticulturalist. The funeral has taken place of Mr Alfred J Creek, of Landithy, Madron.

Mr Creek, who lived in retirement for the last 15 years, was 87. Going to Cornwall in 1906 to take charge of the gardens

at Trengwainton, he was instrumental in introducing the cultivation of anemones and polyanthus for winter flowering into West Cornwall.

He exhibited at the Royal Cornwall and Penzance Spring Shows, and for several years acted as secretary of a flower show at Madron and Heamoor.

His services were in continual demand as a horticultural judge. Later he was responsible for raising and propagating many of the new rhododendrons and other plants sent home by the Forest and Kingdon-Ward expeditions.

He was for many years a church warden at Madron, a governor of the Daniels Foundation, a school manager, and secretary of Madron Men's Club.

Among those present at the service, which was conducted by Rev. H. M. Hocking, were Lt Col E. H. W. Bolitho (Lord Lieutenant of Cornwall) and other prominent parishioners. Mrs Creek and her daughter received a message of sympathy from Queen Mary.

EXTRACTS FROM ALFRED CREEK'S LETTERS

Treng. Jan 1934 (written before retirement)

We have been busy planting up a new piece which has been taken in the back of the old gas house ….

Madron May 1935 (written after retirement)

On Sunday afternoon Trengwainton Grounds were open in aid of a new motor ambulance for Penzance, I have not heard what the takings amounted to, the rhododendrons were very good but some were past their best. The gale last Friday did some damage at Trengwainton, the fine old Grisolina tree on the bank in the Ladies' Garden was blown down and several large beech trees on the place, we had snow showers but no frosts so the potatoes, beans etc. were not cut.

Rhododendron
'Creek's Cross'

Madron Apr. 7th 1936

…. Went down to the Gardens on Monday, Thomas was cutting some rhododendrons to send up to the fortnightly meeting of the R.H.S.

I must look in the Times tomorrow to see if notice was taken of them, one was a sino-grande variety borealis, it flowered for the first time last year but this year it has some good trusses. Another one is a cross between neriflorum & blood red Arboreum, a lovely colour, if it is placed in a good light it is really vivid.

Madron Feb. 28th 1938

…. Want to go to the gardens tomorrow as Thomas sent a word that Magnolia campbellii and Rhodo-macabeanum were flowering, the first named was planted ten years ago and it's flowering at Trengwainton for the first time, it has been flowering at several places in Cornwall for many years, the rhodo is one which Kingdon-Ward sent home seed, we raised quite a number, in fact a lot were not pricked off, it is one of the big-leaved sort a fine plant even out of flower ….

…. Saw the magnolia this morning, it has 3 flowers the size of a saucer, pink in the young state turning white later. The Rhodo-macabeanum flowered last year for the first time and got the R.H.S. award for Merit, it has several trusses this year which are larger, a light yellow with prominent red stamens.

Madron March 29th 1938

…. The Western Commercial Show did very well, there was a good report in the Daily Mail. I was talking to a man about the Rhodo-macabeanum and found afterwards that he was Mr Issard the D. Mail reporter, the Colonel exhibited it at the R.H.S. the previous Tuesday and they gave it a first class certificate, it was shown last year when he got an award of merit, then it was only a small piece, this year it had a fine truss. Trengwainton flowered it first, it was raised about ten years ago from seed sent home by Kingdon-Ward ....

Madron May 12th 1938

Colonel Bolitho did well at the Rhododendron Show last Tuesday week taking eleven firsts, three seconds, two thirds and the Maclaren Challenge cup, no doubt the frosts upset the up country flowers ....

Madron April 24th 1939

.... Truro Spring Show was last week, Thomas showed several things, I see by the papers was 3rd. for flowering cherries & some prizes for rhodo's one or two 1st. among them, and 3rd. for anemones, Lord Vivian Glynn was 1st., suppose he got my strain ....

Madron July 24th 1940

.... so far Jerry has not worried us much, two or three nights lately have heard planes passing but cannot tell if they are our own or German .... Went to a Women's Institute Show in St John's Hall of vegetables and other produce, some women speakers from the Ministry were holding forth, on what the Institutes should do, some decent stuff was shown. Mrs Thomas [presumably the Head Gardener's wife] showed honey in comb and run, also for eggs no prizes only certificates given. I went down to the gardens and picked out a section, a good one which took first, the run was very clear and light but not ripe enough. The section was sold for 3/- and several orders for others, they have only one hive in the old bee house and have taken nearly 60lb from it.

Also saw a seedling rhodo flowering for the first time, a cross I made 8 or 9 years ago, the plants are a nice size, ~ now it's a nice thing and useful, flowering so late ....

Madron March 30th 1945

.... Last Sunday afternoon I went to the gardens; after going round below we walked up to Trengwainton to see a magnolia, it's in the garden at the back of the old gas house, we planted it about 15 years ago. Now it's a fine tree, one mass of flower the var. is M-sargentia it has white flowers flushed pink in the centre, am now looking at one which Thomas picked in the bud state. It has opened in water, it is as big as a tea plate, when fully out the petals curl outwards, it was a sight worth seeing as the tree was one mass from top to bottom ....

Madron Feb, 13th 1948

.... Have written to the Spring Show Committee to retire from it on account of old age cannot attend meetings now. Mr Thomas is leaving Trengwainton is going to Hereford to manage his sister's farm, he told us at the Church meeting, when the weather is suitable shall walk down and have a chat with him ....

Madron Aug. 16th 1948

.... The group of Rhodo guissonianum I raised about 3 dozen and planted them in a group in the Jubilee, it's a lovely colour but they have made a mistake by cutting it back like a common hedge, if I had seen the Colonel I would have told him they had made a great mistake ....

GEORGE WILFRED THOMAS

Head Gardener (1934 – 1948)

John Thomas, son of George Wilfred Thomas, from filmed interview, 2017

"My name's John Thomas, my father named me John Edward George Thomas, after my grandfathers, and I'm here because this is the house I was born in. It's a long long time ago but my memory's still pretty good. My father was George Wilfred Thomas, G.W. Thomas. He was Head Gardener in Trengwainton Garden, and this is the Gardener's Cottage, and we lived here with my sister and my mother. I think my father was born in about 1905, and of course he was a farm worker. He lost his parents very early on, his father died when he was only about 3 or 4, his mother died when he was 14. She died of the Spanish Flu which was a real killer after the First World War. So he was brought up on a farm, and farm labouring was hard work and not very well-paid.

He worked with horses, and he had a friend from his school days that he went to school with who was living down in Kent, working for an estate in its gardens. And he said to my father 'Why don't you come down? You'll get much more money and be much better looked after', and so one hot day when my father had had enough of things he took the horses to the end of the row in the field, he took them out of the harness and he took them back home, and he went, and left, and he caught the train down to Kent to his friend. He was then a journeyman gardener in an estate. In those days you've got to remember that there was a big hierarchy of private service. So you had your butlers, you had your upstairs and downstairs, you had all that...demarcation. So he started off at the lower level as a gardener. Of course he enjoyed it, and he was very good at it.

G. W. Thomas and
Sandy the dog

Interview undertaken at Trengwainton's Head Gardener's cottage. Started a new head gardener today, Thomas.

Obviously a man who won't let the grass grow under his feet.

Extract from Col Bolitho's diary (1934)

Then, his first job lasted I don't know how long, but it wasn't many years before a Labour government came into power and so he lost his job. And he found another job almost straight away on another estate with the Kindersley family at Plaw Hatch Hall, which is in Kent, and from there he went to Kidbrooke Park, which I think belonged to Olaf Hambro of Hambros Bank, and he worked in the gardens there, and he worked layer by layer. He lived in a Bothy with all the other young men, and worked in the gardens.

Eventually he then got a job with Sir William Lawrence. While he was there, living in the Bothy, he borrowed the notes from a friend of his who was doing his RHS Wisley exams, and so he studied in the evening and took the exams and passed! Then he became qualified. So then he started looking round for a job, and of course you got a job then not by applying for it so much as by recommendation. Recommendation was the utmost...if you got a good recommendation then you got a position. So he applied for the position of Head Gardener here in Trengwainton Garden, Cornwall.

He was recommended and Sir Edward Boiltho, who we knew as Colonel Bolitho, took him on in 1934. He would only take him on providing he was a married man. Well my mother was also in private service as a nanny for the Kindersley family, and they met there and obviously they decided perhaps it might not be a bad idea to get married, so 8 o'clock one morning they got married in London. They caught the Cornish Riviera, and they found themselves in Cornwall!

Early Memories

My earliest memories are of, well, austerity of course during the war years, and the pram that I had with a kind of al fresco round the outside, a Grecian al fresco, I can remember that as a little one.

We had a dog called Sandy, and one day apparently I tried to take Sandy's bone from him and got bitten. So my father decided that was that, the end of Sandy, and from then on we had Corgis. I remember going to school here in Madron, and also going with the other children up the road, walking to school every morning. My mother would pack a lunch here and I would meet the others outside and we'd walk up to Madron school.

We were given pretty well free reign around the garden, but there were limits, and you were always wary at the back of your mind that you've got to watch your step. So there wasn't too much screaming and shouting, or throwing things, certainly not that, no playing football as such. I had learnt to ride a bike down from the Bothy to the house, and I had a tricycle which I used to pedal about the place.

We had a motorbike and sidecar, because that's all he could afford. Eventually he did buy a Morris Ten off Colonel Bolitho, I think he paid it for him on the never-never…that was his pride and joy. The car was polished up and we had the luxury of a family car, but it was a motorbike and sidecar for a long time.

My mother and I would walk into Penzance to get what groceries we needed, or we would go to the clinics for the children, because during the war years you had to make sure you had your vitamin c. We had orange juice, and cod liver oil was another awful thing we used to have on a regular basis, so you were always going to these clinics where other kids were.

From the early days life was as it is when you're a child – it was all exciting, things were going on… the war was on. We had to look after ourselves as best we could.

One thing that stuck in my mind which I remembered last night – we had a saying in our family which went over the years, and it was one really wet winter here at Trengwainton, at the cottage. My mother used to get a delivery by horse and cart once a week, with groceries and things like that when she couldn't get into Penzance. One week the chap turned up, and it had been pouring with rain and he was thoroughly fed up, and he said to my mother, 'Well what with the weather, and the war, and our firm packing up, and this old horse', he was right in the pits. That saying stuck in our family for many years after.

PROPAGATING RHODODENDRONS AT TRENGWAINTON

My father's time here was propagating rhododendrons, I think that was his main job. He had a very good relationship with Sir Edward Bolitho, later Colonel as we knew him, and they propagated a lot of the plants here. I remember him telling me that there was an expedition to Burma called the Kingdon-Ward Expedition, which the Bolithos and others financed, I think the Rothschilds as well, and so they got varieties of rhododendron brought back to Trengwainton to propagate. My father crossed several rhododendron varieties you see now, that was his main job. It was a time when there were a lot of gardeners in here, I think there must have been seven or eight, a lot of men working here in the gardens. At times they'd go and work on the farm at Trengwainton, most of the time they were here with the gardens. He knew that the plants he got back were quite unique, and he knew he had to create those conditions that you get in Burma, where the Kingdon-Ward was, to get the propagation right. He didn't talk much about it, except I think he was very proud to have been part of that expedition, and I think he was very proud to have been one of the cogs in the wheel that got the thing moving.

One of the rhododendrons he bred was called *taggianum*, it was a white one, and he took it to one of the shows, the RHS Wisley show, and they refused to believe it'd been grown out of doors. That was a bit of a feather in his cap! He talked about *taggianum*, and he talked about how difficult it was to propagate the magnolias. He used to layer them; they would plant the stem down into the ground and then move soil away from the top and wait for it to root from underneath, when it would become a separate plant. I don't remember him ever having a problem with the rhododendrons. They didn't keep a record of all the crosses that they used to do, so I keep looking through my father's papers now to see if there's anything I can find, but I haven't found anything yet.

It would have been very interesting to look at which different varieties they used to produce the results they got. They found the ones that worked. I remember one expedition he did with the Colonel, and I think I tagged along to sit in the sidecar, and he got some cuttings from somewhere which the Colonel had spied, and dad went and got the cuttings while the Colonel kept watch and made sure no one else was looking [laughs], and I can remember that. What he did with them in the Bothy I can't remember, I can always remember lots of trays and

John Thomas with his sister Jennifer and father, G. W. Thomas 1948 outside the Victorian greenhouse

propagating frames and things that were going on, but as a kid then I would never know exactly what it was.

Everything was by rail, so he had to pack up the best specimens carefully and go with them to the shows.

The RHS Wisley show was I think once a year, and they would display them there. It took a lot of effort, and a lot of gardeners would do it. The Royal Cornwall Show was a great place where they showed things, wherever they got the chance to show they would. In the Bothy there are prize certificates on the ceiling, and it's still going on today which is lovely, and you see these certificates from 1937 and realise what they used to do. Yes they were to do with my father, it would be his job. I think *Rhododendron macabeanum* was another one, but that was bred by the gardener before my father which was Creek, Mr Creek. He had a great respect for Mr Creek.

My father was a propagator but he could see Creek was a proper gardener. But my father also had to produce the veg for the big house, and he used to pick the choice strawberries and the choice vegetables for the house, which went up every morning.

He also took flowers up, and he did the decorations in the big house as well, so that was his chore. So sometimes I might go up with him, but most of the time I was kept out the way, being a 'seen-but-not-heard' child, if you like, but heard quite a lot!

He would start at seven o'clock in the morning, and he usually finished by four in the afternoon, and that was Monday to Friday, and I think we had Saturdays for relaxing. He always met Colonel Bolitho on a Sunday morning and they would walk round the gardens and discuss what they were going to do the following week. Usually we went to church at Madron.

When we came back from church he would then meet Colonel Bolitho and go round and discuss different things with him. That would last for an hour, perhaps two hours, and then there was Sunday lunch and probably off to the beach in the afternoon if the weather was really nice.

He had a very, very close relationship with the Colonel. He was a great admirer of him. Some years later when I was shown the entry in the Colonel's diary where he'd put 'Started a new head gardener today, Thomas. Obviously a man who won't let the grass grow under his feet', [laughs] so he could judge men very well, Colonel Bolitho.

We always knew him as the Colonel and were sort of in awe of him, kept out of the way, but my father always said they had a very very good relationship, they didn't have a misword the whole time from 1934 to 1948. In fact Colonel Bolitho, I remember, did say to me, when I visited in 1958 to see where I had been, "I'd have liked your father to stay on and become manager of the estate."

I think my father would have enjoyed that, but he'd got it in his head to be on his own, so that was that, we'll never know. He spoke very warmly of them all, of the whole Bolitho family, he loved them to bits.

I think what he enjoyed most from this was the education he got from it. He knew a lot about the gardens, he knew the varieties, he could reel off the Latin names of any of the plants you liked to name out, he never missed, and I think that impressed Colonel Bolitho. He would say, "Now here Thomas, what's that there?" and my father would give the Latin name straight away and he could also give the background to it.

THE WAR YEARS

I always remember my own personal feeling was I wanted the war to go on so I could be old enough to be a soldier. I remember my father saying, "Oh, we're fed up with this war, when is it going to end?" and I remember thinking, "Oh no, please keep it going because it's so exciting." There are these men in uniform coming home, and stories to tell. Nothing happened very much, it was very gradual as things came off the ration.

Here in Cornwall we didn't experience that much because by 1948 we had moved to Herefordshire and it was still quite restricted then, lots of things were on restriction. Sweets, chocolate, that was unheard of.

Also 'Dig for Victory' was a big campaign, and I think I remember in my mother's house, I've still got the picture now, of a sort of embroidery they all did, 'dig for victory', with a woman with a spade and a carrot [laughs], and one of those slogan things they used to pin up, yes.

BEING IN PRIVATE SERVICE

When my father went into private service – which they were very proud to call private service; all the big estates employed a lot of people and if you could get into a position with them you were made – so my mother and father used to talk a lot about 'those years between the wars' when they were in private service. The families they met were looked after very well, they were paid well, but of course they worked quite hard but they had a good social life. My father would remember the parties that these fabulously wealthy families would have during the roaring twenties, with champange and cigarettes. The young men in the Bothy knew when to creep around at night and nick the cigarettes when no one was looking! Also if they could snaffle some champagne, they would!

Then those war years, the Second World War, broke all that up. Everything finished, that was the end of it. He could see that these estates weren't going to last much longer like they were, and it was time to get out. And that's when he had the chance to go farming in Herefordshire, where his home was, on his own account.

FINAL THOUGHTS

My father used to say that they were happy times. There was a lovely attitude about Trengwainton, the people were friendly. Both my father and my mother got on well and got in with the people locally, the community. He would talk about things that went on at Trengwainton that you couldn't do in Herefordshire. The climate here in Cornwall is very good, but in Herefordshire we had strong frosts, and that was always a big problem.

We were here in Cornwall during 1947 when there was snow for the first time I can remember as a kid. We had about six inches of snow which closed the village school, closed everything, which of course in Herefordshire wouldn't have made any difference at all, because it would have carried on. Colonel Bolitho was a very philanthropic bloke and he helped my father start off on his own farm – I don't know whether he lent him the money or whether he guaranteed him to get the money from the bank. My father never said that as such, but I know, looking at what my father spent, he must have got some guarantee from somewhere.

Snow at Trengwainton
1947

In 1967 when our farm in Herefordshire was hit by the foot and mouth outbreak of course it was quite devastating, my father lost all his stock. Knowing he'd lost nearly everything, the Colonel lent him nearly one thousand pounds to get started again, and I think that was wonderful. I think my father never forgot that."

GEORGE HULBERT

Head Gardener, 1948 – 1961

George Hulbert was the Head Gardener at Trengwainton while it was privately owned by Colonel Edward Bolitho. Colonel Bolitho opened up the stream which runs alongside The Drive and meanders through the heart of the garden. Hulbert was instrumental in planting up the stream garden, one of Trengwainton's key features that takes centre stage during the summer months.

Below are some memories of George Hulbert, recounted by his daughter Kathy McPhee.

"George Hulbert was born in Badminton and did his journeymanship at Westonbirt Arboretum and surrounding Gloucestershire area. Prior to moving to Trengwainton he was at Spetchley Gardens in Worcestershire.

My Dad was definitely a plantsman, so was attracted to Trengwainton for the unusual plants and had numerous books on the subject. We still have a book of Kingdon-Ward's early expeditions.

He was asked to judge at quite a few of the local horticultural shows – Ludgvan, Falmouth, Newquay, Camborne and Penzance. At the time we were friendly

with the Head Gardener at Morrab Gardens, Joe Haines, and I remember them both going judging on a Saturday.

Dad went to Tresco once, to exchange plants with the Head Gardner, in the days when you had to travel across on the Scillonian.

He also used to go to St Michael's Mount to exchange plants with the Head Gardener. Once on a visit there, he put his keys and notebook on a table and came back home without them! Unfortunately Mum and I had gone out, so Dad had to wait for the next boat across to fetch the keys, as by then the tide had covered the causeway!

When Dad was Head Gardener, there were about six garden staff working with him. The Assistant Head Gardener was Billy Hicks, and I can remember Andrew, Frank and Sandy who were all local from Madron.

The garden was only open to the public a few times a year, Bank Holidays I think, and I remember walking around the garden with Dad, helping him put up wooden stakes with names on like Long Walk.

Early anemones and daffodils were boxed and sent to Covent Garden. Also hydrangea heads when they were going over were sent to Covent Garden (presumably to be used dried for flower arranging).

On Sundays, Mum and I walked up the back lane (the lane which is now part of the car park) with an aluminium milk churn to collect our milk from the farm.

What is now the car park was a wood with a path running through it to the back lane. In the two cottages near the present car park lived Mrs Quick and Mr and Mrs Penberthy, who worked on the estate.

By Trengwainton House was the cottage where the chauffeur, Mr Jenkin, lived. Nearby were the stables and yard where the Bolitho family kept their horses and ponies. I played quite often with Catherine and Hester Bolitho and they let me ride their ponies.

To the left from the chauffeur's cottage was the land to the farm. To the right, behind the stables was the Zig-Zag, where motorcycle races were held. We went to watch each year, as it was quite exciting.

At the top of the main drive, near the Bolithos' house there was an avenue of very tall trees. The rooks used to congregate in them at dusk and make a terrific din!

Towards the end of the time at Trengwainton, Dad bought a moped to save the constant walking up and down the drive. It caused much amusement!

Main house – with antique car 1957

Stable yard with
clock tower
1957

Clock tower in the
stable yard
1957

The Head Gardener's
cottage
1955

Dad retired at the end of 1960 and we moved to Chippenham, Wiltshire.

The Head Gardener's cottage is now the National Trust second-hand bookshop. When we lived there you went in the back door and immediately in front of you was the bathroom. I'm not sure when the room became a bathroom, but I seem to remember it was not long before we moved in. The telephone was installed in 1949, also shortly after we arrived.

To the left of the back door was a scullery with a long narrow storage room leading from it. This room had a large marble slab worktop at one end where we kept the old wooden 'safe' containing meats and cheese, in the days before fridges!

To the right of the backdoor was a kitchen area, which had a Rayburn. Leading from there was another living room, which had built in cupboards and a door

leading to the staircase. Beyond that was the front door with porch, a small hall area and then another living room. Upstairs there were three bedrooms and a landing window, from which you could see the Bothy. Floorboards had to be taken up to move some larger pieces of bedroom furniture in and out.

Past the back door there was a washhouse, which had a large copper boiler used for washing days. It was very steamy! Chopped wood was also stored in there. Next were some low storage containers with corrugated lids.

Whilst talking to an aunt recently, who stayed with us often in the cottage, she said my Dad had told her that originally the cottage had the windows at the back, but it was too dark, so they put windows in the front of the cottage and blocked the back windows up, except for the landing window. I must admit I always thought it strange that the front door with porch was at the back of the cottage."

The cottage today

Back entrance to the cottage, with Mum's bike against porch! Rockery and lawn area fencing porch

View through walled gardens and path leading up to cottage 1957

The Gardens

Looking straight across from the back door in the cottage, there was a small grass area enclosed on three sides with hedging. To the left of this, opposite the front porch, was a grass area with a rockery in the centre. This had hedging at the back and on one side. Behind the hedges were apple trees and a large Kitchen Garden area, used for vegetables.

Archway into the walled garden next to the cottage, 1957

Front of cottage, 1949 (My pram outside window)

Nerines against wall

Behind the wall with the nerines were steps leading up to another smaller enclosed area and then on to the path by the Bothy. Just here there was an enormous compost heap!

Standing at the front porch, to the left was the first door in the Walled Garden and under the wall was a large border with blackcurrants, redcurrants, white currants and gooseberries. Alongside the path leading up to the Bothy and greenhouses, on the left hand side also, there were more apple trees, seasonal vegetables and a palm tree. At the top of this Kitchen Garden area, towards the Bothy, there was a large bed of globe artichokes. For some reason I particularly remember them, as they used to fascinate me as a child! Also under the wall, near the globe artichokes, was a long narrow bed of nerines.

It doesn't look as if the Bothy has changed much. The tools were all kept in the same room along with the garden staff croust (snack). As you entered the Bothy, my Dad used the room to the right as an office and I think he kept rainfall records all the years he was there. Upstairs was kept for storing many racks of apples, pears and so on.

Walking to the right from the Bothy there was a hen coop, and a big shed that stored much larger tools. At the back was a hen run and boiler room (which Dad used to call the stokehole!). Beside that was a small greenhouse. It was a constant battle to keep foxes out of the hen run!

Selection of plants in the greenhouse

Amaryllis in the greenhouse, 1960

Behind the Bothy and greenhouse there was more utilised land and the carthorse from the farm, called Winston, came down to pull a plough to cultivate the land – which I used to love as I was allowed to ride the horse back to the farm!

Looking from the front of the cottage, the sloping garden bed was used for early lettuce, carrots etc. In the adjoining walled gardens were strawberry canes.

The remaining walled gardens had and probably still have a wide selection of unusual shrubs and trees and of course the famous *Magnolia campbellii*. I must confess as a child I wasn't too interested in the names of plants, I think I was more interested in food produce!!

Colonel Bolitho opened up the stream on the drive, and my Dad made his mark by planting moisture-loving plants to make a feature of the stream."

clockwise

Magnolia campbellii,
1960

Primula stream – Main
Drive, 1960

Path leading from
cottage to Bothy/
greenhouse. (Our black
spaniel that followed
my Dad around the
garden)

View through walled
gardens and path
leading up to cottage,
1950s

When my father was Head Gardener, bamboo canes were often cut and sent to London Zoo to feed the pandas.

Kathy McPhee, George Hulbert's daughter.

PETER HORDER

Head Gardener 1970 – 1999

"I was very fortunate and privileged to be appointed as Head Gardener at Trengwainton in the autumn of 1970, following nine years of practical horticultural training at the Garden House in Devon, the Hillier Nurseries in Hampshire, and Ingwersen's Alpine Plant Nursery in West Sussex, culminating in attending the two year student course at the RHS Garden at Wisley in Surrey.

I was interviewed by Major Simon Bolitho and Jimmy Scobie, the Trust's local agent. For the next 29 years, with five permanent members of staff, the garden gave me a fascinating and rewarding challenge to help care for a wide variety of tender plants, in a unique setting and generally favoured mild climate. From the start the main project was to maintain and strengthen the crucial windbreaks along the SW to NW boundaries of the garden, essential in providing shelter from prevailing winds. This proved to be an ongoing process, especially following storm damage where fallen trees opened up the defences.

Our walled gardens, with their sloping SW facing beds, provided micro-climates in which to experiment and cultivate many plants from the southern hemisphere amidst an impressive collection of well-established Asiatic magnolias and tender trees. These and a wealth of rhododendron species were the main representative

Sloping south west facing beds in the Kitchen Garden

Peter Horder c1970s

opp
The Terrace in winter

Rhododendron 'Loderii King George' in Azalea garden

64

plants for which Trengwainton is renowned. In a mainly spring-flowering garden, which can last from late January/February to mid-June, we were constantly aware of the need to provide interest and colour to summer visitors, without changing the character of the woodland garden. To this end we added summer flowering shrubs and perennials in landscaped borders alongside the lower lawns in front of Trengwainton House – under the watchful eye and guidance of Mr Graham Thomas, the Trust's Gardens Adviser, who was not impressed with us for taking on an extra area of garden near the entrance, to mark the Queen's Jubilee Year. "How would we manage to care for it with our current staff and trainee volunteers?" he asked! Other clearings along the woodland walk were planted with suitable subjects to blend with the broad swathes of mainly blue, plus green and white Hydrangeas, an eye-catching feature up and down the old carriage drive.

The use of water played an important part at Trengwainton – the main stream being fed from springs to the west of the Carn on higher ground. A new feature was proposed in the 1980s – to direct some of this water under the main drive, to feed a large landscaped pond at the higher part of the woodland walk. This proved to be a very successful project, which helped to draw visitors to the area, and onwards across the lower lawn to the highest point on The Terrace with fine views to The Lizard, and long borders planted for summer colour. Tree ferns are much in evidence around the new pond – the largest specimens are a prominent feature to the south of the lower drive. Gardens have to evolve in a sensitive manner, and I am pleased to see new areas being open to visitors, especially the orchard and gardens around the very successful tea room being used to their full potential."

IAN WRIGHT

Q&A with Ian Wright, Head Gardener at Trengwainton 2000 – 2006

How long were you Head Gardener at Trengwainton and what was it like then?

I arrived in 2000 from Hampshire, after a vigorous but (for me) successful interview process, with my wife and two children. Trengwainton had been a garden on my wish list of Head Gardener positions after visiting a few years earlier.

I wanted to work again with some of the more tender species which I was introduced to in the early part of my career whilst working on Tresco. The garden had had a period of limited resources so a backlog of work existed.

That said, the previous Head Gardener Peter Horder had done a great job in building the content of the plant collection. Addressing the much needed woody plant management was key, alongside not doing everything everywhere and spoiling the spirit of the place, which was a challenge.

I remained Head Gardener until 2006 when I started a secondment as Garden Adviser, firstly for Devon and Cornwall, then also leading on plant health management for the whole National Trust. I eventually moved on in 2009. I took on a role of National Specialist for Plant Health then Garden Adviser in the South West region.

I found Trengwainton had a certain character of its own and all that worked there were proud of it being 'a bit different'.

Kitchen Garden

What were your favourite areas/plants and why?

My favourite area is the low stream area. This is where the tallest tree ferns grow. I also like the five sections of walled garden that are home to the woody plant collection…a surprise around every corner!

My favourite plant has to be *Magnolia campbellii* bought from the Veitch nurseries in Exeter for 10/6… great value for money and on a good year starts flowering in February, well before many other gardens with the same plant. I also love the Bee House which is a rare servicing example and still in use!

Were there any high points or low points that affected the garden?

Low points were the battle against *Phytophthora ramorum*, and the ongoing challenge of securing funds to address the backlog, but I have to say that the National Trust did a fantastic job of supporting the garden and finding the much needed funds.

Were there any significant changes made during the period?

Introducing volunteers in number… they made a big difference.

What is your current role within the Trust?

I am a Consultancy Manager and I am the specialist lead for gardens in the South West and Wales. I also manage a team of other specialists that advise on archaeology, houses and the care of collections.

Anything you would like to add?

Trengwainton is a fantastic garden but you need to be brave to tame it as the speed of growth can quickly overtake all the effort you put in.

What had been your focus for the gardening during this time? Was there a vision for the garden?

The focus was improving the infrastructure…new drainage, paths, growing facilities. In the garden dealing with overgrown woody plants, restoring then managing the tree shelterbelts, tree planting and the restoration of the terrace planting. I also secured funding and restored the Kitchen Garden and Orchard area.

We also restored the Foliage Garden and upper well area. The vision in my mind was to get Trengwainton's profile back where it deserves to be, as one of the country's most exciting gardens and plant collections in a beautiful setting. A 'must go destination'. I believe we achieved this.

SPRING

Phil Griffiths, Head Gardener

As the garden starts to spring into life, here are some of the jobs we would do in spring.

- Start to protect plants from slugs and keep an eye out for other pests as they wake from winter hibernation.

- Plant summer-flowering bulbs, start planting out summer bedding at the end of the month.

- Mow the lawn on dry days.

- Hoe and mulch weeds to keep them under control.

- Watch out for late frosts on tender plants.

- Keep an eye on watering in the glasshouse on those hotter days, recycle water when possible.

- Regularly hoe off weeds.

- Open greenhouse vents and doors on warm days.

- Check for nesting birds before clipping hedges.

IN THE VEGETABLE GARDEN

Ian Willsdon (Kitchen Garden volunteer)
MARCH

Most organic gardens don't just contain vegetables but also a good selection of herbs and flowers.

These not only beautify the garden but can be useful in other ways. Herbs and flowers are perfect for bringing pollinators into the garden to ensure good crops.

The plants will also attract other insects which will attract other good garden predators such as birds and frogs. Many herbs are attractive to bees such as thyme, marjoram, sage, fennel, chives, hyssop and lavender. All of these are easy to grow from seed and can be sown under cover this month and will be ready to plant out in May. They can be planted in a separate herb bed or used as edging plants or intercropped with vegetables.

Flowers that are particularly effective in the garden for attracting a wide range of pollinators and predators include the following which you will find in the Kitchen Garden at Trengwainton.

Borage *(Borago officinalis)* – an excellent bee plant that flowers over a long period. It can renew the nectar in the flowers within 2 minutes of a bee visit.

Poached egg plant *(Limnanthes douglasii)* – bright yellow flowers that will flower early if sown in autumn. They also tend to be good self-seeders as are many of these flowers.

Phacelia tanacetifolia – a quick growing plant with numerous blue flowers that are highly attractive to bees. It can also be used as a green manure and can be sown from spring through to autumn in our climate.

Pot marigold *(Calendula officinalis)* – large orange or yellow flowers that attract many beneficial insects.

Garden nasturtium *(Tropæolum majus)* – can be found in an array of colours and can be grown as dwarf plants or climbers.

Sweet peas *(Lathyrus odoratus)* – worth growing for the colours and scent alone but thy are also good pollinator attractors.

Angelica *(Angelica archangelica)* – good for early nectar. The birds will like the seeds later on.

Rhododendron macabeanum

Illustration by
Dominica Williamson

APRIL

Our sloping beds at Trengwainton often feature in photographs of the garden. A main feature of the beds is ordered rows of multi-coloured lettuce.

To achieve this look sow varieties of lettuce such as red and green salad bowl or Lollo Rosso and Lollo Biondo in modules this month. Lettuce germinates best before temperatures get too high and can fail to germinate in a very sunny spell unless kept shaded and moist. Let the lettuce grow to a reasonable size before putting outside to harden off for a few days. If the plants are larger, healthy and in good condition before being planted out there is less risk of slug damage (as organic gardeners we don't use slug pellets).

Other ways of reducing slug damage are to check the weather, don't plant out if rain is expected, plant out in the mornings and water in well (an evening watering can make it easier for slugs to attack plants). Make patterns or rows to your own design.

MAY

May is the month to be sowing tender outdoor plants such as squash, sweetcorn, French and runner beans. These are best sown in the greenhouse in modules or pots ready to be planted out next month. We use peat-free compost with a good proportion of coir which helps with germination and watering and is environmentally friendly too. Most of these plants don't like too much root disturbance when young so you should choose bigger modules like root trainers or sow individually in pots no smaller than 5cm. Larger plants like squashes and pumpkins will need to be potted on into larger pots before they are planted out as they will grow quickly indoors and need more room to develop strong roots

before it is warm enough to plant them outside later on in June. These plants need to be kept well-watered indoors, particularly if the weather is sunny because if the plants dry out they are unlikely to recover and produce strong growing plants.

Timing when to plant out squash is crucial. If they are planted out too small they can be a target for slugs and snails, particularly if the weather turns wet. Also, if the weather turns cold after the squashes are planted out they can stop growing and rarely recover well.

When planting out squash it is a good idea to put some well-rotted manure or compost in the planting hole to increase moisture retention in the soil as these plants are greedy for water. This also means watering them in well straight after planting and ensuring they do not dry out if there is a prolonged dry spell. Most squashes need quite a bit of space and should be planted out 60-100 cm apart.

Pumpkins

opp

Sloping beds in the Kitchen Garden

RHODODENDRON MACABEANUM

Artist's notes

Dominica Williamson

Its native home is India in the states of Manipur and Nagaland. It was first found by George Watt in Manipur in 1882 at altitudes of between 2440 and 2740 metres.

It was introduced in Britain by Frank Kingdon-Ward. Its name commemorates Robert Blair McCabe, an Indian civil servant, who at one time was Deputy Commissioner of Manipur, and later the Inspector-General of Assam. McCabe came to an untimely end in the Shillong earthquake of 1897.

Ros Smith, a microprogator manager at Duchy College, works with Trengwainton as well as other heritage gardens across Cornwall to ensure that their plant collections continue for generations to come.

She has the rare *macabeanum* safely deposited in a walk-in fridge.

It takes years to grow into a magnificent bush with large glossy leaves that grow up to 30cm in length. They have a fawn down on their underside.

I totally fell in love with the large flowers. They sit in dense rounded trusses, and are a pale but rich lemony yellow bell-shaped form with a purple blotch in the throat. The stigma is the real showpiece though.

It's as showy as an elephant trunk, with a glossy orange mouth! I'd love to get it under a microscope and dissect it.

WELLS

Barbara Santi

At Trengwainton Garden you can find three wells:

Mally James' Well, accessed via the Lower Drive.
Unfortunately nobody knows who Mally James
was but the name can be seen written in maps and
documents by the surveyor Henry White in 1883.

Ladies' Well is found beyond the Upper Pond and
Bridge going towards the house lawn.

The following extract is taken from private documents
of the Bolitho family by the surveyor Henry White
in 1883. '*In the plantation between Flower Garden and
Carriage Drive there is a shoot, approached by a flight of steps.
This shoot was constructed by Sir Rose Price in whose time it
was known as the 'Ladies' Well.' From it water was procured
by the Baronets daughters for the purpose of watering flowers
to which then grew in a small garden near the shoot which
had been laid out for them exclusively.*'

Around the corner from *Ladies Well* as you take the
path to the right you will find a third well (name
unknown). Gareth Wearne, Trengwainton gardener for
29 years (as of 2018), was once told that the well could
possibly have been used for washing the horses' hooves
and carriages before approaching the house as it is
situated on the original drive. However its true origins
have been lost in the mists of time.

> *The Hydra was abundant in the ponds at Trengwainton; it is only found in
> a few places on the cliffs at Penzance and Marazion and not in any
> other parts of the county.*
>
> **The 1845 Penzance Guide**

Ladies' Well

Mally James' Well

Well

ORAL HISTORIES

GARETH WEARNE

From filmed interview, 2016

EARLY DAYS AND WORKING FOR THE NATIONAL TRUST

"I used to come up here as a tacker[28], my family have always been involved with the gardens, my mother's great-uncle, great-great-uncle and auntie used to help in the gardens. Great-uncle used to work on the farm and his son used to work in the gardens. I used to come into the gardens with my cousin Roger, and my uncle when they had open days. Even from the days I could walk, I used to come in the gardens, with the family. I used to go off round the farm and the house with my uncle. I was just amazed at the colours of the rhododendrons mainly. Even as a tacker, I could look at them, just couldn't believe the colours.

As soon as I went to school I thought I wouldn't mind being a gardener at Trengwainton, and all the way through my school life I had that at the back of my mind. Then one day I had the time to study for horticulture, so I did, went off to college, and got my qualifications. I thought, I don't suppose I'll ever get a job there, but it was in the back of my mind. I worked on a local farm, in a market garden for a while, and I managed to get a job on Bolitho estates at Trewidden gardens. They always sent a person across in the summer to help at Trengwainton, so I worked at Trewidden in the winter, for one year, and then came across to Trengwainton and a job came up here and I applied for it, and managed to get the job. They've been stuck with me ever since.

Gareth Wearne

I couldn't believe I got the job working for the National Trust. When I was asked to prune a bush, I was scared to prune it because it was the National Trust's bush and it felt like you was vandalising something that belonged to the National Trust.

I still can't believe it in all honesty you know, working in the gardens like this for the Trust, it's pretty amazing really.

I remember the first day I was here I was pulling bamboos out on the top. Bamboos died all over the world at the same time.

We thought it was voodoo or something happening or global warming but it wasn't, most of the bamboos were cultivated from the same stock, as they all came into the country at the same time.

They all reached maturity at the same time, and they all flowered at the same time. That was my first job digging them out. I remember a lot more bamboo in the garden; you could get lost in it, and walk in between the clumps.

Riley told me there were tigers in them, my cousin said "there's tigers in ere, you got to be careful."

A total change of emphasis is that at one time when you worked in the gardens you didn't work with anyone else, that was it, you were the gardener here and you did gardening, and that's all you did. If a visitor asked you a question, I was told to keep looking down, keep working, but answer the question politely but don't engage with them, you're wasting too much time.

Now it's the other way round, the customer comes first. You go out of your way, and the people you meet are fascinating, I never thought I'd be working with schools doing the Dig for Victory here, exploring wartime, it's just amazing all the different gardening clubs, different people you meet through all these events.

That's another thing, we never did events, you just came to the garden and went home. Now we have different events, the Pumpkin Day and the Christmas do, it's brilliant, total change.

ANCIENT LANDSCAPE

To me Trengwainton is at the centre of a very ancient landscape, so even two/four thousand years ago there was stuff going on in this area, so I think there has always been bits and pieces going on.

Just up over the hill there are mines, clay works and so on, so it's quite busy and the families have been very busy in industry. The Bolitho family with the tin smelting and stuff, and involved in Newlyn, it's quite a list of industry around here with the mines. At one point we were clearing up tree damage from a hurricane that came through the garden about twenty/twenty five years ago and the chap I was working with just leant over and pulled out this massive great flint knife from the Bronze Age so there was something here a very long time ago. (Please see page 19 for more information and photo).

TRENGWAINTON GARDEN

At one time there was the Head Gardener, myself and Brian with no volunteers. Hardly any kit, we used to bring in our own kit to mend the mowers, we had an old mower that came from the 1950s. It was so worn out, it used to cut on one side so you had to be careful how you cut or you got ridges in the grass. That broke down mysteriously one day and we had to have a new one, but it's certainly changed. Now we've got all modern kit, all modern machinery, you couldn't ask for anything more, it's really good.

I was told that Trengwainton was an experimental garden, so I suppose now, this is the time with all these new diseases coming into the country with different insects and pests, it would be nice to bring it back to an experimental garden to see what we can grow.

The garden's quite linear; you've got The Terrace right at the top which backs onto the old steep hill climb, which a lot of people remember. It's an ancient trackway which goes up that way. Our boundary goes round the back of the house, and then it comes down a drive, quite a long drive, with the garden both sides. Then you get to the bottom and you have the Walled Garden and Jubilee and areas like that. If you forget something when you leave here by the time you get to the top you regret it, because you either do without it or it's a long jog back. I can get down the hill quite quickly, but going back up I think it's getting steeper.

The Terrace up the top has beautiful views over Mount's Bay, the sea and the hill fort, you can see the Lizard and all over there. Then you come down through the wooded area and the top fern tree glade and you got the historic wells.

Down through the stream, then the lower tree fern area and Jubilee Garden which was made in the Queen's Silver Jubilee that was just woodland there. Then you've got the walled gardens just here, vegetables and tender plants, it's got a bit of everything, got a stream garden, got walled gardens, got semi-formal gardens around the house and The Terrace so it's nice, there is a bit of everything and not just one thing.

TRENGWAINTON PLANTS

Frank Kingdon-Ward went to Assam and Burma on a plant collecting expedition, and what would happen was the families would give him money and sponsor him, but he would have to bring back cuttings and seeds for them and then there would be a bit of shuffling around to see who got what, and we've had some of the Kingdon-Ward's plants from Assam and Burma. He was one of the last plant collectors, because a lot of them who went in Victorian times and before were sponsored by the big families, so you're talking about the 1800s, whereas Kingdon-Ward was in 1927/8 when he bought the specimens back to here. A lot of wealthy local families chipped in and put in money to it to bring stuff back.

We're on the Camellia Walk, which is the lower walk, and it branches out there and goes onto the other Camellia Walk, and it's all different camellias and fantastic to see when they're all in flower. Again, we have had to cut these back a little bit because last winter was so wet they had a disease called *Pythium* which is what's killed all the escallonia off in the area, and it's just a fungus caused by the humid weather. So we cut a lot of the greenery back, and hopefully that will give the roots a chance to establish themselves again.

The rhododendrons are my favourite. The magnolias are absolutely fantastic and obviously the camellias. Some of the tender plants we grow come from the Sudan and Zaire. Up until these last couple of frosts we've had them still flowering in January. To be able to grow plants like that... you just look at it – it still amazes me.

Another change I have seen is the sudden oak death that's come through the gardens and killed a lot of the rhododendrons off, that's quite upsetting to see as some of them were like old friends. You see them flower and they go on, but all of a sudden they're dead, and you've got to drag them out and burn them.

Rhododendrons have a bad name because the *Rhododrendron Ponticum* that everybody knows, which is the wild one, is slightly hybridised which is why it goes ballistic everywhere. I'm not saying this for sure, but I was told by the propagator at the National Trust that what we think of as a wild rhododendron isn't.

It's a beautiful ground cover, not much good for wildlife, nothing lives under it, or in it, or on it. It's poisonous; it will kill goats and horses. The problem with it is it does host *Phytophthora* (sudden oak death) so that's why places like Madron Carn had a ground that was all grubbed out and burnt, which in the long run is good because you get more wildlife on the place. I think that might be one of the reasons it's spread down through the gardens, it was all around in all honesty, it's everywhere. *Ponticum*, it was a beautiful thing and to stand on Madron Carn and see that in full colour was absolutely fantastic, you couldn't have painted a picture that beautiful really, but unfortunately it was a host for this disease so we had to get rid of it.

The trouble being we're still not sure which rhododendrons have got ponticum genetics in them, so we don't know if that ponticum gene is bringing the *Phytophthora* even now. There's research being done into that, although unfortunately Ash Die Back came along, so Defra are going into that, and leapfrogging from one disease to the next and I think *Phytophthora* is on the back burner for the moment.

It sounds soppy but some of the rhodies when they're going you do everything you can, like cut them back, prune them, mulch them, it's like putting a friend on a life support system, you're hoping he'll come through but, eh, I don't know… yes some do respond, some don't… we've had some successes but a lot more don't, so it's very sad. Camellias are nice but they are all basically red, white or pink, whereas rhodies you can get any colour, from almost a blackish purple, right through to the whites. You've got the oranges, you get vireya rhodies which come from hot countries like Cambodia and Vietnam which I've tried in the gardens. I'd love to try them again because they are almost like a lilly

flower, a totally different rhodie. If you planned it you could get a rhodie to flower in your garden every month of the year.

The Bolithos were instrumental in breeding some really nice rhodies at some stage and they got awards of merit and medals from London and everything for the colours. There's one called *japonica*, there's *macabeanum* that's in the garden at Trengwainton. There's a whole lot of rhodies that were bred at Trengwainton, some of which we've lost, and there was one called 'Ding Dong' named after the engine house on the hill. Mr Alfred Creek, was the Head Gardener at one stage and he was an intensive plant breeder and he bred a lot of different plants, mainly rhodies, and there's one called 'Creek's Cross' but we've still got to get it recognised by the RHS and get it registered hopefully. There's a massive great large pink head on it like that, beautiful. He bred a lot of stuff and he named it after local villages like Madron, Morvah, it's quite nice.

I remember the last 'Ding Dong' in the garden, but to be able to breed it again, you can never be sure what you actually put into it to get the results, that's the trouble, so there's a lot of history of plant breeding at Trengwainton, which would be nice to bring back.

The big *Magnolia campbellii* is one of the record trees in Britain. It's a massive tree and it's got a bromeliad growing in it, which you don't see very often in this country. That was planted in 1927 or around that era.

Now so far as I know there's a horse buried under it, because one of the Bolithos died and his horse was buried under that tree. I think it came from Treseder's Nursery up at Truro. That's quite a large one, but we've had problems with it because to force the flowers we've got to cut the water shoots off and that makes it get a fair old withey on it. Now years ago, they would have kept them up with the wires to tension the branches up, well that causes them to get very thin but keep growing, so now we've got nylon straps that stretch so you can get a little flexing in the stem and the trunk and it makes it a stronger tree. My favourite one is called the 'Lanarth', it's a very dark purple that's named after 'Lanarth' out on the Lizard, that's a beautiful one.

THE STREAM

I can remember the old Major, Colonel Bolitho's father, Major Simon (he was a colonel, that's where it gets confusing!) telling me that before his time the drive was a field, and the river was roughly where the draining ditch was. It could've explained why during the summer when there was very little water coming down, the moles were going into the banks for worms, and then when the river did start to flow again it goes down the mole holes and disappears, so we're forever going on plugging up little holes in the side of the stream and so on.

I was told by the old Major that there was quite a deep drainage ditch there at one time. I would have said it was the same time that the drive was built, that was way back because the Old Walk used to be the main drive at one time. The Head Gardener Hulbert planted up the stream in the fifties.

THE HISTORIC WELLS

The bottom well is called Mally James' well but that's all we know about that one. We didn't even know that the top one on the inside, the more woodland one, was a well. I always thought it was a shaft because we used to go in there and burn rubbish.

At one time, it was just solid woodland, and we used to stay clear of it because we thought it was subsiding.

Then the Colonel wanted a bit more privacy around the house so we moved all the paths down slightly because at one time you could walk right round the house and it wasn't nice for him bringing up a young family with people looking in the windows.

Well, when we moved through with the digger we scratched away the top to see what it was and uncovered a well. From reading between the lines and from what I've heard people say, at one time the ladies of the house wanted a little bit of a garden up there. It wasn't trendy to be a gardener in those days and if you had a suntan it showed you worked outside, you had to have bleached skin, so the garden was under the trees so you wouldn't get a suntan and I think that was their well. The other well I was told was for washing the horses and carriages because that's on the original drive up to the house, so if you were coming to present yourselves at the house you washed the carriages down and perhaps the horses' legs and so on.

THE BOLITHOS

Colonel Simon was known as Major, and he said "I'll stay Major until father dies," but by that time everybody knew him as Major so it stuck, so I've worked under two family members, Major Simon and now Colonel Edward. The old Major was a very dignified chap; I used to see him coming down through the gardens and my blood would run cold and I used to feel guilty but I hadn't actually done anything. If he looked at you, you'd think "I'm in trouble here," but you weren't necessarily, it was just guilty conscience I suppose. He was brought up in different ways.

Colonel Edward comes around now and you talk to him face to face and don't feel intimidated, whereas the old Major had that persona about him, that he would talk to you and was nice as pie, there was no problem with that but I was always scared of him to be quite honest.

I remember when we were blasting the stubs during the storm we were all hiding behind trees and lying down so as we wouldn't get any shrapnel and I turned around and there was Major Simon beside me just standing up looking at us and I felt a bit stupid really [laughs].

He would come round once or twice a week with the Head Gardener and say what he wanted done in the garden, and he was really hands on and would layer a lot of things. If the old Major saw a rhodie or something that was dying which he wanted to propagate up he would get us to layer it and that's why a lot of the old rhodies haven't got any lower branches on them because they are all layered to propagate up again and we haven't done a lot of that for a long time what with the diseases and stuff like that.

Colonel Edward still comes around, he comes with Phil once or twice a week perhaps, whenever he's here. Has a walk around the garden, hears what's going on. The family still have input into the gardens. The National Trust discusses it with them so they are in the loop and the family might come up with an idea, and swap it around.

Dig for Victory Plot

We get certain projects every year as part of the overall planning, and one of them might be education, and school children, or vegetable production or whatever, and you've got to sit down once a year and go through it with Phil, the Head Gardener. A few years back the schools were doing the Second World War so I thought of this project 'Dig for Victory' whereby you could get the school children in and show them how to produce vegetables. It frightened me a little bit when some of the children couldn't recognise basic vegetables, because they'd never dealt with them before.

So it was nice to bring the children in here. I'm in a Living History group, so every now and then I put on a Home Guard uniform and show them the rations and give them the outfits and tools they would have used in those days. I've had some good feedback from that and really enjoyed working with school kids.

The Walled Gardens

Sir Rose Price came here and started planting up the garden as we see it now. He made a lot of his money out of slavery in the sugar plantations in Jamaica, and built these walled gardens here with the red brick walls – it's a fair old status symbol for this area because everything else is granite. Now how true it is, I don't know, but I was always told it was built by Napoleonic prisoners and I've always wondered ever since I've been coming here why the walls just stopped dead there (at the beginning of the Camellia Walk), and I've always wondered whether it was when those prisoners were repatriated.

They built up to here and then they went home, and the wall stopped there...or whether Rose Price died? There's got to be some reason why the next compartment being built here just stopped. It doesn't make sense, but I don't suppose we shall ever know really.

When I first came here I was told by the old Head Gardener that the vegetable production areas in the walled gardens were exactly the same size as Noah's Ark, as mentioned in the Bible, measured in spans and cubits. I believe it's from a man's elbow to his forefinger, depending on how big the man is and if you look it up there all different lengths anyway, but roughly between 10 and 21 inches or something like that I think it is. We measured it and it's within a few inches of what's mentioned in the Bible so it does lean that way a little bit. I was also told that the Cornish hedge that runs around the top was the same size as Solomon's Temple. We don't know why he did that either. Whether he was trying to buy his way into heaven as he had a guilty conscience, I don't know.

Well the gardens are open to southwesterlies and the entire garden is designed against southwesterly winds, so all the wind break is heavily planted on the south-western side of the garden, and it does stop a lot of battering. Over the recent years we've noticed there's been a lot more northeasterlies coming in which sneaks into the back of the gardens and knocks the trees over. When it comes off the back, the taller trees are open to storm damage so we're having a few problems with that.

It's nice to have a bit of tradition, but gardens are, how can I put it, they're a rolling project really, nothing stays the same forever and especially a living plant.

A lot of the garden, because they've got a conservation plan, people like to see them the same year after year after year. Keeping that balance is hard going really, but nothing stands still, that's the trouble, and then when you do start knocking some of the plants back people get a bit upset. It's just one of those things, it's the way it works. I should like to see some of it stay the same and some of it change in all honesty.

HURRICANE

About twenty-six years ago we had a hurricane and we came to work in the morning at half-past seven, and by eight o'clock we had trees down. Brian, who used to work here, and myself, we went out on the drive to see what was happening.

We thought we'd better get back in quick because there were branches flying, and we looked up across the field here, towards the farm. There were Evergreen oaks and the tops of them were like massive trees just snapping off and sailing through the air horizontally.

We couldn't comprehend what was happening, so we thought we'd better get back in, why, I don't know, as there was no more protection there than anywhere else. By four o'clock we had about two hundred trees down and another hundred damaged, so we had to cut them down and had a lot of the tree surgery done on them. I was on chain saw for about a year, every day for a year, just cutting timber, just cleaning through the gardens bit by bit.

Some people did take photos, but I didn't want to look at them because it just reminded you of how much damage had been done, and we didn't like looking at them. Now, I wish I had taken more photos, because you look back in time and think you can't actually remember how much damage was done, it's just beyond belief!

THE FUTURE

I would like to get my thirty years under my belt, that's another couple of years and we'll see then, see what happens. I've been here all my life really."

DAVID MCINTOSH

Trengwainton Beekeeper (retired in 2016)

From filmed interview, 2016

"I started beekeeping with my father when I was seven. When I got married we went to Canada and lived on an Indian reservation for five years. Then we came back and I worked in a mainstream school for seven years as a science teacher. I then got a job as a Deputy Head at a special school and on my first day there a swarm of bees landed on the window. So I went down to the woodwork shop and made a hive, and that's how I started again.

My father kept bees in the garden, just two hives, he didn't bother with a veil or bee suit or wellingtons, he would go down dressed as he is. When I was little I went down with him and I got stung so we came back and got a piece of netting I think from the window, put it round my head and off we went – that was the start of it. No gloves, no bee suit, no wellingtons, just a veil to keep them away from my eyes. He kept bees till he died at 86. I first started keeping bees myself probably when I was ten. My father said, "these are yours, look after them." So I did.

He took me to a hive in his garden and we worked the bees, just played with them really. They were his pets. He loved them. He taught me the basic handling skills of not being clumpy and how to be gentle with them and he always said that the danger of handling bees is when you kill the first one, because when you squash it, it gives off a pheromone and then all the others will attack. If you get stung you have to scrape it out quickly and smoke the site otherwise the bees will come and sting the same place.

David, the bee keeper

80

first built, that's why there are so many entrances. A skep is what they used to keep bees in years ago.

They'd sit the skep on the table in the bee house, the bees would go in, build their own comb in there, natural comb, and then come the end of the summer they'd sit it on top of another skep and turn it upside down and drive the bees to the top, and then scrape the honey out. That's one way. The bee house at Trengwainton was designed to house 12 skeps.[29]

If you hurt a bee then they'll start to get alarmed and give off a smell of…bananas…and if you smell bananas and you are demonstrating you close the hive straight away because they can get very aggressive.

A fellow called David ten years ago came to me and said would I help renovate the bee house at Trengwainton, so I came over here, and it was tumbled down, but I said no I won't, I didn't want to get involved in the building of it. I said if you renovate it then I will put bees in it. The house was designed to have skeps in it when it was

I try and stop the bees from swarming, keep them healthy and get some sort of a crop. But mainly it's fun.

My wife is not very keen on honey and even less when I try to process it in the kitchen. There was a particular occasion when my extractor, which I had on wedges, tipped over and 70 pounds of honey went across the kitchen floor. Which she was not best pleased about."

BILLY BARR

From filmed interview, 2016

MY FATHER AND TRENGWAINTON

"My name is William Barr and my connection with Trengwainton is when I left school in 1941 my father worked on the estate as a mason and obviously in them days where the father worked they usually tried to get the boy a job. I wanted a job on the estate as a general worker but the only job that was going at the time was working in the garden so I worked in the garden from

1941. I stayed then till 1944 and then I joined up and got demobbed in 1947, and then I came back here and worked at Trengwainton for about another 12 months. I think having been in the forces and mixing with a lot of different people and enjoying a different type of life I felt a bit restrained working in the garden then, and I wanted to go further afield.

My father was Richard Barr but was known locally as Dickie. When my father came out of the forces I think he went back to mining for a while, he was mining before joining the forces but then eventually he met Colonel Bolitho and got a job on the estate. He was then working as an assistant to the estate mason. He used to work all over the estate on all the farms that the Bolithos owned at that time which were many, he would go out to outlying places doing roofs, drainage, well everything you can think of. I think the mason was called Smith and when he died I think his wife was moved out into some almshouses and then my father moved into that house which was West Lodge, near Tremethick Cross, so we all moved in there. We didn't live in a Trengwainton property all the time. Prior to my father moving to West Lodge we lived in Heamoor. He was doing the same job till he died actually. At a guess I think it was about 25 years working on the estate.

One job he did do which is quite interesting, as I understand (I wasn't involved), a lot of the water at Trengwainton House and the farm came from up on the Carn and the hilly parts and there was a water course that they laid with pipe work that went right down to feed Trengwainton House and the farm, and I think I'm right in saying some of the water came down to the garden as well. One of his jobs was to look after the watercourse which was quite involved because it was right up in Madron Carn, so you are going between rocks, ferns and gorse bushes and quite often he couldn't find it, he'd have to spend some time looking for the manhole covers. Apparently it used to get blocked and two or three men would have to go up and unblock it.

We had six-hour days then and got paid on a Saturday lunchtime. Saturday dinner-time was a long way off because we all wanted our money. I was only 14 then, so it was a matter of going home on Saturday and handing your wage packet over to mum and then she used to give me 2s 6d to enjoy myself for the rest of the week.

I think in a way it was a little bit of a disappointment because when I had visualised working at Trengwainton I thought I was going to be working on the estate and be a general worker with a bit of travelling around, visiting various farms and different areas. And then when I was told I was going to work in the gardens I don't think it was quite as attractive to me at that time as it would have been climbing a ladder and clearing some gutters.

It was hard work a lot of the time because where you use tractors for various things now, in them days most of the work was with a Cornish shovel. Anyone will tell you that in work today you quite often say 'pick and shovel', but in those days it was literally pick and shovel. All the ground was turned with a Cornish shovel.

You dug your trenches, put your manure in, turned over another trench and so on and so forth. It was pleasant doing it because in the end you saw a nice bit of turned soil and also you were ready to plant then and it gave you a certain amount of satisfaction.

In them days we used to go up to the ponds and keep the ponds clean and certain areas for the shooting because they used to have shooting parties and that was all done around that area.

THE LAND GIRLS AT TRENGWAINTON

We had Land Army girls at Trengwainton as well. We had quite a few men working here and I think we had three or four Land Army girls at different times, they were all involved with most of the work. It was quite good actually, to put things into perspective, if you got a group of men then you've got a group of girls working with you, you always had more fun. So we all wanted to work with one of the Land Girls!

GARDENING JOBS

A big thing that we did then was to send a lot of produce up to Covent Garden market, and to the navy, army and air force institutes at Pall Mall London. We used to send away lettuce for instance in crates, leeks and that sort of stuff. We grew quite a few potatoes. That was a big job actually because that involved digging the trenches for the Land Army girls to put the potatoes in, then of course we used to harvest them as well. A lot of the produce was sent from the farm. They were in it in a bigger way than we were.

The gardens used to supply the house with vegetables. We used to take food up to the house everyday. One thing I do remember is that we turned the ground up at the lawn in front of the house and grew various vegetables up there. When the Land Girls were here two Land Girls used to collect the produce that the cook said she wanted for the next day and then they would pull the goods up the drive with a four-wheeled trolley – one girl pulling and the other girl pushing and then they delivered the produce in the kitchen and they'd get a note of what the cook wanted for the next day. That was a regular job for the girls, that was a couple of hours in the morning.

child – it was quite nice really. And of course we all had to make a fuss of the corgi dog.

One of Mr Thomas' pastimes was bees. In them days we used to get swarms of bees and Mr Thomas would always have a phone call to say there was a swarm of bees somewhere and at that time he had a motorbike and side car and Clifford went out with him once to collect a swarm. It was unfortunate that when he got stung by a bee his face swelled up, quite serious, and he couldn't do it after that so the next swarm of bees I had to go! It was something we never looked forward to doing, we would go out with Mr Thomas with his short ladder, he'd have his ladder up and you'd be underneath with a basket while he shock the branch to get rid of the bees.

> *Everything was more free then. As a young man or a boy – we always had ropes and trees in the woods.*

There was the Head Gardener George Thomas. There was another chap called Sydney Hall who used to work four days a week. He had his own smallholding actually, he was quite important here, he was a good gardener. Then there was an old chap called Ross King, lovely fella, he used to walk down from a place up on the Carn everyday, I think he was about 70 then. Quite a hard man. Then there was Clifford Pollard and Tom Pollard his brother. Then Leonard Simmonds, he went in the army as a dispatch rider, he was from Madron. There was another chap called Guy, that was his surname, and another boy called Edgar, then we had several Land Army girls most of the time. Clifford Pollard was the same age as me. Then there was another chap called Roy Trembath, he was another young man, and Edgar – we were the only four young men.

Mr and Mrs Thomas had their first child while I was at Trengwainton and that was really a big deal at that time. When Mrs Thomas had the baby we went in to the Head Gardener's cottage in turns to have a look at the

In the open shed that's where we used to sharpen all the tools, that was a young man's job to turn the wheel for the Head Gardener to sharpen all the sheers and anything you wanted to sharpen, especially on a wet day. You would probably spend the day turning the grinding wheel.

I recently came up to look around which I hadn't done for a long time and when I went down to the garden and looked at the beds, I thought, hello there's seaweed! In the old days you always saw seaweed on the ground, in particular in the Gulval area. Farmers used to use it a lot because they were nearer to the sea and we used to have seaweed occasionally as well. I remember seeing the horse and carts in the forties going out onto the

beach at Ponsandane. They'd put too much seaweed on the cart and the wheels would sink down and the poor horses were struggling. Then they would have to bring another team of horses that someone else had and tow them out. That happened quite often. The main time was around October after the spring equinox tides when all the seaweed broke up and was washed up on the beach. There were tonnes of it on the beach and the farmers took advantage of it, it was a natural fertiliser.

Threshing was a time we used to go up to Trengwainton farm and also lopping sugar beat we used to send away a lot of that time, so they were jobs that took us from here to the farm. In them days we had a little pony and trap that used to go between the rows of broccoli. We used to trim it then throw it in the little cart and of course we'd go to the end of the field and tip it up in piles and some of the girls and men as well would pack the broccoli.

We had various fruit, we had nectarines, peaches and that sort of thing and obviously grapes in the greenhouse and we grew a lot of tomatoes then as well.

Once you harvested the plants then the ground had to be manured and turned so that was all with a shovel so it was all time consuming. We were going to and fro with wheelbarrows all the time and spreading it and turning it in and then when you planted it you had to dig it again with a shovel to make trenches to put the potatoes in."

A regular thing we used to do is pick snowdrops, bunch them up and send them away.

TRENGWAINTON HILL CLIMB

A personal view

Linda Collins, Project Volunteer

As a child, I remember being taken to Trengwainton Hill Climb events in the 1950s and early 1960s. My father was a General Practitioner in Penzance from 1947. His name was Dr W.J. Turney, known as Jack. He soon became a member of the West Cornwall Motor Club which organised the Hill Climb events. His name is on the programme covers for 1950 and 1951 (spelled incorrectly) and listed as 'Time Keeper'. I believe this is an error – he was the Medical Officer on duty in case of accidents. In subsequent years his senior GP was the Medical Officer. My memories of the events as a young girl – lots of men and boys with cars and motor cycles and tool kits, very loud revving of engines, and the strong smell of Castrol oil! We were instructed by parents to always stand on the inside corner of the Zig-Zag, without understanding what the 'inside corner' meant! Apparently this was the safest place to be in case anyone skidded off the track. Everyone cheered the riders and drivers as they went past, but we were soon bored with the adults' sport, and would run off and play in the woods, climbing trees and building shelters, until the picnic came out!

The West Cornwall Motor Club was created by the amalgamation of the Euny Lelant Motor Club and the Penzance Motor Club in 1933. The purpose was to run trials, rallies and treasure hunts for both motor cyclists and drivers of cars. (*The Cornishman*, 25 January 1934). In 1938 Col Bolitho kindly granted permission for the club to use the steep Zig-Zag cobbled track through the woods at Trengwainton for a speed hill climb for the first time. The event proved very popular and was quickly established as part of the motor sport calendar, with Easter and August Bank Holiday meetings each year. These attracted drivers from many parts of the country to West Cornwall to participate.

Over 80 competitors took part in an evening event in August 1939, including Donald Healey, the famous international driver, and W.P. Uglow from Callington, and a large crowd of spectators cheered them on. (*The Cornishman*, 17 August 1939).

Naturally the war years brought an end to motor sport activities, but they were resumed in 1946 in appalling weather conditions, when the two-wheeled classes had to be cancelled. The BBC were in attendance to record the event.

The following year members of the club prepared the track and laid a concrete surface, with special corrugated areas on the corners to aid tyre grip and thus avoid accidents, especially in wet weather when there was a higher risk of damage and slower times. 1947 also saw the retirement of Leslie Pascoe, the President of the West Cornwall Motor Club. Arnold White of Madron was elected in his place, and this marked the beginning of a remarkable dynasty of prize winning motor cyclists, with the whole family engaged in the sport over many years at Trengwainton.

Sadly, the last Trengwainton Hill Climb took place in April 1973 following an inspection by the RAC. Today the track has returned to nature and the woods are silent, and the evocative sounds and smells of past events are preserved in the memories of those who organised and participated in the sport and their enthusiastic audience.

My thanks go to Mr Roger White
for his help with this article.

Snowdrops

PETER SCRASE

From filmed interview, 2017

LIFE AT 'POLCLOSE'

"My whole early life, from my birth in 1937 through to 1945, was spent at Trengwainton proper. There were connections after that period of time when we moved into the centre of Madron, at Fore Street, Madron.

The house that we lived in, Polclose, was off Whitegates, which was the entrance to the farm from the crossroads that included Wishing Well Lane. The house itself consisted of a front porch, a sitting room, off of which was the staircase, which we called 'the little road to Bedfordshire' as children, a kitchen with a Cornish Range to one side and beyond that a scullery, which had the copper for boiling the clothes. Outside there would have been a mangle and a privy – an earth closet which my father emptied, once a week, into the front garden. The front garden, in our time, had vegetables in it. There were three bedrooms upstairs.

There was an outside water tap. There was no electricity; we had oil lamps and candles for going to bed, which we did like. We loved the flickering of the candles and the changing shadows on the walls.

To the rear – we kept hens – there was a chicken coop. We used to enjoy going in there; we found it very soothing when the chickens were roosting and were making their sounds. We found it very comforting. To the rear of the house, beyond the privy, there was a hedge which we jumped over and two fields away took us to Madron Carn.

In the house, we lived with my parents, me, my sister, Sally who was three and half years older than me

Norah and Harry Scrase en route 1930s

and latterly from 1943, my late brother Martin. My mother's father came in 1943 from Belgravia Street, Penzance and my father's mother came from Sussex in 1931, where she had been housekeeper for a literary parson. So, we were 'packed in' somewhat. Therefore, in the bedrooms we had separate rooms for the paternal grandmother and maternal grandfather.

The three of us, my brother would be in a cot and my sister and I had camp beds, were near our parents' double bed.

TRENGWAINTON

Trengwainton was a wonderful place. My mother loved it and we all did. 'Hats off' to Trengwainton from that point of view. In those days, you had access to the Carn, now it is totally overgrown and I'm saddened by that, it should be accessible. You'd get up onto the Carn itself and you'd look down to where there were rhododendrons and through them were growing conifers and they were very closely knitted together. There was one point you could climb and because it became so trodden down us children were able to walk on top of the rhododendrons.

I was talking to someone who is slightly older than me and he recalls that it was at least one hundred yards and you looped around these conifers that were growing through them and it was called 'The Burma Road'. That relates to, obviously, wartime experiences. We were all fed lines from the radio and cinema and newspapers about the campaigns in the Far East and one of them was the route between China and Burma. So, we named our route 'The Burma Road'. It's well known among the elderly now in Madron who clambered all over those trees. We also went on the Carn to bake our potatoes. We would light a little fire and put our potatoes on sticks and eat them semi-raw.

WARTIME

You have to put me in context. I was two when the war started, I was eight when the war ended and therefore during my early life, all at Polclose, it was the centre of a great deal of activity. We were allowed to roam freely, I seem to recall the old Colonel giving me bamboos to make bows and arrows. I saw the New Zealand ferns and all the other exotic plants as being 'normal' plants and was surprised when they weren't elsewhere. So, yes, it was quite a privileged upbringing from that point of view – we roamed freely all over the place. Occasionally we got shouted at, like my sister recalls. We collected primroses and daffodils and wandered down and got crab apples near the ice-house and rambled around

the ponds, freely, and all over the Carn. So, yes, it was quite an experience really. We saw the back of The Big House; you got a sense of your position within the hierarchy, a little, although we weren't employed by Trengwainton. I think the other Trengwainton Houses were inhabited by people who worked for the Colonel. Why we became tenants in 1931 at Polclose, I'm not sure, but my guess is, my father was big in the founding of The British Legion in Madron, which was very important to returning servicemen from the First War.

He became, eventually, Vice Chairman of the Madron Branch. I think there may even have been a connection with the Colonel through the Mesopotamian Campaign that my father was in, in 1916. I've got a feeling that the old Colonel, who was a professional soldier, may have been out in that region and so may have looked sympathetically on someone who was looking for a house that had similar ex-service connections.

My father was registration officer. One of the reasons that he was registration officer was that he had a car. We went to exotic places like Heamoor and the Bone Valley up to Carfury, across to Newbridge, and so on, right up above Madron Carn.

My abiding memory of the car was very joyful. You would sit on the back of the car, it was an open car, you'd be driving maybe into the setting sun, up towards what we called 'Ding Dong turn' up at Bull's View and the countryside there still blows my mind away. It's very, very special. So, sitting on the back of this marvellous car, chugging along through open roads was just a wonderful experience.

I have many recollections of wartime. I have one vague memory of people camped between Madron Carn, our house and Home Farm, Trengwainton.

All I can remember is going down to Home Farm and hearing "Toot-tootle-toot-toot-toottoot, toot-tootle-toot-toot-toot", and I believe it was a bugle call that came from the cookhouse door calling people in for grub. I don't know whether that's right or whether that's some sort of figment of my imagination as a child. Also on the field opposite, two down, a light aircraft caught its wheels in a hedge as it was coming in to land, and it crashed. I can remember security soldiers being all around Polclose and not being able to go down the lane for a while. That was quite exciting.

We used to go onto The Carn and chat to the Americans who were there from, I suppose, late 1943 early 1944. This is above Carn Lodge, you've gone past Carn Lodge and there was a gateway on the left, it was there for many, many years, put there by the Americans. On the other side of the road on what we call 'Forest Carn', there was a 'rab' pit. 'Rab'[30] was a kind of clay.

I think it was used for driveways and so on, and there were caves there which were obviously created when they took the 'rab' out and we saw old shamrock-shaped shell cases, so it was clearly used for storing ammunition at that time. Also, I can remember the jeeps coming down from the Carn. American soldiers with white helmets on, I think they were military police, to prevent too many skirmishes with the local men.

My father, being a First World War man, didn't really overly respect the Americans. In fact, he probably echoed the comment, 'over-paid, over-sexed and over here.'

My father also said that they couldn't march properly; lots of unreasonable prejudices because many of those men, of course, went away and were lost on the beaches on D Day.

My father was in charge of the Home Guard at Madron. They were billeted in The Workhouse at Madron. They were drawn from Trengwainton and Madron and often they were either too young to join the Army or they were too old, but had served in The First War.

Camellia *japonica*

THE AUSTIN 7

You've got to remember that in those days there were probably about three cars in Madron. So, you would mention about someone motoring out fast and of course, my father's car would motor at about five miles an hour.

When my mother was expecting my brother Martin, her waters broke in the middle of the night. My father's car was a very early Austin which had a magneto rather than a dynamo. It didn't have a battery, so if you couldn't start it on the handle, to generate the high voltage, you had to push it. Mother, by now, had her feet probably covered in mud from the field and she had to push the car down the lane towards Home Farm which was on a slope to try and get it to catch. My father would then put it into second gear and hope the engine would start, but he carried on down because

it's quite a slope. The old Colonel, probably due to his wartime duties, allowed him to use the drive so he then turned left into the drive at Trengwainton House and I think the engine caught somewhere down near Boscathnoe Lane. Mother, having pushed the car, gave birth promptly afterwards in Penzance Nursing Home. That was one exploit I remember with the car.

The top of the lane down to Home Farm at the Wishing Well crossroads is called Whitegates. The gates were white, except in the war they were not white, they were black gates, because any kind of recognition they wanted to cut out, so that German planes wouldn't identify any particular areas. My father had obviously been in The King William and had a couple of pints and came back and forgot that the gate was closed and drove through it and took the gate with him down the lane. I don't know what it did to the car, but it certainly didn't do any good to the gate. My mother only drove it once, by the way. She put it into a wrong gear and reversed it into a wall and banged her head on the dashboard and cut her head. She never drove it again after that.

By wartime it was in bits, its back had broken. My father was a very clever welding engineer, he'd welded angle irons from bedsteads that were being discarded. You often saw fences with bits of bed irons in them and the bed irons were quite strong. He welded those to the chassis to keep it going.

TRENGWAINTON HILL CLIMB

I think on the occasion of the photograph Dad was on
registration at the bottom of the Zig-Zag itself, hidden
away, most of the people were further up towards the
end of the Zig-Zag and therefore they wouldn't have
seen him and this is quite significant. So, the cars would
be registered at the bottom and there would be some
organisation about the sequence in which they went
up, because they went up individually in their timing.
There could well have been motorbikes there as well, of
course, and in the case of the photograph it was at the
end of the Speed Hill Climb. The loud-speakers were
on trees right the way up through the Zig-Zag.

An announcement came to say that there was a special
vehicle coming up and there was the brrrm brrrm roar
of a powerful motor engine and then some time later,
tottering up, that's the only way I can describe it, came
my father's ancient Austin 7 with the registration table
on the back and one or two numbers that would have
been on the vehicles. Of course, that was tremendously
hilarious for everybody that was there.

They thought it was absolutely wonderful and of course,
he was well-known and his car had a reputation for
all sorts of things, so there was loud applause. The hill
climb is quite steep and I think it would have gone
up something between five and ten miles an hour,
that would have been about the maximum speed that
it would have gone up. There would have been a lot
of people shouting out his name and him waving at
everyone and all the rest of it.

It was a big event, I mean, for example, it was
something that everyone looked forward to.
There were things like gymkhanas that went on
at places like Nancealverne[31] in those early 50s."

Photograph of Dad
in his Austin 7,
registration table on
the back, tottering up
the Zig-Zag at the end
of the Trengwainton
Speed Hill Climb in
the early 1950s. The
crowd were expecting
an extra special racer
as announced by the
loudspeakers!

ANN FOREMAN

From filmed interview, 2016

"In 1968/1969 I had just come down to Cornwall with my elder daughter for a few months thinking I would go back to the village I was brought up in. I put a notice in the Cornishman that I wanted a job, anything to do with horses, and that I'd been a farmer's wife. I just got one reply back that was from Lady Bolitho at Trengwainton on a scribbled piece of plain paper unheaded with just Trengwainton scribbled onto it saying "I saw your advert and would like somebody to come and exercise my horses. I do have a girl and she's been working for me for a while. Just to start with if you would like to come over and meet me and help me

Stable yard

Trengwainton

1957

Ann Foreman

exercise the horses." She had two hunters because she was the master of the hunt at the time. She said "One hunter the girl can't make go and the other she can't stop so I'm not really happy with her out with them on her own." After we'd been talking for half an hour she said "I'd love you to come and work for me."

She found me a cottage on the farm and I was in that cottage for about 14 years. I worked for Lady Bolitho for about 11 years – 6 years at Trengwainton and the rest when she moved to near Land's End.

It was awe inspiring to me having come from Essex which is just farms and not many big houses, so of course when I first went in up the drive I thought "Oh my golly I can't come and work here," but of course you go up the top and into the yard and suddenly you are in the yard with lots of horses. We just always saw eye-to-eye because we both had the same old-fashioned ideas about horses – the sort of feed and the way you cared for them.

She was just known as Lady B. I noticed that other people like her friends called her Dizzy but I never felt like doing that. Later on when I wasn't working at Trengwainton I could have easily have said to her "is it alright to call you Dizzy now?" but I never did because I respected her very much and worked for her for 11 years and it just stayed as Lady B.

Everything grew well at Trengwainton and it has always been a very well-known garden and they say it was the Queen Mum's favourite garden – she used to come down here and stay. The Royal family used to come quite regularly. The Queen Mother used to love those gardens because everything was so early in comparison to up the line.

I do flower arranging and one time I was told to do the flowers and Lady B used to say to me "We've got some flowers for you to do, it's in two weeks time, Princess Anne is coming down." I felt that was quite an honour to be in there doing the flowers and it was lovely to have those gardens to get the flowers from, great big things on the side board."

> Trengwainton farm had a bull and this girl was in the yard with the bull and it went for her and Lady B was there. She sort of dashed in and rescued this girl from it.

MARGARET TREMEER

From filmed interview, 2016

Margaret Tremeer

Life at Trengwainton

"I was born 1 May 1940 in a little row of cottages where the bungalows are now. There was a little row going inward from Fore Street, called Hillside Row. I was born there and I lived there until just before my ninth birthday when we came here to Trelawney to live.

My connection with Trengwainton began with my father's brother, George Roberts, who was the farm manager. I went to school with quite a few children whose fathers worked on the estate. One was the Head Gardener's son and a couple of farm workers' children and there were two sisters, whose father, Mr Sivier, was the butler at that time. My next association with the estate is Ernie Hill, who was the next butler. I went to school with his daughter, Jenny, and his son. Jenny and I were great friends and I used to go over there to stay sometimes. They lived in a flat opposite the back of the Big House.

The lower part of the building wasn't occupied, so we used to open the window and go in there and play. It was full of old furniture and we used to play house and we also used to play in the woods. If the cook was on holiday or was ever sick, Mrs Hill used to do the cooking, so Jenny and I would help her to do the washing up. When I think about it now, I dread to think if we'd ever dropped and broken one of those plates. They were probably worth thirty or forty quid a piece, but Lady Bolitho used to come in and say, "that's all right," she used to say "so long as you put them to work." If it had been the Colonel's first wife we probably wouldn't have been allowed over that step. The cook would probably have got the sack for letting us in.

Lady Bolitho (Dizzy Bourne) was a Land Girl at Trengwainton and then she ended up being farm manager. She used to work in the fields with the men and she really was ever so nice; she was so 'down to earth'. My mother liked her very much and of course my mother knew the Colonel's daughter by his first wife, Miss Anne, and their son Major Simon, because Miss Anne was about my mother's age. She always used to come home for Madron Feast and she would always make herself known to my mum and go up and speak to her. I didn't really know the Colonel, we didn't see him very much.

The only time you saw him, perhaps, was when he came to church and he always had the front pew. You were in awe of them, you really were, especially when he was with his first wife because she was a very grand lady. I think the second Lady Bolitho, as she'd worked on the farm, was much more 'down to earth' and you could sort of almost stop and have a conversation with her, but you couldn't have done that with the first wife.

My mum used to work at Trengwainton in about the late '20s, not permanent, but just as and when she was

wanted, when they were short staffed. It was always classed as The Big House, and you sort of showed them respect, but it wasn't quite so respectful in my day as when my mother was a young girl and you met them. The boys touched their hats and the girls curtsied, because if you didn't you were in trouble. My mother used to work, on and off, at Trengwainton; she worked a lot in the laundry. The lane from the back gate into Trengwainton Gardens, up to the top by the fir tree,

was known as Laundry Lane, because the men used to bring the big baskets on trolleys from the Big House that way, to have the laundry done. Then they'd take a basket of freshly done laundry back.

Mother said the gardens by Laundry House were strewn with (washing) lines. There is a great big long garden on the side, that's where the (washing) lines used to be. We went for walks round there and mum she used to say, "gosh, this garden is overgrown" or "this is where we used to hang all the washing out in these long gardens. Line upon line upon line we used to hang them out and all the clothes props that pushed the lines up a bit higher."

They boiled up the sheets in great boilers and everything was starched. They had tiny irons with a little stone to go in them to do the lace collars and the babies stuff, I've heard her say. They'd keep them on the stove getting them hot – 'box heater' irons, that's what they were called. It was a lot more manual labour then, nowadays, everything is done by machinery; for cutting the grass, you had the old push mowers, and all the digging and everything was done by hand. During the war, my mother only went to Heamoor to do her shopping. You had to be registered with a grocer. If you went to Penzance you only went once a week; the buses weren't, well it was like it is now, the buses weren't very frequent.

My mum and I always used to decorate the church at Easter with the Easter Garden. We would go up to the

Dizzy (Lady Bolitho) on left hand side
Margaret at the back
Mrs Jenkin on right
1950

Big House and ask if we could go into the woods to pick primroses, so that if anybody saw us doing it we could tell them we had permission. Lady Bolitho always gave us permission to pick the primroses.

We didn't go in the gardens because they weren't open in those days. I didn't really know much about it. It was only when it was opened up by the National Trust that people got to know what the gardens were like. It was private up until then. We used to play in the woods behind the house when I used to go over there with my friend.

Douglas Tremeer
building pergola
commissioned by
Major Simon Bolitho
1989

They used to tell me about the Bothy, where they used to go for their cups of tea. It was supposed to be the potting shed, wasn't it? It was a bit dark and spidery and that's where they used to go and have their cups of tea or their bit of 'croust'[132] as they called it.

Oh, it was lovely. I can remember them building the race-track, the Zig-Zag, when I was young. If there had been a storm and a lot of the trees came down in the woods, and if you got permission, you were allowed to go there with a horse and cart, but only with a hand saw, and saw up logs and bring them home. We used to go up to the Carn to get firewood and small wood for kindling. The ladies used to go off with their carts and their children, a flask of tea and sandwiches and make an afternoon of it, collecting the wood and sitting down and having a cup of tea before meandering home. They were good times. Kids played in the road; there weren't many cars in those days.

FAMILY CONNECTIONS (DOUGLAS AND JOHN TREMEER)

My uncle was farm manager and like my father, he had an allotment which was rented from the estate. You had to go to the estate office to pay the rent for the allotment. My husband Douglas Tremeer worked on the estate for quite a few years. He served his carpenter's apprenticeship at Trengwainton when the workshop was still at Trengwainton in the stable yard.

It was only in later years that the workshop was moved to Trewidden. Then Douglas worked for somebody else and then for the old Penwith District Council.

When he was made redundant he went back to work for Trengwainton again but at the workshop at Trewidden. So, he came a full circle really, and his brother John ended up at Trewidden as well. They had quite a few carpenters and they had their own masons.

My husband spent a lot of the time in his younger days in farmhouses up in the roofs that had woodworm and replacing them. He got emphysema, because in those days they didn't wear masks to stop them breathing in the dust.

My brother-in-law, John, who was deaf, used to work at Tomlins,[33] when they had a flower farm where the Long Rock bypass is now. The foreman was Polish and as my brother-in-law was deaf, they just didn't understand each other; they just didn't 'stable horses' at all. So, one day John had a row with the foreman and walked out. His mother was quite a bit older than my mum, and she was quite upset with John.

He wouldn't go and 'sign on', but my mother got him to go into the office and he 'signed on' and a job came up at Trengwainton in the gardens.

John didn't go to deaf school until he was eight and he left again at fourteen. He was trained as a shoe repairer but he didn't like being indoors, so a lot of his gardening skills were self-taught. He was there for many, many years and when it was taken over by the National Trust he stayed there and he had his 30-year gold medal. John and Gareth Wearne got on like a house on fire. John liked to work by himself. He was such a good worker because being deaf he didn't chat while he was working, so nobody wanted to work with John because he worked too fast. So, he used to work by himself a lot of the time. I can remember my brother-in-law used to clear the stream, clearing it of weeds so the primulas would grow. When he came to retirement age he went to Trewidden to work for three days a week, then he dropped it down to two days a week and he was there until about six months or so before he died."

Madron school 1958

Margaret as May Queen at 18

ROGER CURTIS

Trengwainton's Gamekeeper for forty years, retired in 2017

From filmed interview, 2017

"I'm Roger, I'm employed as the estate Gamekeeper for the Bolitho family at Trengwainton. I've been on the estate for forty years. Before me, there was a chap called George Mitchell. I think George was here for eight or nine years, and before George was a chap called Claude Skinner. Claude was here for lots of years, but how many exactly I don't really know, and then poor old Claude, he died here. Before Claude was a chap called Tommy Woolridge. I think he was here for lots of years.

First thing in the mornings I get out at quarter past six, take all the dogs out, give them a good run for three quarters of an hour, clean the kennels out, and then I come in and have a cup of tea. Then, when I was working full time, out in the woods all day cutting, doing this and doing that, and back home again in the evening same thing, take the dogs out, feed them and clean their kennels out.

The job is the same. One year you're cutting tracks, then the following summer they've grown up again, so you're back in there. It's repetition, you're doing the same thing over and over again.

Trengwainton is a woodcock shoot. Woodcock are birds which you cannot breed, so what we do on the estate is to try to look after and improve their habitat, which is keeping the woods fairly clear,

keeping gun rides open, cutting beaters' tracks so that when we are shooting in the winter beaters can get through the woods. There is a lot of ground, a lot of ground to cover, and it's all chainsaw work, big brush kind of work and the majority is done by hand. Most of our covers, down in the valleys, are withies, blackthorn, hazel, hollies, there's some gorse down in there too. Over the years we've planted several thousand trees on the estate. You've got to look ahead to the next generation.

The Carn now is completely different to when we first come here. When we first come here, well I suppose eighty/ninety percent of the Carn was *Rhododendron ponticum*, and then they got a disease, and five or six year ago we had contractors come in and cut it all out.

They took all the rhododendrons out and if you go up there now and look where the rhododendrons was it's surprising what is actually growing. There's different grasses coming up, there's gorse coming up, there's heather growing up, it looks completely different. There's not so many people go actually on the Carn now.

Roger Curtis and his long service medal

There is a public footpath across it, it's in the 'right to roam', but we don't see that amount of people up there now that we used to years ago. Why, I don't know, but you still get the odd one or two up there, come from the village, walk a dog or two up there, but nothing like there used to be, nothing.

In a nice morning it makes me feel happy to be alive, and be up there when you see the sun coming up on the cairn, it's a lovely place, lovely place, especially on top of the Carn, what a view. You look out to Marazion, the Mount, the Lizard and look all around; it's a lovely view from up there.

The ponds haven't really altered much since we been here, originally there was three ponds down there, the middle one now is overgrown. It's been taken over by withies, the bottom one is overgrown as well. The top one, what we call the main pond that is fairly open, obviously there's trees all around it. Several years ago it was a Sunday morning and Colonel phoned me up and said "Do you know the pond is empty?" I said "Which one?" He said "The big one down the covers." Well, I thought he was joking! I said "No, that can't be empty." He said "Well it is", he said "it's bone dry!" So I went down and had a look and it was. At the bottom end there's a big waterfall there, and bottom of the waterfall there's a nine inch pipe going through the wall which had a wood bung in it, and the wood bung

had rotted out over the years, and it had completely drained right out. It's quite a bigish pond I suppose, two acres.

Well, even now I'm coming up to seventy one, I still feel pretty fit, but being out all day with a chain saw and a big heavy brush-cutter, it was hard going, yep. My work is my hobby, you know I'm not into golf or anything like that, but, well, time will tell, we just have to wait and see when I retire. It's been my life for forty years, yeah it has, it's been my life, and when we got to go I shall miss it, I will miss it."

The Western foxhounds at Madron moving off after the annual Feastentide Meet. Lt Col Edward Hoblyn Warren Bolitho, Lord Lieutenant of Cornwall is on a white horse at the front of the hunt. 1935.

ROS SMITH

Duchy College

From filmed interview, 2016

"My name is Ros Smith and I look after the micro-propagation laboratory at Duchy College at Rosewarne, near Camborne. The micro-propagation laboratory works with rare plants or material that is threatened with disease, so that we can conserve it. Propagation takes place in laboratory conditions that are sterile because everything has to be clean. We can start with just a small bit of plant material and propagate hundreds of little plants from it.

Instead of growing in compost in a plant pot, we grow them in a nutrient jelly which contains all the ingredients needed for growth. It has sugar for energy and plant growth hormones which are important for the direction in which a plant grows, which is why we get a lot of shoots coming from a flower which would not normally happen in nature.

Micro-propagation is useful if you have got something that is rare. You are not going to need a lot of the plant, you only need a small portion. Very tiny flower buds, for example, with the application of plant growth hormones, can produce hundreds of plants, so it's a good conservation tool. We don't want to see any flowers because then it is a bit too late. Usually between November and March time is a good time to collect. The buds come to me and we take off the outer layers of the flower bud so that we can almost see the tiny little flowers that are developing and then we sterilise the outside with a dilute household bleach solution. It's not very high tech, but it works. We use a cabinet where sterile air is coming through and we take out the flowers with scalpel tweezers and then pop them into appropriate gel. In time those flowers will produce little shoots right at the base, which wouldn't normally happen in nature. Just using the mother plant tissue will regenerate more material of the same.

It all started in about 2005 when there was a threat from a disease that affected rhododendrons and what we wanted to do was to try and save some of those very old historic varieties or very early introductions to Cornwall. Because the rhododendron plants were very old, they were very difficult to root from cuttings. The threat of disease made it important that we had clean plant material. So, micro-propagation ticked those two boxes; we could produce disease free material and work with old plants. As long as the disease wasn't in that bit of material, which generally was the case, you could find buds that are high up on the plant that were disease-free.

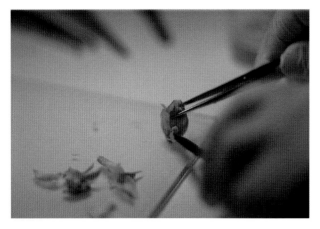

When the problem started with *Phytophthora*, which is a disease that affects rhododendrons, we got involved with some material from Heligan Gardens, because one of our students, who was looking after their collection, realised that rhododendrons could be micro-propagated quite easily. From then on it went to Trengwainton and

we produced quite a lot of plants from there as well. We had funding from Europe and also from DEFRA and that gave us the boost to enable me to work full-time with the micro-propagation and conservation of rhododendrons. From then on it sort of expanded around the country. Now a lot of National Trust properties send in material, as well as other gardens where they have something of historic interest but which is not of commercial value. These gardens may only want a few plants produced, so this is an ideal situation to be in.

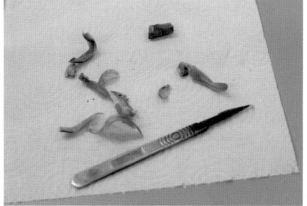

left
Micropropogating

right
Rhododendron
'Morvah'

It can take up to two years, it depends. Some things like the hybrids are faster growing than the species, the wild collected seed, which take a lot longer. The aim is to produce a lot more than the one rooted plant that you would get from a normal cutting.

Initially I think it probably took about four years from when we first started to take plants back to Trengwainton. They've planted quite a lot of different ones around the site and some of them have now been flowering for about four of five years. It's very rewarding to go and see that they have grown really well. They've almost been rejuvenated, are very strong growers, and they are looking really healthy and happy.

I think for some of them we get up to two hundred plants but they don't really want two hundred because they don't have a lot of commercial value and are only of historic interest. We don't want to produce hundreds that are wasted. Usually we try to get about fifty and that's enough to spread around or at the National Trust plant propagation centre they can propagate those by conventional cuttings.

I leave it to the Head Gardener to find the most suitable plants that they want to be conserved and they collect the flower buds. We don't work with shoots because we get too much fungus; too much contamination in the little pots of gel and you lose the culture altogether. We found working with flower buds was the best way forward. The gardeners collect what they need and send them up to me with labels and I work with them here. It's really up to them to choose the most important rhododendrons to work with.

You can propagate all sorts of other plants, but with Trengwainton the focus has been on their historic rhododendrons. There were some that were bred there, names like 'Creek's Cross' and 'Morvah', spring to mind and there's a very important species rhododendron, one that would have been collected in the wild and grown from seed at Trengwainton, named *Rhododendron macabeanum*. I'm sure there are lots more there but those are the few that spring to mind.

I think that the one that appeals to me the most and looks the nicest is one called 'Johnnie Johnston', which is a double one. The flowers are pale pink, so it's a 'girly sort of a flower', but not a particularly strong growing plant. It's just such an unusual flower because most rhododendrons are single florets when you have a look at them, but this has got a small, almost misshapen, but unusual centre to it as well as the pale pink flowers. It is scented too which is another attraction.

I like the idea of conserving things, saving things, especially things of historic value. I'm the sort of person who likes things from the past rather than more modern plants and things like that. I like something that has got a history behind it. This is why I think the Trengwainton plants are so interesting, because a lot of them are named from the Head Gardeners who actually bred them there. They've got a bit of history and I find that fascinating."

TONY RUSSELL

Independent Garden Consultant and Author

From filmed interview, 2016

"We're at Trengwainton today cataloguing the collection of plants digitally by mapping them using GPS and trying to identify them at the same time. We make notes about whether it's failing in some way or whether it's diseased and capture as much information as we can about each individual plant. The machine that I have here is incredible because it 'talks' to about 13 satellites and it pinpoints every plant within a metre by metre square on the ground. All that information will eventually appear on a map, digitally, so people can interrogate it, even before they come to the garden, find the plants that they want to look at, print their own map, bring it here and wander around until they find them.

The first thing to do is secure a GPS signal, so I will go and stand by the plant and I will actually click a

little button and all the satellites will 'talk'. It will put a dot on the ground and that dot will be within about a metre-by-metre square. Then it brings down a form which I fill in. I'll put down the name of the plant and all of the information that I can find out about it. It varies, some plants you can do very quickly in a couple of minutes, some might take you 10 -15 minutes just to do one plant. It is astonishing just how accurate it can be. If we had satellites on us now it would have two dots a metre apart between you and me.

What's particularly interesting about Trengwainton is that there are plants here which really have no right to be anywhere near the British Isles, because it's such a mild climate. So, there are things here for example like this *Rhododendron* 'Fragrantissimum'. In most parts of Britain that would be a conservatory plant but here it's just outside all the time. Just in this one small area we have probably got plants from literally every continent including Antarctica. If you dig down below the ice into the soil and you look at the seeds and the pollen which is in the soil from millions of years ago, there are representatives of those same genus of plants actually here in this garden.

So, it's an incredible collection and a very old collection as well. For example, there is a wonderful magnolia over there, *Magnolia doltsopa*, which was probably one of the original ones introduced into Britain from China just before the First War in about 1913. So, to have trees of that size as well as rare and unusual plants just makes it an amazing collection. It was collected by a plant collector called George Forest, and it was just before the First World War, about 1913, and we know that he had quite a lot of associations with various gardens within Cornwall: Caerhays Castle for example, Trebah, Trengwainton. All the landowners at the time would talk to each other and so when these plants came back they would be grown-on and then they would be swapping them round. Each landowner would have some and undoubtedly, that would be one of the ones that was planted here before the First World War.

At Trengwainton I'm concentrating on what we call woody plants, things that are there all year round. Obviously, some plants come and go – the herbaceous things – but even with just the woody plants we are probably looking at somewhere between 6,000 and 7,000, probably even more than that.

That fern over there is the Black Cyathea and that comes from New Zealand and again it is a very tender plant. You would normally find it under cover if you are growing it within Britain. Here it grows perfectly well outside and that's pretty old, but not everything that is old has to be big. Some plants may not grow very big but they may have been here for decades, centuries sometimes and that fern is a good example of that.

With all the tree ferns, in fact, they originally came into Cornwall as ballast on ships. The ships from here went around the world taking cargo. When they came back, sometimes the ship's hold was empty or sometimes it had other material or cargo in there and they needed to secure it in the ship so that it didn't move or roll around, so they used the old tree trunks of tree ferns. They were coming in from Australia, Tasmania and New Zealand and the first ones arrived here just as ballast. They were thrown out onto the dock at Falmouth and some sharp-eyed plantsmen who were around at that time – we're talking about the 1850s/1860s – were members of the Fox family. The Foxes were a big Quaker family in Cornwall and they had lots of gardens, like Trebah and Glendurgan.

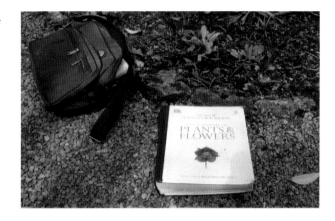

They realised what they were and they took them from the quayside and planted them in their gardens. Some of those original ones are still in those gardens today.

The biggest tree in this area of the garden is the *Magnolia campbellii*, it's otherwise known as the pink tulip tree because when it's in flower it has big goblet pink flowers on it and again that is around 100 years old and could be one of the first introductions into Britain. Even in the wild you rarely see them to that extent with that kind of spread of branches on them. It's a magnificent specimen. The great thing about it is that it's a garden in its own right now because when you get up close and look at it you can see that it's got all ferns, lichens, mosses growing over it so it's got its own garden in amongst the branches.

Something which you can't capture on film, but in fact is all around us at this moment in time, is this amazing fragrance. Most people think of rhododendrons as not having any fragrance but several of them do and one of them, appropriately enough, is called *Rhododendron* 'Fragrantissimum' and that's what we can smell. To be working in this environment with that around me all day is just wonderful."

BETTY DAVY

"I was born at Polteggan cottage and my grandparents lived at Polteggan House on my father's side and then we moved across when they were selling up the house. My granny bought the house and we went there to live till the late '60s. We had a big garden and my dad he kept us all going during the war because he provided fruit and vegetables for us and all our relatives. They used to come with their baskets and mum would fill up the baskets with fruit and veg. We had a wonderful diet really. We used to collect milk from the farm we used to go with our bucket, a pale full of milk and mum made cream and butter and stuff from that.

We are at Trengwainton Lodge, the old lodge and this is where my granny lived, Bessy White. After living on a farm and after her brother died they gave up the farm and she came to live here.

It has a lot of happy memories. I remember sleeping under one of those Morrison shelters during the war. It had a steel table and we used to sleep in that in the lodge here when we visited.

It was in the '40s, we thought it was our woods and nobody else's. We always used to play here up through the woods and on the tree ferns. I remember my brother being told off by the Colonel for climbing up the tree fern and telling him to come down. As children, even after my granny wasn't living here, we used to climb over the wall from the field and we still played at Trengwainton garden down the paths and things. I don't think the Bolithos knew about it but it was fun, it was lovely. I was a great tree climber and I always wanted to be at the top of a tree. I still like that idea actually. The stream was lovely, we used to have a pole and try to vault across the stream but often we'd miss and land in the middle of it. We used to follow the stream and pretend we were explorers. It was fantastic, just freedom. It was a really good childhood and although it was wartime it wasn't too dangerous or anything from a child's point of view, obviously the adults were concerned about it.

During the war they used to drop aluminium foil and we used to have a little basket and all the children would pick it up because it was radar jamming, so we had to pick it up for them and filled our baskets – I don't know who we gave it to.

We were aware that there was a war because Tregavarah chapel got bombed close to us. There were several bombs dropped in the fields because they were trying to bomb Cable and Wireless that goes to America. We had evacuees as well. Dad was in the Home Guard and my uncle was in the army.

One very strong memory is with my friend, we must have been 5 or 6 I suppose, standing on a hedge down at Chy Noweth and a squadron of Lancasters came over and they were so low and we were two little girls standing there waving at them. I often wondered how many of those came back.

Later on my mother and sister used to pick soft fruit, we knew the Head Gardener Mr Thomas quite well and the soft fruit would get sent off to London.

We spent a lot of our childhood playing at Trengwainton woods by the ponds. We used to be up there almost all day sometimes climbing under rhododendron bushes and following the streams, it was a wonderful place for a child really.

My favourite fruit were the raspberries – they used to have yellow raspberries which you don't see very often. They had a lot of soft fruits, black currants, raspberries, gooseberries.

Mr Thomas had two children, John and Jennifer and they were our age so we used to play with them and at the cottage, we used to have good fun the four of us."

SCHOOLS PROJECTS

Our Trengwainton heritage project has worked with five schools. Different themes inspired by Trengwainton's history were used by each school.

Newlyn School's class 5 and 6 visited Trengwainton and learnt about WW2. The workshops explored the 'Dig for Victory' campaign, the 'make do and mend' ethos, the different roles men and women played during the war and how the war affected Trengwainton and Penzance. In 1943 Land Girls were employed at Trengwainton

Trying on WW2 outfits

garden. The main lawns and the Terrace were ploughed up and planted with vegetables, the produce being sent to London to feed the troops.

Gareth, one of Trengwainton's full time gardeners has a large collection of wartime memorabilia and ran for us an inspirational workshop to highlight the war effort. At Trengwainton a 'Dig for Victory' area is now dedicated to that period of time.

Air raid shelter, Trengwainton

Gareth Wearne, Trengwainton gardener, dressed as a Home Guard

A week after Gareth's workshop Angie Butler, a local writer and poet, ran a captivating Womens' Land Army workshop with the same classes. The workshop looked at WW2 from a woman's perspective.

SOME QUOTES FROM PUPILS AND TEACHERS

"The best part was when we got to hold and wear the helmets and bombs. When we got back to school we all couldn't stop talking about it. It was the best workshop ever!"
Newlyn School pupil

"The trip was fantastic. It was amazing to see the bomb shelter, I think to actually sleep in one would be freezing, damp and uncomfortable."
Newlyn School pupil

"The children had first-hand experience of artefacts and came back with a wealth of new ideas and local stories from the past. They had a much better idea of what life would have been like for ordinary Cornish folks. It lead on perfectly from our immersive learning evironment – it was the outdoors part!"
Newlyn School teacher

CLAIRE PENLERICK

From filmed interview, 2016

Father was Mr Jenkin, chauffeur to Sir Edward Bolitho (1920s – 1969), and mother was a parlour maid.

"My name is Claire Penlerick and I was born in the chauffeur's cottage at the top of the drive. My father was the chauffeur and my mother worked there as a parlour maid. Dad was Sir Edward Bolitho's (also known as the Colonel) first chauffeur, or driver as he was called at the time. Dad came there in the 1920s after having an hour's driving lesson in Heamoor and got his car license. He had to see to the cars because they had their own petrol tank there, he filled the cars, valeted them and did whatever was needed. He did the repairs and mechanics and tyres because there weren't the garages or the people

to do it so you had to be self-sufficient.
That happened in lots of cases no matter what it was. There wasn't the throw away society there is today.

I can't remember when mum came there but I do know that they met on Penzance station and he threw her trunk onto the loaded coal on the lorry they had at the time and that had to be driven up the drive backwards as it wouldn't come up forwards! They married in 1940 and I arrived in 1947 and we lived in the cottage by the stable yard. I left there when I got married in 1969.

Our source of drinking water came from the moors, came down to the middle pool to the farm and down to the stream that's on the drive and then it goes down to Penzance.

My mum would go and get the groceries in Penzance once a week and when I was a baby she would push me in the pram. The drive, being half a mile long and up hill on the way back, was not easy with all

Claire Penlerick

Claire and Dad
with Rover 60
1954

In the gardens there were several different ones over a period of time and then you had the keeper up on the Carn, Mr Woolridge.

Mr Hulbert, the Head Gardener, was very meticulous and very fussy. The gardens, don't forget, supplied the big house for flowers, fruit, vegetables. There was hardly a weed in the place. He worked with the Colonel to cross lots of rhododendrons, camellias and worked with Caerhays a lot. And also the Queen Mum had a lot of interest in the garden and she came here when she opened the Saltash bridge.

Caerhays is an estate the other side of Truro owned by the Williams's and they brought a lot of the camellias into the country and they have a lot of connections with Trewidden. The Colonel and I used to go there occasionally.

Mum and Dad outside cottage 1966

William Thomas Jenkin

the shopping, especially when it was not tarmac, the drive was gravel.

Dad used to take the flowers from the garden to market down to the station, the cows from the farm to market, take the carpenters and masons to all the outlying properties and whatever was needed, like cut the wood, take the wood into the sawmills and gather the kindling wood from the Carn. He collected the coal from Penzance and put it in the coalhouses and tended the Aga in the kitchen and boiler in the cellar.

The masons' store was behind our cottage so I spent time with them, learnt about the gardens and knew all the plants. There was three carpenters: Mr Simmonds, Mr Williams and Mr Tremeer and there was a chap that used to come from Newlyn, Mr Hoare, who used to mend the furniture. There were three masons, Mr Hicks, Mr Barr and a mason's boy called Tony Nicholls.

Sometimes he would go on his own and other times he would tell Dad and he would put mum and I in the car and we would go wandering around the estate.

In the lower walled garden at Trengwainton is a magnolia tree called 'Lanarth' – it was one of the first mauve flowering magnolias and I think that was in the late 1960s that it was propagated. It is still there, the Colonel told me about it. He had propagated that one with I think Mr Hulbert. It was ready to go out and he asked dad to show me being planted because he thought he would never see it flower but I'm glad he did actually. There were a lot more of the rare tropical plants then, not the ones we see there today.

The Colonel was interested in everything and everybody as well. His bark was worse than his bite. Even a lot of the tenants on the farms would say that they could go in and approach him and talk to him about anything. He himself would go up in the hay field and sit on the hedge and chat with the men.

The Land Army took over the farmhouse and mum had a couple to stay there. Dad was in the Home Guard. A lot of the Americans were around at the time as well. It was a very difficult time because it was all hard work and there were hardly no men left on the estate because they went to war. My dad had to help with the harvest. Mum and I would take the teas up in the field and sometimes have a picnic – yes we were free.

There was always one man on the threshing machine and somebody else doing the bags of grain. Trengwainton had its own mill so the grain was put in the barn for milling. Using the water from the main water source, dad would spend all day, collar and tie up, pitching the sheaves up to the threshing machine. If it was hay harvest they would build 'pooks' and then 'mows' before it was carried in on a wagon and put in the Dutch barn.

Cottage in Stable Yard where we lived

Claire on Winston 1953

right

Claire and Ross
King, Trengwainton
gardener, 1950

below
Dad on duty

Everybody helped each other, it was a very friendly time in history – if you needed help you just helped and that was it.

Apparently years ago, before I was born, the old lady of the house used to take the horse and carriage on a Sunday morning and the Head Gardener and go around all the paths, along the Zig-Zag and up to the rings which isn't there anymore. If there was a weed she would make him get out and dig it up.

In the summer, this was even before I was born, the Bolithos would take a hunting lodge in Scotland for grouse shooting and salmon fishing and they would go up by train and my dad would bring all the staff. They would stay about a month there.

> *The estate was self-sufficient, there wasn't the big conglomerates you got today and everybody worked together.*

At times all the staff in the house had so much fun, it was hard work but they made their own fun. You didn't have all the entertainments like you've got today and people were a lot happier.

My dad and the Colonel were good pals. They had their differences like everybody does. Then just before dad died when the cricket was on, the butler, dad and the Colonel were in the smoking room watching the cricket together.

Ross King used to live in Trewern Farm up the Carn and worked in the gardens and he walked down to the gardens everyday and walked back. My uncle actually made his boots and he never had a damp foot. He was a very philosophical man – he used to say about the weeds 'keep terrifying them and everything will be alright.'"

TOMMY TUCKER

From filmed interview, 2016

TRENGWAINTON GARDEN IN THE 1930S/40S

"Mr Creek, who we called Pa Creek, 'Pa' for father, was revered and when I knew him it would have been just before he died. I used to go and sit with him with my uncle who was a gardener. He was considered a god. He wasn't well at all, a very frail man when I knew him. I think the Head Gardener that took over from him was called Thomas, George Thomas. Mr Creek was a very knowledgeable and well-trained gardener and he came down to help Edward Bolitho – Sir Edward Bolitho – to whip the gardens into shape, Trengwainton Garden. I think he was credited with all the imports of shrubs.

My uncle would take me in and sit me in a corner and they would chat. I was six when he died and he was a lonely old chap but he had a hell of a reputation as a plantsman and horticulturalist.

I think Colonel Bolitho moved into Trengwainton rather unexpectedly because I think the people who were first and second in line to take over were killed in the 14-18 war. I think he was the third or fourth in line. He started to build the house up and the gardens and I think Creek was brought down as the adviser. I wouldn't say a lot of people of my age knew him really, it was rather secluded in that little cottage beside of Landithy Hall.

I think all the kids worked in Trengwainton before they left school and I worked there a bit during wartime. We weren't gardening, we were in the middle of a big field of sugar beet and kale that was bigger than us. We had no clothes because there were no waterproofs or anything then because it was wartime, one pair of boots, so what you got wet today you had to wear tomorrow.

So there wasn't a lot of good feeling about, even when we were kids working. "Go on boy, you can carry that!" We were carrying hundredweights down the field. "Go on you can carry that boy, go on!" and of course at that age…the more I look back, the more I'm surprised at how people took advantage of lesser people, whether they were smaller or younger or what.

I was working at Trengwainton at eleven, 1940 'til I left school at fourteen, so three years. We had leave from school which was all the summer. The evacuees went in the morning and we went in the afternoon but because we were working on the land we were registered as horticultural workers – we couldn't do anything else. You couldn't leave school and go and get an apprenticeship as a carpenter or anything because you were registered as an agricultural worker. I think it lasted until after the war.

So, we had no schooling and we had no choice of jobs. I mean, if somebody came to school and said "Trengwainton are picking up potatoes tomorrow" you'd go, but you wouldn't be recognised as a regular. They would take you because they thought you were reliable or something, perhaps. Every boy in Madron worked for Trengwainton at some time or another. I think my uncle, who was like my father, nudged me along the road to get away and go into a nursery.

I don't ever remember having a wage packet, the Head Gardener always paid pennies-in-hand. There was always the harvest time and then potato picking or beans to pick. Sometimes you went in Saturday mornings to sweep the drive, that sort of casual work, but I was always picked up for the shoots and did other jobs.

You would stand in line and walk through to beat the birds up. The guns were at the other end of the wood and they would shoot them as they came over and then, if you had a dog, your dog would go and pick-up and would go and bring the dead bird to you. That's picking-up. So, I always did that.

Colonel Bolitho, when war broke out, said to all his gardeners "Get out and join the army," every one of them. I know one of them had been in The Old Contemptibles which was the regular army in 1914 and he had gone through the war – hard war. He'd got out, he got a job at Geevor and the second day he was there the mine engine went down. He walked home and he said he wasn't going to go mining and he went to work in Trengwainton Garden.

It was a really hard time. A lot of the agricultural workers had gone into the army so we were encouraged to leave school and go to work. I must have been there regular for him to offer me one of the prime cottages that was on the Carn. It must have come vacant and he wanted somebody reliable to go there. Madron Carn, one of the keeper's cottages. I was, as I said, picking-up then and doing odd things like that and one day I was with another bloke in the front lane and he called me in.

He said, "You've got married?" and I said, "Yes Colonel." He said, "Well, would you like Carn Cottage?" I would not have swapped that for paradise – beautiful! And then I got involved with the keepers that were there, next door. They would get a bit behind and I would go there with the power saw. If they got a bit behind clearing out drives I would give them a bit of a hand. Oh, fantastic! I'm a dog man, kennels around the back and I'd have a day off for the shoot. Hard work! We went to Lord St Levan's, Caerhays Castle and places like that, at weekends. Most of them gave you a fiver, but nearer to home the less you got. I loved it, it's the sort of job I loved, but I was in a good job then. I could have been a keeper at Trengwainton, but no money, no money and not a lot of joy.

FAMILY LIFE

My grandfather had a blacksmith's shop at Heamoor, Newbridge, and I think, Gulval. I know he had three at one time and quite a business but was too fond of cricket. The second son was an extremely good cricketer, playing for the county. He had two sons playing for the county, the other one was not a blacksmith but between them they managed to lose the business and my uncle, who took over as my stepfather, was the one who didn't play cricket. He is the one who tried to stop me. He said, "Cricket has lost us a good business," he said, "you're best not to do it."

I was a child, he was in his 70s or 80s then, my grandfather. He was in the blacksmith's shop a lot and my mother moved down here and kept house for my grandfather and the one bachelor uncle. So, I was brought up with the bachelor uncle and my grandfather. We used to hear the stories of the times when they used to play cricket and one of the Bolithos used to ride down on a horse and say, "Edwin, we're playing cricket tomorrow," or "today." He would drop things and go.

He was an extremely good cricketer. He would do things like order iron fencing for the fields, he'd make them but then he had to pay for the steel and then they'd say, "Well, we don't pay 'til the end of the financial year." My grandfather stuck it, but my uncle who took over the business, when war broke out he was desperate. I can remember him not being able to smoke because he had to buy steel before he could make a living. He got a job in Devonport dockyard.

During the war, we didn't play. There was no football or anything. As an eleven-year-old, we worked a forty-eight-hour week plus all the overtime we could get. My mother was born and reared in Tretorvick Terrace, Heamoor, the last row of houses going up Madron Hill. She was living with grandfather who had quite a business, but by that time he had retired. She was a widow and it was a hard old life.

Trengwainton Life

I remember the ponds and this was just before the war and it was drained and 'puddled' – put clay in

them and walk cows over them and that would waterproof – then they had gravel in. They had a boat house put down the bottom, they had a diving board and a house put half way up. I can remember all that being done.

We used to go there and sit down and watch them. They had a lot of people working there then, all hand tools see, all wheelbarrows and horse and cart then.

Miss Anne she used to have swimming parties there and everything. That must have been 1934 or '35 possibly. Anne was Sir Edwards Bolitho's daughter who of course was one of the stars of the '20s and '30s. I mean, they had great parties at each other's houses didn't they?

She was a nice person. I think this was done for her more than anybody, but it was a lovely pond. I've seen an otter there.

The Colonel

Edward Bolitho got a knighthood. If we found a strange grub or an unusual butterfly we used to take it out to him and he'd give us a penny and chat over it with us, tell us what it was. So, I think he was trying to educate us a bit.

We used to go out there Christmas to sing carols when they had their dinner. Do you know Hartley's jam? Well, Miss Hartley stayed there most of the war. She used to sing Children's Hour on BBC. I was a bit frightened of her but my cousin, who was in the Girl Guides, said she was wonderful.

In the front of the drive a tree fell down across the hedge and we cut it up and left the stump lying on the hedge. The Colonel came down and with an indelible pencil wrote, 'Rome fell, I fell.' I'll always remember that."

CHRIS ELLERY-HILL

From filmed interview, 2018

Janie and Betty
1948

Betty taking two
granddaughters to see
the Laundry House
1985

My grandmother, Janie Uren, lived and worked at the Laundry House at Trengwainton in the 1940s. She was born in Carnyorth in 1902 and she was a miner's daughter. In 1923, she married Arthur Uren who was a butcher's son from Penzance who became a miner. They had three daughters born in 1923, 1926 and 1929. Within a few weeks of my mother being born in 1929, Arthur moved to Canada to work in a mine where there were already other people from the village working there. He travelled out there with his brother-in-law (Janie's sister's husband). I think after a few years he decided he wanted to settle out there and I think he

probably tried to persuade Janie to join him but she didn't want to go. Then he basically disowned the family and stopped supporting them so Janie then had three young daughters to support on her own.

Janie's father had died when she was about fifteen years old – he'd been a miner in South Africa. To support the family Janie's mother, who also had younger children, was working as a midwife and also laid out the dead for people. They were living in Carnyorth and moved to Tregeseal. My grandmother was doing cleaning, taking in washing and doing whatever she could. She always had trouble with one arm which had been broken but had been set badly and she always suffered from bronchitis.

I don't know how it came about but in 1940 a position was advertised at Trengwainton and they moved into the Laundry House which is now rented out as a holiday cottage. It was a fine house and a great contrast to the little miner's cottage where they lived before. It was in the woods, up a lane near Madron. My mother enjoyed

117

down Lesingey Lane picking rosehips and anything else that was forageable, I guess.

Janie's two older daughters went off to do war service, one in the ATS and one in the WRNS and my mother was still at Madron school. There were a lot of land army girls on the estate and evacuees. My mother met quite a different mix of people in comparison to living in a mining community, it was quite a change. She found it difficult at school in Madron because she had never known her father and felt put upon in many ways and was a bit more vulnerable to pressure from teachers.

My mother, when she was nineteen in 1948, married my father in Madron - he was a farm worker. They came to live in the Laundry House as well. The view of the estate in those days was that the head of the household should be working for the estate but my father didn't work for the estate so they were encouraged to leave. Although my grandmother worked for them she was no longer regarded as being head of the household. There were new council houses built in Mousehole in 1950 (which are now extremely valuable houses) and my parents moved into one of those. I think the Bolithos eased their move there because they could pull some strings. My mother certainly and my grandmother as well had some very fond memories of Trengwainton and the community. My mother had correspondence for the rest of her life with some of the evacuees she had known at school.

Laundry House
2018

moving there – I think they had five bedrooms in this house – it had a garden and woods all around. I remember my mother saying it was a lot of hard work. I don't think they were doing laundry every day but probably a couple of days a week – it was very heavy work. I think Janie's mother sometimes would come over and help. There was the big double height room at the end which was the drying room and when the weather was bad the drying would be done in there. There was a whole range of flat irons called 'etters' which were heated on the slab. There was a lot of ironing to be done – everything was ironed. I guess all the laundry from the house and the estate as well as the laundry of workers of the estate was done there – it was one of the perks of the role. With the land girls and evacuees, I imagine there was quite a volume of work.

I know that my mother and her sisters were terrified of the bats and of course there are loads of bats on the estate. They were scared stiff of the old wives' tales of bats being caught up in your hair. They also used to go

My mother told me once that the Boscathnoe reservoir, which is between Trengwainton and Heamoor, was emptied for some sort of maintenance work and my mother described it as 'a plague of frogs' - apparently there were hundreds of frogs everywhere and the road was covered in them!

HEATHER BRAY (NÉE HODGE)

Memories of farming at Trengwainton and the estate

above
Albert John Hodge with Winston and Duchess, 1945

right
Albert John Hodge ploughing Trengwainton

My father Albert John Hodge was born 9th June 1910 in the workhouse at St Austell. He was married at St Merryn Church on the 6th May 1937 to Doris Louvoin Ead, originally from Goldsithney and the daughter of a policeman.

My brother Keith was born first on the 1st February 1940. I was born long after in West Cornwall Hospital on the 2nd Feb 1950 and my first home was cottage Nº 2 near the farm at Trengwainton.

Dad worked there from 1945 to 1952 and was a general labourer looking after the horses and worked two horses called Winston and Duchess. With these he ploughed and did general work, milking the cows at weekends, and when Mr Kerrigan left Colonel Bolitho offered him the tractor work. My Dad said he had never driven one but the Colonel said he would be alright and he even won a prize for his ploughing!

Dad worked with Paddy Kerrigan, George Roberts and John Hall. Miss Bourne, who became the second Lady Bolitho after the first wife died, loved looking after the cows. Later on, Ivor Stains came as a foreman. Annie Love was mauled by a bull but survived. Paddy Kerrigan, his wife Flo and his two boys, Nigel and Dennis, lived in the next cottage to us. Vegetables and milk were plentiful from the farm and later my grandmother, Annie Ead, came and lived with us and she sang in Madron Church Choir.

When young I remember taking our terrier, Judy, up on Madron Carn and collecting wood but I had to walk home as the pushchair would be full of wood.

I was baptised in Madron Holy Well, the first baby for 30 years, and the Madron Old Cornwall Society cut the path back for the event.

We left in 1952 and after a tough time in a farm near Kingsbridge, South Devon, we returned to Luthergwearne Farm next to Boscathnoe Reservoir where Dad was the Manager for the Pill family. We were very happy there with Dad milking the Jersey herd, farming pigs and chickens while Mum had a big allotment growing flowers, vegetables and selling eggs.

A memory: my brother was given a large, very old and tatty Teddy bear from the Bolitho family which became mine later on and really was my favourite over all the dolls. I would go up into Trengwainton Garden and play with Kathleen Hulbert, the Head Gardener's daughter. If Colonel Bolitho came along in his car he would stop and ask what Teddy was wearing and I would have to get the bear out of the pram and show him. Teddy had better clothes than I did – he was dressed in a sailor suit and lots of hand knitted things, some from the Church jumble sale. This greatly amused the Colonel. During my time playing with Kathleen in the gardens we often were asked to have a photo shoot for papers and magazines under the trees and shrubs sometimes holding flowers.

Mum was always on about learning to drive as no one liked going out with her in the car; even the dog, who loved travelling in the van, went indoors when Mum got in the car. She could never reverse and one day came up too fast through Heamoor in a hurry to get back to the farm, turned the corner by the school too wide and hit Colonel Bolitho's car. I put my hands over my eyes. He was very nice about it but Mum wished the ground would open under her feet as she had taken the front wing right off. Even after passing the test no-one liked riding with her, poor Mum!

Albert John Hodge at St Austell, pre 1945

WATER

TRENGWAINTON & PENZANCE'S WATER SUPPLY

Robin Knight, Project Volunteer

In the 18th century Penzance relied on a number of private wells and pumps for its water supply but with the expansion of the town these were becoming inadequate and as there was no drainage system the town was becoming extremely filthy and un-hygienic. In 1750, to try to improve matters, the Corporation approved the construction of a new leat (a man-made channel) to bring water from Madron Well to the town.

Madron village also took water from the Well and that not used in the village flowed down the hill from near the church towards Hea(moor) where it joined water flowing from Nanceglos, near the present day Mounts Bay School. Another stream which arose near Poltair Moor also fed into the leat and from here the water flowed in an open or partially covered channel, about 1¼ miles to Causeway Head and into the town. The reliability of the water supply was improved in 1757 when a reservoir, an open brick basin and holding about 11,331 gallons, was built at the top of Causeway Head at a cost of £132. A plaque of the wall alongside Clarence House records the site of the sluice that controlled the flow of water into the new reservoir at 126 feet above sea level. From here the water was taken down Causeway

Old sluice gate

Head in open gutters and pipes to the town shoot by the site of the present HSBC Bank, near where the old market cross stood and then via Chapel Street reaching the sea by the Battery Rocks.

The Royal Commission on Municipal Corporations had noted:

Corporation funds are frequently expended in feasting and in paying the salaries of unimportant officers. In some cases, in which the funds are expended on public works, an expense has been incurred beyond what would be necessary if due care had been taken. These abuses often originate in negligence ... in the opportunity afforded of obliging members of their own body, or the friends and relations of such members. [35]

Under the 1835 Municipal Corporations Act, the newly elected, reformed Councils could take over social improvements such as the water supply, proper drainage and street cleaning. Only 20 years earlier, in 1816, the old Corporation had proposed seeking statutory

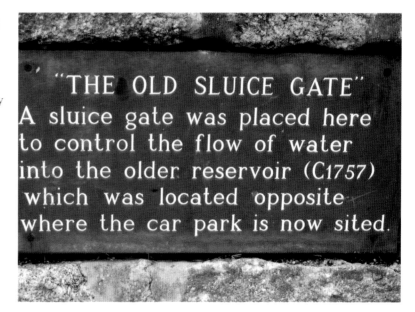

powers for 'paving, lighting, cleansing, watering, watching and improving' the Town, but a meeting of the townspeople rejected this, mainly on the grounds of expense.

However, the water supply of 1757 was, by 1847, inadequate. Plans were soon drawn up for the Corporation and also by a privately owned company to bring more water to the town from a new source, the Lariggan Stream which flows down the valley on the west of the present Trengwainton House. This stream is elsewhere called the Hendra or Alverton River, Stream or Brook!

A set of plans and maps drawn by a Mr Brunton CE [36] dated 29 November 1847, for the Corporation, shows how it was proposed to take water from a diversion of the Lariggan stream to Polteggan Mill and then into a new storage reservoir nearby. From here a new leat would connect with the Nanceglos Stream and the existing one from Madron, taking the water to the reservoir at the top of Causeway Head.

The other set of plans and submission to Parliament were drawn up by M Laxton, Engineer, London, for a private scheme and also dated November 1847. The scheme also proposed to take water from the Lariggan Stream; build a small reservoir at Polteggan from where the water was to be piped alongside the Lariggan to the Green Market and Market House in Penzance.

With the proposal there is a reference document, four pages of details in a table showing who owned the land along the course of the proposed pipe, and its then current use. Henry Lewis Stephens of Grice, the owner of Trengwainton, seems to have been the major landowner.

The book of reference accompanying Laxton's maps gives details of the proposals in fulsome legalese:

...to take and use water of a certain stream, rivulet, or brook called the Larigan river, and also certain streams, rivulets or brooks near to Trengwainton, and other streams, rivulets or brooks near to Polteggan Mills, ... powers to purchase by compulsion or otherwise, or take on lease all such lands and houses, reservoirs, streams or other hereditaments as may be necessary for constructing and maintaining the said intended waterworks... To raise, levy and collect rates, dues and rents for the supply of water.

Nanceglos shoot

A Public Enquiry

In January 1849, George T. Clark, Superintending Inspector of Public Health, visited Penzance for four days, during which time he held a one-day public sitting in the Guildhall.

His findings and recommendations were published in his detailed *Report to the General Board of Health on a Preliminary Inquiry into the Sewerage, Drainage, and Supply of Water, and the Sanitary Conditions of the Inhabitants of the Town of Penzance*, dated 14 April 1849.

This important document not only gives a review of the sanitary conditions but also background information about the town, and concludes with his recommendations of how to improve the poor, unhygienic conditions he witnessed.

Clark recommended that the Corporation scheme of 1847 be adopted and that a supply 121/2 gallons (57 litres) per head, per day, would be sufficient for domestic consumption (current guidelines suggest about four times as much: 55 gallons or 250), and double that allowance to cover street cleaning, other sanitary purposes, and 4,500 gallons for shipping in the port.

Therefore it would be necessary to source 250,000 gallons (1,136,500 litres) daily and to be prepared to supply a much larger quantity, if the need arose in the future. Clark calculated that even in the driest periods the proposed scheme would provide a daily supply of about 158,760 gallons; which, in addition to the quantity in the reservoirs, would amount to a supply for about a month. In 1850 the Council agreed to borrow money to enable water to be brought into the Borough.

The main source of water for the new scheme was to be the pond at Polteggan Mill, fed by the Hendra or Lariggan Stream and then into a new storage reservoir at Brick Kiln Moor, or as we now know it, Boscathnoe.

The priority was to obtain the necessary rights from Henry Lewis Stephens, owner of Trengwainton, the Polteggan property, and other riparian (river bank) owners along the Lariggan stream to take water from this stream and divert it into a new reservoir and water course.

Mr Stephens, when he was told of the proposal in March 1850, raised many objections; but in order if possible to avoid the delay his agents were instructed to ask for a rent of £20 a year and allow the scheme to go ahead!

By 1852 all objections and problems had been overcome and the works were completed. Although virtually the whole town was being supplied with water from the new reservoir at Boscathnoe, a second, larger reservoir was soon built on adjacent land, bought from General Tremenheere for £400, to improve the reliability of the supply.

The two were united on 10 October 1860 at a ceremony attended by the Mayor and the entire Corporation, who proceeded to a reception held in a large tent erected on the hillside above.

Shortages continue

Even with the two reservoirs now in use the growing demand for water from the growing population of Penzance was soon causing problems in dry summers, when the water supply was often turned off from 6pm

Lariggan stream was insufficient. A letter of 3 July 1901 from his solicitors says:

Mr Bolitho would of course rather not have any works of this kind so near his entrance, but, if the Council consider it likely to really improve the Town water supply, he will grant liberty to sink the shaft and erect engine on the following conditions:- Terms to be 2000 years, yearly rent of water £10, in addition to surface rent at the rate of 25/- for a quarter of an acre...

On 16 April 1902 the Seal of Penzance Town Council was affixed to a lease for 2000 years with Mr Bolitho and the Town Council with respect to land on which a line of pipes from the reservoir at Hendra were laid, at 10 shillings per annum.

The first well was dug in 1901 and during 1903 a second well was sunk and the weir at Hendra was altered and a high level tank installed at Boscathnoe to take the water from higher up the Lariggan valley at Hendra, at a cost of £807; the pipes costing £60.

In 1905 plans were approved for a building to house the pumps and this was duly built the next year by one Mr J.H. Nichols at a cost of £204. Messrs Tangye Ltd were contracted to supply a double cylinder engine and boiler fixed complete, at £292. Every summer thereafter, water was pumped from here into the reservoirs to maintain a steady supply to the residents of, and visitors to, Penzance. The pump house still stands and has recently been renovated as workshops and studios.

ALL'S NOT WELL WITH THE WATER

With the new inlet from Hendra to the reservoirs and the new wells and pumps, all seemed to go well until December 1912 when a letter from the national Local

to 6am to save water. The question of improving the supply was regularly raised at Council meetings over the next 30 years, but little was done to remedy the situation.

However, on 25 September 1886 the water in the reservoir was so low the Council gained permission from Mr Bolitho, who by then was the owner of Trengwainton, to increase the supply to the Hendra (Lariggan) stream, that supplied the reservoirs, by lowering the water in his pond above Hendra by 12".

After two reports into improving the water supply the Council did start to take action. In 1900 they again approached Mr Bolitho, this time to take water from higher up the stream on the Bolitho estate (field 1343), and pipe it directly to the reservoirs bypassing the pond at Polteggan Mill.

Mr Bolitho, through his solicitors agreed providing that the pipe was buried so that there was minimal interference. The other proposal was to sink a well near the Boscathnoe reservoirs from which water could be pumped in summer when the flow of water in the

Government Board, LGB, was received in response to a request from Penzance Council for a loan to improve the water quality:

... it appears to the Board that the progressive deterioration in the quality of the water yielded by the well at Polteggan which is shown by the chemical analysis and is specifically indicated by an increased amount of chlorine, can only be attributed to the presence of the Trengwainton soakaway cesspool, and, in the circumstances, the Board do not consider that they could properly sanction a loan...

Polteggan mill 2015

The Council minutes do not give any indication of how this was resolved but one assumes it was as there is no further mention of this problem. All seemed well until 1928 when in February the Penzance Sanitary Committee meeting considered various letters about proposed cleaning of lower pond and leat at Trengwainton.

The Borough Surveyor, Captain Frank Latham, expressed the desire for the work to be carried out immediately.

Col Bolitho's agent had suggested some time previous that it might prove cheaper to compensate the Bolitho estate at £200 to divert the water permanently into a leat to bypass the lower pond. We hear no more until 1937 when the leats at Tregwainton were to be cleaned.

A letter to the Council from Bolitho Estate Office offered for sale between 100,000 and 200,000 gallons of water in the bottom pond of the estate for the sum of £10.

Although water was now being taken from higher up the valley, and the upper pond was also being used as a primary reservoir, there were still summer shortages of water.

By this time plans were well underway to build a large high-level reservoir at Chywoone with water pumped from the Newbridge Stream, also known as the Newlyn River, at Drift Mill.

Although the new high-level reservoir was in use by the outbreak of the war in 1939, and plans had been adopted to build a large impounding reservoir at Drift, the problems were not fully addressed until the Drift dam and reservoir were completed in 1962.

The Lariggan Stream as a source of water for Penzance and the reservoirs and pumps at Boscathnoe then became redundant.

SUMMER

Phil Griffiths

- Plant and regularly pinch out side shoots on tomatoes.

- Harvest lettuce, radish, other salads and early potatoes.

- Plant out summer bedding.

- Stake tall plants. Doing this before they flop over can save time and anguish.

- Prune many spring-flowering shrubs.

- Shade greenhouses to keep them cool, this also prevents evaporation of valuable water.

- Pick courgettes before they become too large.

- Clear algae blanket, weed ponds, keeping them topped up to allow late emerging amphibians and insects to not get trapped.

- Summer feed your lawns.

- Give light prune to apple trees.

- Continually deadhead plants to keep that colour well into the autumn.

- Collect seed from garden plants, we would be collecting Primula seed from the stream garden now.

- Harvest sweetcorn and other vegetables as they become ready.

- After bouts of summer rain keep on top of the hoeing, it doesn't take long for the weeds to take control.

Dicksonia antarctica

Illustration by
Dominica Williamson

IN THE VEGETABLE GARDEN

Ian Willsdon

JUNE

Early June is the best time to plant outdoor tomatoes. If you grow your own from seed you have a much wider choice of varieties. For Cornwall it is best to choose varieties that are more resistant to blight for outdoor growing because of the humidity of the climate which helps blight to spread quickly and much earlier than further north or east.

Cherry tomatoes or certain bush tomatoes are better than larger varieties and do seem more blight resistant. My favourite varieties are Sungold or Black Cherry for cordon tomatoes and Red Alert or Sub Arctic Plenty for bush tomatoes (these last two varieties are quite early and will give relatively early outdoor ripe fruit. All these varieties need to be sown indoors in February or March and potted on into larger pots at least once or twice before being planted outside. Plants need to be about 30cm high before they are planted out and should be developing their first truss of flowers.

Cherry tomatoes will need support such as canes as they produce the best fruit from one main stem. This means removing sideshoots from the plants as they grow to avoid having too many small tomatoes. Remove each new stem shoot that grows from the main stem just above the main leaves on the stem.

If you dig in well-rotted manure or compost when you plant this will help to retain moisture and produce better fruit. For outdoor cordon plants like these it is better to stop the fruit production in late August to allow fruit to ripen before the weather turns colder. To do this simply take the top off the main stem and keep on removing any sideshoots. Bush tomatoes are much simpler to grow as you do not need to remove sideshoots from the plants – you can just let them grow. However, they will still need some support to keep the heavy crop of tomatoes off the ground. Wire hoops or canes tied horizontally on either side of the plant are good ways of doing this.

JULY

July is a good time to plant out leeks although you need to start much earlier for good crops. Leeks are best sown in March or April, initially in deep boxes of seed compost or modules indoors. If the compost is deep the leeks can be grown to a decent size without disturbance and there is no need to prick out into modules.

If the leeks are started off indoors in an unheated greenhouse you will need to start hardening them off by putting them outside before planting out. Leeks can be a good follow-on crop to early potatoes.

When planting out you can trim the leeks top and bottom to stimulate early growth. Plant out about 16cm apart (closer planting will produce smaller leeks).

The best way to plant out is by using a dibber to make a hole about 10cm deep and then dropping in the trimmed leek plant.

For many years accepted wisdom was to fill the holes with water to settle the soil around the plants and not backfill. However, backfilling can produce more even results and minimise plant loss.

After planting the leeks need to be kept well-watered, especially if the weather is hot and dry. Harvesting time will depend on what variety of leek you have sown and how big you want the plants to grow. It can be a good

idea to sow a few different varieties that will be ready at different times of the year from early autumn to late spring.

A good early variety is King Richard and a good maincrop is St Victor. With careful planning you can harvest leeks from early autumn right through to the following spring.

AUGUST

August is a good time to sow green manure in your beds as they become empty after being cropped.

Green manure has several purposes from helping to build up organic matter in the soil to improve fertility and water retention, to restricting weed growth (weeds will inevitably colonise bare soil).

Other advantages include producing late flowers for pollinators if you choose a green manure like *Phacelia tanacetifolia* which is greatly loved by bees and also looks good in the plot with its lovely blue flowers.
It will stand through most winters in our climate.

Its advantages include quick, easy germination, rapid growth and an ability to self-seed easily if wanted while being relatively shallow rooted and easy to remove and unlikely to become an invasive problem.

When the bed is wanted again you can quickly rip it out and compost it or leave it on the soil as a mulch to rot down slowly.

Another good green manure plant good for ground cover is *Limnanthes douglasii* or poached egg plant.

This can be sown in September or October to give early flowers for pollinators the following spring. It can be effective as a companion plant under fruit bushes.

FERNS

Artist's notes

Dominica Williamson

Gareth the gardener led me to the Tree Fern glade in the summer and said 'spot the difference' between Tree Fern *Dicksonia antarctica* and the Silver Tree Fern *Cyathea dealbata*. Wow yes, the former is scratchy – full of texture, whilst the underside of the Silver Tree Fern lives up to its name. The brown sori look incredible against the silver colour of the leaves. I can't wait to capture in paint the differences between these beautiful plants.

Tree Fern *Dicksonia antarctica*

Tree ferns are scratchy to feel unlike other ferns such as the Male and Lady fern, which are soft to the touch. This tree fern is indicative of Trengwainton and other Cornish gardens. In Trengwainton there is one plant whose growing habitat is different than the other – the leaves waving down to the ground like the shape of a weeping willow. They don't know why this is, it must be genetically slightly different. Also, this plant has self-seeded in the hedge, something they have not seen elsewhere in Cornwall.

Silver Tree Fern – Ponga (Maori) *Cyathea dealbata*

The Silver Tree Fern is rare in Cornwall. It is the unofficial emblem of New Zealand. On the underside of new shoots, when the plant is 3-4 years old, you get this amazing silver colour. Although not a main feature of the garden, it is rare and there are several plants that you can see growing in the Tree Fern glade beside the other varieties.

Dominica Williamson doing Tree Fern research

THE BOTHY

Phil Griffiths

Extract from filmed interview

We know the Bothy has gone through various changes. It started off life as a barn we think. There were some remnants just above the orchard wall of some building footings, so we're not quite sure what was there prior to Rose Price, we think he was responsible for building the orchard and landscaping that side of it.

So the Bothy was a barn, then it was said to be a journeyman's cottage. A journeyman was somebody who travelled round the UK over various seasons or various years learning their trade, so they might have been sent by their sponsor to come to Trengwainton to learn about propagation or learn about the plant collection from the Bolithos. Then some time in the mid-Edwardian period the Head Gardener's office was put in downstairs, upstairs they put in some fruit-drying racks, so that was to over-winter the apples, pears, plums, anything from the Kitchen Garden.

Downstairs was their potting shed, and that was the same right up until the late 80s, early 90s.

The first year I came here one of my first winter jobs was to take the drying racks out of upstairs to turn upstairs into the office.

When the garden first was handed over to the National Trust, we might have had a couple of thousand visitors a year, at that point we were getting towards 45 thousand visitors a year, so with all those extra visitors, extra health and safety, there's the booking of coaches, school groups, and we'd just outgrown that little office downstairs.

The Bothy has had various different incarnations and now we still use what was their little potting-on area, we use that as our little snack room, it's where we meet with the volunteers in the morning. Sit down and have a cup of tea, make sure we have lunch in there as well, sometimes it's really riotous in there and you can't hear yourself think.

I think it's one of the things that really adds to the volunteers' experience, because we sit down as a gardening team with them every day, and we have lunch with them and are able to talk about what's going on, what projects have been happening, what we've got in the pipeline.

The Bothy

PEOPLE
CHARLES DALE

1870 – 12 March 1960, Groom at Trengwainton from 1889 – 1942

Nancy Carter, Project Volunteer

Charles 'Charlie' Dale was a first cousin to gardeners James, William and Walter Howard Dale. He was born at Madron in 1870 and began working for Thomas Robins Bolitho in 1889 and remained in the employment of the Bolitho family at Trengwainton for the next 53 years.

Charles married his wife Elizabeth in 1898 and they had four children. They lived initially at Nanceglos Lodge but later moved to the property known as Park Lodge. The family attended the Wesleyan Chapel at Madron and Charles was a member of its board of Trustees until 1949.[37]

Charles Dale of Trengwainton. Centre horse wearing bowler hat

He was highly regarded for his horsemanship both at Trengwainton and with The Western Hunt where Charles's son Reginald 'Reg' Dale was the whipper-in until 1921.[38] Horses remained Charles's lifelong passion. His love for his horses was not dinted when in 1903, he was injured by one of them. This was newsworthy and was reported in *The Cornishman* on 4 June 1903:

We are sorry to hear that on Wednesday Charles Dale, coachman at Trengwainton, Penzance, was kicked by a horse in the stable, the blow fracturing his jaw. Mr Dale was removed to Penzance Infirmary and is suffering severely.[39]

George James was a carriage boy at Trengwainton from 1922 to 1923. This is an extract from his memoirs which are in the keeping of the current owner of Trengwainton, Col Edward Thomas Bolitho:

Mr Charles Dale was the head groom and always rode to hounds. He was a great horseman and everyone in the district knew him. He was held in great respect and lived in a lodge on the estate. His daughter was one of the servants in the big house. Whenever Mr Bolitho was unable to go to a meet, Mr Dale would come to the house after dinner and give Mr Bolitho an account of the day's events. He was a very fine man and Mr Bolitho thought a lot of him.

His loyalty, hard work, love of horses and sunny disposition gained Charles great respect. When Thomas Robins Bolitho died in 1925, his will, which was published in *The Cornishman* newspaper on 30 December 1925, instructed that Charles should receive the sum of £1000 'in recognition of his long and faithful service'.[40] In the book about Madron Daniel School, *The Story of Our School*, a paragraph describes how, at T. R. Bolitho's funeral, Charles walked in the funeral cortege, leading his employer's 'big beautiful shining horse, Barum.' Schoolchildren who witnessed

the procession said that 'Mr Dale was crying all the way.' [41]

I have been told that when the artist Sir Alfred Munnings RA visited Trengwainton he painted Charles riding his horse. The painting is entitled 'Black and White.'[42] An illustration of the painting is in Alfred Munnings's autobiography and below it is written: 'Dale in his cockaded hat, black coat, leather belt and boots.'

Charles continued as groom when Lt Col Edward Hoblyn Warren Bolitho inherited Trengwainton following the death of his uncle. Charles often accompanied Sir Edward's daughter, Miss Anne Bolitho, when she rode out on the estate.

Miss Anne recalled her relationship with Charles Dale many years later, in a conversation with her nephew Col Edward Thomas Bolitho:

When we arrived at Trengwainton, Dale stayed on in the stables. He continued as groom, and lived in the cottage on the right just before you get to the Farm.

I adored him; he was my sort of nanny. He was lost when Uncle Robins died as he'd looked after him, so Daddy said, well now you've got to look after Miss Anne and he was like the superest Nanny but a bit tiresome at times. "No, you're not to come hunting, you're not to get onto that pony again until you've had a change of clothes. You're wet through."

T.R. Bolitho died in 1925, by then I was seven. I didn't go to his funeral, but I watched it with somebody else so that I saw the procession going through, from Madron down through the back of Heamoor. I was somewhere there and remember Barum, his horse, led by Dale and Dale had Treacle the terrier at his heels. Dale wasn't a big walker, because he was very small with short legs to boot.

In 1942, when the announcement of Charles Dale's intention to retire was made, *The Cornishman* newspaper publicised it to the wider community in their issue of 22 October:

One of the most popular and well-known horsemen in West Cornwall is shortly retiring after a lifetime of service for the Bolitho family on the Trengwainton Estate. Mr Dale's cheery disposition and bright smile, coupled with his diminutive size, made him an outstanding figure in the local world of horsemanship, whether it was in the hunting field, among the agricultural community or at any horse show or race in the county.

Wherever there was good horses on view, there one could always be certain to find Charles Dale, dapper, enthusiastic, a keen and sound judge of the animals among which he had spent his life and which he tended with loving care.

No matter what the weather, however wet and cold he might be himself, his horses always came first, they must be rubbed down, fed and made warm, before he ever gave a thought to his own discomfort. That loyalty cost him dearly, for one winter after such an incident Charles Dale was laid low, and only his indomitable spirit brought him through a long illness. Almost before he was convalescent he was in the saddle again.[43]

Prior to her marriage, Miss Anne Bolitho was presented with a wedding gift at a reception at The Oddfellow's Hall, Penzance. At the same occasion Charles Dale was presented with a cheque for forty-six pounds, as a retirement gift from well-wishers on the Trengwainton estate and from local hunting circles. The presentation was made by Mr W. H. Borlase who also gave an address:

In 1889 Mr Dale had entered the employ of Mr T. Robins Bolitho, that fine sportsman and old English gentleman, and had continued in the service of Col Bolitho. Fifty-three years unbroken service with one family spoke well for both employer and employed. There were a great many who owed their early riding education to him.

Mr Dale had always had a cheery and pleasant word for everybody. He had acted at times as whipper-in, as huntsman and in teaching the young ideas. Now the time had come for him to retire or, at least slack off, and the cheque which he was to receive was a token of the regard and esteem in which he was held. Mr Dale was a faithful servant, a keen sportsman, a good friend and loyal Englishman ….

Returning thanks, Mr Dale (who was accompanied by his wife) said that his first gratitude must be to God for the health and strength that had been given to him to carry on his work; then to his employers throughout all the years.

He had begun work in 1889, on a Sunday, and he had worked every Sunday since. (Laughter). "I love horses as much as I do people," declared Mr Dale, adding the fervent hope that all would attend to their horses properly. He would also like to thank all his farmers and other friends, and apologised for any damage he might have caused. (Laughter). In a concluding tribute to his wife, Mr Dale described her as "one of the best partners that ever a man married."[44]

Miss Anne Bolitho married Lt C. Tupper at Madron Church on 14 November 1942 and was driven to church in an open carriage by Charles Dale. I believe he may have timed his retirement so that he could perform this happy but final duty. *The Cornishman* reported the event on Thursday 19 November 1942:

The bride went to the church in a carriage driven by Mr Charles Dale, who is retiring after 53 years' service, and was performing his last function in the employ of the Bolitho family. When the bride and bridegroom were being taken back to Trengwainton

after the wedding ceremony, he had the unique experience of sitting on the box of the carriage while it was drawn by a contingent of Naval ratings, in charge of C.P.O. Smith, consisting of a gun crew of 18 men, all local and now serving in the Navy .... As the sun set the happy couple drove away in their carriage, to the cheers of their friends and Mr W. Pittaway, former huntsman, sounding "Gone Away." A new career started for this popular young couple, while another ended memorably for Mr Charles Dale as he drove them away in the failing light.[45]

In 1943 E.H.W. Bolitho wrote the following in his garden diary: *My entrance gates and about 30yds of railings have been removed and so, a landmark passes for ever. I might add that after Anne's wedding, Charles Dale, who drove her in a single horse drawn carriage to the Church (pulled back by the Navy) retired after over 50 years with Uncle Robins and myself, a great character known to all in West Cornwall. A very loyal servant to the Bolitho family, he, like the railings, was a landmark.*

Charles and his wife Elizabeth retired to Bedfordshire and he continued to keep horses during his retirement. He rode regularly with the Hertfordshire Hunt and celebrated his 80th birthday by riding at their meet at Weston, near Stevenage.

THE DALE BROTHERS, GARDENERS FOR THE BOLITHO FAMILY

James Dale, 26 March 1871 – 28 September 1954, gardener until 1900

William Dale, 30 August 1878 – 24 September 1969, gardener until 1906

Walter Dale, 3 October 1880 – 24 June 1943, gardener until 1906

Nancy Carter

Walter Howard Dale is the gardener standing on the right of four men in their long gardening aprons. He was the third son of my great-grandparents, James and Mary Jane Dale. He was one of 9 children and was born at Madron in 1880 but later the family moved to Poltair Terrace, Heamoor. He stood just 5ft 4.5 inches tall, with blue eyes and black hair. Walter began working at Trengwainton when he left school at an early age, possibly as young as 13, to join his two older brothers

James Henry and William whom I believe were already working as gardeners. Walter and his brother William were known locally for their fine tenor and bass voices. Walter was a member of the Choral Society and also played for Madron village cricket team. The horticultural knowledge that these three brothers gained was to change their lives. In 1900 it was James, the oldest brother, who had been a gardener for Col Glynn Bolitho at his homes, Poltair and then Keneggie, who took the bold step to sail from Southampton to New York on the ss St Paul. His wife Sarah and baby son Sydney remained in Madron.

He headed for Upper Michigan and immediately began to use his horticultural knowledge in an entrepreneurial way. By 1901 James was sufficiently well established, in Michigan's 'Copper Country' on the Keweenaw Peninsula for Sarah and Sydney to join him. His innate business sense and hard work eventually led to him becoming the owner of 50,000 square feet of glasshouses and three floristry shops. He became the largest grower of roses grown under glass in Upper Michigan.

Walter Howard Dale is the gardener standing on the right of four men

Sign for the Dale's flower business

In April 1906, probably at James's suggestion, William and Walter also made the journey to Hancock travelling from Liverpool on ss Celtic. Their departure was reported in *The Cornishman* of 12 April 1906:

Mr Walter Dale left Madron for America on Thursday. Being a popular member of the Cricket Club, Institute and Choral Society, he will be greatly missed, but will carry away (from) all the best wishes for a successful career combined with good health. He is accompanied by his brother, Mr William Dale, for whom also the good wishes are extended. They left Liverpool on Friday by the Celtic.

William and Walter began working with James in greenhouses in the Copper Country. William had also left his family in Madron, but his wife, Harper, and their children William and Margaret, were soon on their way to join him. William was reunited with his family in October of the same year. After a spell working with James in Hancock he was employed as a gardener for a wealthy family in the neighbouring town of Houghton.

In February 1908 Walter made a trip home and on 27 July 1908, he returned to Michigan. He sailed from Liverpool on ss Ivernia bound for Boston, Massachusetts. He continued to live with James and his family, and worked alongside James as a nurseryman and florist.

In November 1910 Walter married Hilda Cotton, whose family had emigrated from Newlyn. The wedding took

Dale's shop

where he continued to work as a gardener. He later moved to Southern Pines in North Carolina. I believe he was the gardener until retirement, on another of the Andrews family's properties at Pinehurst, which may have been their winter residence.

The brothers maintained a closeness with their home village and families in Madron; all of them made several return visits. When James visited he would sometimes follow The Western Hunt on horseback with his cousin Charles Dale, who was the head groom at Trengwainton from 1889 to 1942. James, William and Walter Dale changed their fortunes when they decided to emigrate. However, without the horticultural knowledge acquired at Trengwainton and other gardens owned by the Bolitho family, they may not have had such successful careers.

place at Trinity Church, Houghton, Michigan. By 1913 Walter and Hilda had two children, Gerald and Dorothy. The following year Walter and his family moved to Akron, Ohio, where he was to begin work as a gardener on the private estate of J. H. Andrews, a co-owner of the Quaker Oats Company.

In 1916 Walter, like his brothers, became an American citizen. Walter worked on the Andrews Estate for 29 years and the family lived in a house built for them by its owner. Prior to his death in 1943, he had been in charge of the estate's grounds with a team of 11 gardeners working under his supervision.

In 1920 William and his family also relocated to Akron

In 1925 James purchased a comfortable home in Madron for his unmarried sister Nannie and his elderly parents. Nannie Lawry Dale had also worked on the Trengwainton estate. She appears on both the 1891 and 1901 census working as a domestic servant in the home of Simon Semmens at Hendra Farm.

In 1931 James paid for the installation of electric light at Madron Methodist Chapel. He also contributed to the chapel's organ fund, the Penzance Spitfire Fund in 1940 and the fund to build Memorial House at Madron.[46]

DOROTHY SLATER

The 'baby housemaid' at Trengwainton aged 14

Written and transcribed by Annette Gibbons, Dorothy's eldest daughter. Cumbria, September 2017

Dorothy Slater, my mother, worked at Trengwainton in Cornwall for the Bolitho family probably arriving in 1930 when she was 14 years old.

Dorothy had been sent to stay with her second cousin Emily Georgiana Hogbin in Falmouth prior to being taken on at Trengwainton. Dorothy had been born in a small mining village in Derbyshire and her father, my grandfather had "wanted better than a mill job" for his eldest daughter.

Emily Hogbin was the superintendent of the Girls' Friendly Society in Falmouth and trained up girls to go into service. I believe that Dorothy worked at Trengwainton over two periods, one in 1930 and again in 1935. Dorothy was so young and very petite that she was known as the 'baby housemaid.' While Dorothy was at Trengwainton, the Bolitho family consisted of Colonel Edward Hoblyn and Mrs Agnes Bolitho and their two children, Simon and Anne.

One day Dorothy was asked to take hot water to one of the family bathrooms and was horrified to find Colonel Bolitho lying in the bath, hooting with laughter that he had caused her such embarrassment. Dorothy said if she were to meet him in a corridor she would try to scuttle away in fear and he would again boom out his laughter (she did a great impression of him!). The staff were all invited to stand on the mezzanine floor to watch the arrival of guests on the occasion of Miss Anne's 21st birthday party.

Dorothy remembered Mrs Agnes Bolitho in a gold lamé dress looking glamorous! When Major Simon Edward went away in military service he brought all the staff a small present. I still have the tapestry that mum received.

Dorothy used to go to village dances in Madron village hall and women wore long dresses. Particularly on the day George V died (the current Queen's grandfather). Dorothy remembered that she was with Sybil in a white gown and Dorothy wore blue. It was announced during the early evening that George V was dying – not that they cared that much as they were more interested in the boys.

In the year 2000 I contacted the family at Trengwainton and mentioned that I was coming to Cornwall with my parents and that Dorothy would love to visit. The family were delighted to meet her and we were invited to tea one afternoon. The present Bolithos had invited their great aunt Anne to attend as well who was a similar age to Dorothy. We did a tour of the house with Mum telling stories as we toured. Mrs Ali Bolitho took notes as she spoke. As we sat in the drawing room, Mum said quietly to me "I used to clean out that fire place!"

Mum had been engaged to Ronald Harvey, from Lincolnshire, who was the Whipper-in for the hunt at Trengwainton and we visited the hounds and found a gentleman there who had known of Ron Harvey. Ron was taken as prisoner of war in the first week of September 1939 and spent most of the war years in Stalag VIII B. I have a Christmas card that he sent her. Mum was still engaged to Ron Harvey and was wearing his ring, when she met my father, Geoffrey Pain, on Empire Day, 20th May 1941. They married in February 1944.

THE STAFF AT TRENGWAINTON IN THE 1930S

Mum told me about people who were at Trengwainton including:

- Head housemaid was Joan Morrison who married Mr Mitchell.

- Other housemaids were Sybil Andrewartha with Dorothy Slater, Nellie Jenkin (half time) and Muriel.

- Pittway (possibly from Yorkshire) was a parlour maid, Iris Buckingham was a scullery maid.

- Marjorie Williams shared a room with Dorothy during her first work term at Trengwainton.

- Dorothy called her Madge.

- There were three staff in the pantry: the butler, Mr Mitchell, a footman, and Nellie Jenkin did half time there.

- The chauffeur was Bill Jenkin.

- There was a dairymaid who lived separately in the nursery wing so as not to wake the others when she was up early milking cows and churning butter.

- Mr and Mrs Calder were a married couple in their 70s who acted as odd job man and woman.

- The cook was Mrs Warner who had her own sitting room and was asked to put out hot milk and cake for staff when they came in late from their day off.

- Mr Calder beeswaxed the floors, going down on all fours with hessian type sacking material on his knees to polish up after he had waxed the floor with his hands. He made his own beeswax polish. The ground floor of Trengwainton had beautiful parquet flooring.

HOLIDAYS IN SCOTLAND WITH THE BOLITHOS

Every year in September the house would take a 'holiday' to Scotland to the estate of Balnacoil beyond Inverness in Sutherland.

In the year Dorothy was taken with them, she went by car with the chauffeur Bill Jenkin. The journey took at least two days and others in the Colonel's car were Edgar, the butler, and Sybil Andrewartha with whom Dorothy shared a room at Trengwainton.

They stopped off at least once according to Dorothy (surely it took more than two days for that journey) and stayed in Crieff when she was offered Cock-a-leekie soup, the first time she'd heard of it. Others went up by train, including Anne who enjoyed the train.

Dorothy said that the servants all had a lovely time at Balnacoil, particularly being with the 'ghillies' (a Scottish term used for a guide on Highland hunting/fishing trips) and were invited to Gordonbush estate owned by Colonel Tyser to a dance for both sets of servants.

Another year, Dorothy stayed alone in Trengwainton with just Mr and Mrs Calder for company. Dorothy was told by the Colonel that she could choose any room in the house to sleep as long as it wasn't Mrs Bolitho's or his rooms. She chose the best guest room with all its windows and loved it, though was always scared of being alone and in the dark. Dorothy was very shy at 14 and when told that Mrs Bolitho would ask her what she wanted for Christmas, she didn't know what to say.

Sybil told her to ask her for whatever she wanted and Dorothy was delighted when she unwrapped a beautiful red dressing gown, the first she'd ever owned.

CHARLES WHITE

Gardener At Trengwainton

Carol Partridge

William Thomas Ronald White married my aunt in 1934 in West Ham, London. Ron, as he was known, was a policeman with the Metropolitan Police. Ron was born 10 May 1906 in Madron parish; his sister Evelyn was also born in Madron parish in about 1910.

Ron and Evelyn's father was Charles White. Charles was baptised on 4 May 1873 at Madron. His father, John White, had been a tin miner (possibly Ding Dong mine as this appears to be the closest) living at Gulval but by 1873 was a dairyman. The 1881 census shows us that Charles, his parents and siblings, were living at Luthergwearne, a farm in Madron. In 1891 the census shows us that Charles, now 18, is still at Luthergwearne and appears to be helping to run the farm for his mother, Honor Jelbart, who has become a widow by this time. Charles continued to farm at Luthergwearne until at least 1901 but it is interesting to note that the 1901 census also shows his brother, Thomas White, working as a gardener. But where? Was he working at Trengwainton but living 'out' in 1901?

On 14 Dec 1904 Charles married Rhoda Mary Retallick at Gulval. The banns give Charles' address as Luthergwearne once more but a notice in *The Cornishman* 29 Dec 1904 tells us that he is now a gardener at Trengwainton. In 1911 the census shows:

Charles White, aged 38, domestic gardener
Rhoda Mary White, aged 32
Evelyn white, aged 1
William Thomas Ronald White, aged 4
(Even at this age he appears to be known as 'Ron')

The address given is: Nanseglos Hea Moor, a dwelling house with five rooms (including a kitchen but not counting bathroom, scullery etc.)

Charles died in 1941 and the funeral was held on 16 Jul 1941 at Madron.

Red Camellia

JOHN GRENFELL HALL

Gardener at Trengwainton circa 1911

Notes complied by Sophie May Lewis, great-grand niece of John Grenfell Hall, October 2017

John Grenfell Hall's story starts in 1888. He was born on St Mary's Island, Isles of Scilly. The first-born son of Mary Elizabeth Alexandra Moyle, and was named after his maternal grandfather, Dr John Grenfell Moyle.

This man, originally from Penzance, served the entirety of the Isles of Scilly as the archipelago's only surgeon and general practitioner. He had come to the Scillies from mainland Cornwall in 1849 and soon settled down with local girl Elizabeth Nance.

Mary E.A Hall, née Moyle, was their fourth child, she had seven siblings, five of whom were sisters. One of the brothers died aged just 10 years old, leaving Mary's immediately elder sibling as the only son.

As an older teenager, in 1881 Mary had lived away from home as a student teacher at a small school in Devon, and upon return to Scilly she took a position as a school teacher at the school on St Mary's island. She married in March 1888, aged 25. Her spouse was John Hall, a carpenter from mainland Cornwall. It is supposed that he came to the islands for work, but the details of how he and Mary met are unknown.

John Grenfell Hall was baptised just seven months after the wedding, October 1888. Within the next two to three years, the small family of John Hall and Mary, with baby John Grenfell left the Isles of Scilly and set up home in John's hometown of Chacewater near Truro. The census of 1891 (always recorded in April) reveals

Mary with two year old John Grenfell, and two additional children, another son Charles Hicks aged one and four month old daughter Gladys, living in Chacewater. John Hall is not registered in the census however, other than a note that reads 'Husband in U S America'. Three more siblings for John Grenfell were born between 1895 and 1900 (a sister and two brothers, Dorothy, Ernest, and Thomas) during which time the family relocated from Chacewater to the much larger Cornish town of Liskeard.

After 22 years of marriage to Mary, John Hall died aged 42. Within a year, the widowed Mary had taken her five youngest children and left Cornwall, creating a new life in Bradford Yorkshire.

The same census that places the fatherless Hall family in Yorkshire shows that John Grenfell Hall had found reason to remain behind in his home country, as he was living and employed as a gardener at Trengwainton Garden, Madron near Penzance.

Although John Grenfell Hall is certainly living at Trengwainton in gardeners' accommodation in 1911, records of him in Cornwall stop in the years afterwards.

The reason for this is revealed when he is recorded as living in Mildura in Australia when he enlists into the Australian army in 1915. John Grenfell Hall survived active service through WWI, returning to Australia at the end of the war.

He was eventually successful in a land acquisition application, and settled in Mildura on a fruit-farming plot, marrying local girl Ellen May Baker in 1922. John Grenfell Hall died in the 1950s but it is pleasing to note that the family still live in Australia today.

WILLIAM COOPER

Land Agent of Trengwainton 1911 – 1926

Ben Cooper

I have been interested in tracing my ancestry for some time and with the help of the internet and by studying many photographs and documents I have managed to trace my heritage back into the 18th century and beyond.

William Cooper, my great-grandfather, was born in 1860 and lived until 1937. He had a full and active life and served in many land estate positions before retiring to Reading. In his final years when almost an invalid he set down his memories and reminiscences, in pencil, in several exercise books with the help of his wife Caroline.

William starts his memories with the following quote:

It has been suggested to me that being an invalid and unable to read and nearly blind, I write some of my reminiscences, some of which may probably be interesting to my descendants in years to come.

These have been invaluable in providing a fascinating insight into not only his life and our family but of life in the late Victorian era and through into the early Edwardian period and beyond. My family and I are greatly indebted to my cousin Christopher Cooper for his painstaking work in deciphering these pencil recollections, editing and processing the scripts into the text.

Obviously, we are only extracting his life and times at Trengwainton from 1911 to 1926 during which time he was estate manager and had many associations with the local area, these are read as they were written down in the eyes of someone who bridged the end of the Victorian era and Edwardian times.

MEMORIES OF WILLIAM COOPER, LAND AGENT OF TRENGWAINTON 1911 – 1926

I had to look round for a fresh post and a friend of mine who was agent for Lady Smyth of the Smyth estates near Long Ashton told me of a vacancy in Cornwall, where the agent there was leaving, so got into communication with the owner, Mr Thomas Robins Bolitho and I met him at one of the large shows.

My interview with Mr Bolitho was most satisfactory but on asking him what he would allow me for the keep and use of a horse, etc, as of course had sold mine and had not one; for small holdings, he told me, he had generally 14 or 15 in his stables, I could always have one whenever

left
Ben Cooper,
William Cooper's
great-grandson

right
William Cooper

I wanted to get about the property. In many ways this was very satisfactory as it saved me the wages of a groom and there were no stables at the agent's house.

So I left Bath and went to Cornwall, which I found very different to any other place I lived at. I remained for nearly seventeen years until Mr Bolitho's death and as he had no family, all the property was cut up and left to various nephews and by that time, being nearly 65, I was too old to get a new post, so came to Reading and purchased a house there.

Mr Bolitho, I found, was looked upon as a sort of King of West Cornwall, he being one of the wealthiest and best-known men in the county. He was also most generous, giving away vast sums to nearly everything in the county that required assistance, also he had a pack of fox-hounds ('the Western') of which he had been Master and hunted for over 40 years entirely at his own expense, also paying poultry, damage, and other funds. These hounds I found were a very fine lot as Mr Bolitho had always been most particular in breeding and drafting.

Of later years as he was getting older his nephew, Colonel W. Bolitho, hunted them when he had time (on other days the kennel huntsman, Tom Mollard, who was a really good man, and a wonder over the Cornish country, did so), but when the war came and Colonel Bolitho had to go, Mr Bolitho asked me to act as field master and take his place when not out. This I did, so filled the post that many gentlemen would have given hundreds a year for.

The western country was very rough, there being a large outcrop of granite rock everywhere and the fields only about an acre in size; consequently we had more jumping in one day, than in most districts in a month, and wanted a very clever horse.

The whole of the Cornish land, I think, was originally what we call croft, that is, a wild, an uncultivated sort of rough pasture land, uncultivated because it was just a skinning of turf over the rough granite, and when the mining was in full swing, the miners were given a few acres of this and they dug out the large granite blocks which weighed perhaps from 2cwt to 2tons and dragged them to one spot; piling them on one another and so making their cottages, which to present ideas were most primitive. Then they would clear a little more land in the same way and drag the stones to one side of the ground and so make a little field and in this way the district was covered with small farms or tenements, as when one small field had been made, others would be added; consequently all the tenements were small even if in time two were joined together to make one and later on called a farm. The walls dividing the fields were locally called hedges and were built up of these big stones, the general rule was, that, say, the base of the wall or hedge was 5ft, it would be brought up to 5ft high, narrowing at the top, and the centre filled with small stones or earth. Sometimes a row of gorse would be planted on the top – there were very few gateways, and those that were, were quite narrow, and until altered, not wide enough, for any modern farming implement to go through, as in the early days there were no wheeled carts and even the harvest was taken to the mowhays or rick-yard, on mules' backs.

Memories of William Cooper, Land Agent of Trengwainton 1911-1926 (pages 138 - 140) copyright Benjamin Cooper and the Cooper family.

The rest of William Cooper's diary can be read at www.trengwaintonheritage.co.uk

THOMAS EDGAR HOLWAY AND SELINA HAZEL MARY WINTERBOTTOM

Footman and Maid at Trengwainton, 1930s

Tom Holway

Thomas Edgar was born in Uffculme, Devon, on 28th April, 1907. He was always known as Edgar because his father was also a Thomas or Tom.

Selina Hazel Mary was born at Perran Downs, Perranuthnoe, Cornwall on 17th November, 1918. She was always known as Hazel.

I will refer to them as 'Dad' and 'Mum' for the sake of brevity.

Thomas Edgar Holway standing next to Mr Jenkin, chauffeur

Dad passed the selection exam for Tiverton Grammar School but with five brothers and sisters his parents could not afford books, uniform or travel so he was unable to go. My grandad was injured and gassed in France and died on Dad's thirteenth (and uncle Joe's twelfth) birthday. Dad entered an apprenticeship with the village tailor later that year (1920).

The tailor could not afford to employ Dad at the end of his five-year apprenticeship as the country was in a depression. Dad looked further afield for work and found work as a footman for a family in Torquay, probably in mid 1926 as there are a couple of references dated March and July 1926 from Uffculme people.

There is a photo of Dad in his footman's uniform taken at Ponsandane near Gulval in 1929 and I think Dad said the house was owned by a member of the Bolitho family. According to a reference written in February 1943, the Trengwainton Agent and Estate Manager, Mr T. Beamish, said he had known Dad for over 12 years so Dad probably moved from Ponsandane to Trengwainton in 1930 or 31. Dad started as a footman

at Trengwainton and ended up as Butler/Valet. Dad was medically examined for army service at the end of July 1940 and Lt Col Bolitho wrote him a reference in September, so he probably left Trengwainton soon after.

Dad used to relax on his days off by swimming out to a buoy that was about half a mile out from Penzance promenade with his pals. Dad would have been one of the first people in the UK to hear about the demise of the Hindenburg airship when it caught fire in the USA in 1937. One of his pals worked at Cable and Wireless and told him about it when he came off shift.

Mum left Penzance High School for Girls without staying on in the sixth form. On leaving school, Mum went to work as a nanny for a dentist's family in Helston, probably in 1935. I think Mum was at Helston for a couple of years which suggests she probably went to work at Trengwainton in 1937 or thereabouts.

Mum worked as a maid and left Trengwainton to train as a nurse some time after the outbreak of war in 1939. I don't know exactly when Mum left Trengwainton but I remember her saying that the staff were all encouraged to join up or go nursing if not too old. I have a postcard

from Dad posted in Penzance and addressed to Mum at Royal Cornwall Infirmary in Truro postmarked June 1940.

I think the chauffeur was Mr Jenkin and I got the impression that he and Dad got on well and shared a sense of humour. The Bolitho family used to go to Scotland for the Grouse shooting and Mr Jenkin took Dad and two maids in the Rolls Royce while the family travelled by train. On one occasion Mum was one of the maids and I think Dad went several times. I would imagine that there were no trips after 1939.

Mum and Dad were married at Perranuthnoe on 18th August 1940 with Mum getting special leave for the wedding. Dad was stationed with the Army near Redruth and Mum was in Newquay nursing wounded soldiers. Dad used to see her on to the Newquay train at Redruth after they had been out for the evening. On the 20th March 1941, Dad and another chap saw Mum

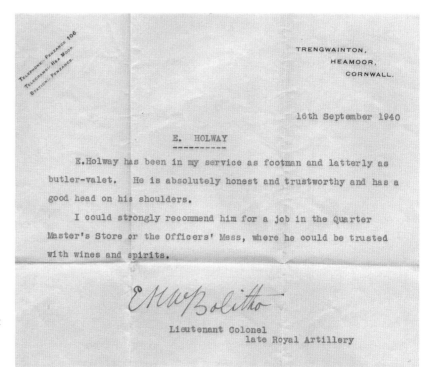

TRENGWAINTON,
HEAMOOR,
CORNWALL.

16th September 1940

E. HOLWAY

E.Holway has been in my service as footman and latterly as butler-valet. He is absolutely honest and trustworthy and has a good head on his shoulders.

I could strongly recommend him for a job in the Quarter Master's Store or the Officers' Mess, where he could be trusted with wines and spirits.

Lieutenant Colonel
late Royal Artillery

and another girl on to the train and then answered the call of nature in the station toilet. At 9:41 pm, according to police records, the station was bombed. When Dad and the other chap were pulled out of what was left of the toilet, Dad had serious leg injuries and the other chap was dead. I understand that if it were not for a lady, and possibly others, donating blood, that Dad would probably not have survived. Dad's right leg was amputated below the knee and he was fitted with an artificial leg and walked with a stick for the rest of his life. When he left hospital he and Mum went to live with his mother and Dad took over the running of Craddock Post Office from her. Dad gave up the running of the Post Office and took an office job with a local company because the Post Office pay was not enough to keep a family.

Thomas Edgar Holway reference letter

Thomas Edgar Holway

MRS VIOLET STEVENS (NÉE TIPPETT)

Land Girl, Trengwainton Home Farm 1942-47

as told to Peter Scrase in the early 2000s

Violet Stevens in
Land Army outfit

Mrs Violet Stevens came from Newlyn East and was 'called up' for war work during the Second World War in late 1942. Her mother wanted her to stay in Cornwall

and she became a land girl, doing her one month training with Mr Walter Tregarthen who farmed at Collurian, White Cross, near Crowlas.

After her training Violet went to work at Trengwainton Home Farm, lodging with Mr and Mrs Bill Jenkin (Bolitho chauffeur) who lived to the rear of the Bolitho 'Big House'.

LAND GIRL UNIFORM

Violet wore the standard uniform which consisted of dungarees and bib, dust jacket and boots for work. There was also a 'walking out' dress consisting of brown shoes, fawn stockings, breeches, fawn airtex shirt, green tie, three quarter length fawn coat and hat.

Violet stayed with Mr and Mrs Jenkin for some time but eventually shared accommodation with another land girl, Annie Love, at Tregoddick Cottage, Madron.

CONDITIONS OF WORK

Violet recalls feeling that she worked all the time! It was clearly a very hard life. She got up at 6.00 am, filled her flask, then off up the lane to Home Farm.

Mr Cyril Guy, from Madron, would by that time have brought in the cows from the fields and Violet would then milk the cows using the milking machines. She then returned to the lodgings and had breakfast between 8.00 and 9.00 am.

Then back to the farm to clean out the cow sheds and sterilise the equipment; brush up the yard and feed the calves and heifers, a big job as there were a lot of young stock in the pens. Violet worked mainly in the farmyard, later she was joined by Flo Jasper, from the St Just/Pendeen area.

Annie Love joined later and helped clean out the cow sheds. Violet also worked with Annie on sugar beet. This task involved banging two beets together to get the earth off; lopping the tops off; bagging up and transporting them for pulping as animal feed.

They were also involved in silage making, a process in which stamped down grass is treated with black treacle in the mowhay. Violet's other tasks included feeding the bull and to do this she had to pass through the pens

to the yard house! At 4 pm she would bring the cows in and milk them again, finishing work at 6 pm. Violet had worked a twelve hour day and understandably went to bed early at 9.00 pm! She spent the time after supper knitting, or making patchwork dolls clothes for the Red Cross.

Beyond the yard at Home Farm was the mowhay and the water mill. A land girl called 'Piskey' operated the mill processing feed; rolled oats for cows and horses,

worker; worked like a man, and with a driver would unload 2 cwt (100 Kg) bags from the lorry! Later on Violet was joined on the farm by several other land girls.

Violet remembered Peter Scrase and his family as, during the war years, they went down to Home Farm on a daily basis to collect the milk. They lived at Polclose, Trengwainton.

and ground barley for pigs. Piskey and Muriel eventually went up to stay with the Woolridges at the Madron Carn Lodge. Violet went home to see her family in Newlyn East once a month.

WAGES

In training at Collurian, Violet received 8/9 (44p) one week and 8/11 (45p) the next week etc. At Trengwainton she received 21/ − (£1.05) per week from which she paid 10/ − (50p), at least, towards her keep.

HELP ON THE FARM

When Violet first started in the yard at Home Farm she did not have any support with her daily tasks, so she complained, saying that she needed help in the yard at 6 am with the milking. Dizzy Bolitho (née Bourne, Col E. Bolitho's second wife) offered to help, however she was not an early riser, so Mr Jenkin cut Violet a very long bamboo from the garden, which she used to tap Dizzy's window in the Big House until she arose! Dizzy was a great help in the cowshed and according to season would go ploughing with horses. She was a hard

AUGUSTA BOLITHO

At Trengwainton 1887 – 1932

Pauline Hope, Project Volunteer

Born in Yorkshire on 15 July 1848 Augusta Jane Wilson married Thomas Robins Bolitho in Westminster on 30 January 1870. Single and under 21, she was the charge of her father. As a married woman she was one of the first generation to benefit from the Married Women's Property Acts, which gave her the same financial independence as a single woman. She would have promised to love, honour and obey her husband but what talents she had she was able to give freely. Her concern for the community, her kindness and generosity towards it, is her legacy.

Augusta was the first woman Justice of the Peace on the West Penwith Bench, which was a remarkable achievement in the day when administration of the law was monopolised by the male fraternity.

Augusta died on 14 October 1932.

CHARITABLE WORK

The West Cornwall Infirmary and Dispensary was built on its present site in 1874. Augusta and her husband played an important part in its development.

Concerned with child welfare, in 1896 Augusta had instigated Mothers' Meetings in Gulval which became in 1903 the Mothers' Union. She was the first woman Member of the Board of Guardians for Madron Workhouse situated less than a mile from Trengwainton. This was reported in The Cornishman of 24 March 1898.

Augusta and Thomas Robins supported the Young Men's Christian Association which was founded in London on June 6th, 1844 by George Williams. The aim being to put Christian principles into practice by developing a healthy 'body, mind, and spirit.' By 2017 it had touched the lives of 57,000,000 people in 125 countries. Its International House in Penzance provides support for many people in need, no doubt not a far cry from the practical help given in the premises they helped to create in Market Jew Street.

Augusta encouraged the formation of Boy Scout and Girl Guide troops which had been inaugurated nationally in 1908 and 1910. These young people were encouraged to fulfill their potential and, being teenagers during both periods of war, provided invaluable service to a community which had lent its young men to the

Augusta Bolitho

military. The Penzance Madron Scout Group flourishes still with enthusiastic leaders and boys and girls between the ages of six and twenty.

Many fund raising events for local and national causes were laid on at Trengwainton, such as one for the Navy League on 5 July 1912. One annual Trengwainton tradition until 1914 was the July free tea treat for school pupils and teachers. Apparently parents and friends paid 6d and 9d each for the privilege of attending in 1898, and in 1906 a total of 384 people from Madron and Morvah attended the event which must have been great fun.

In May 1914 the gardens were open to celebrate the 300th anniversary of the granting by King James of the Charter to Penzance.

Augusta had encouraged the foundation of Madron Women's Institute in 1918, the first in Cornwall. It had been formed to encourage women to share their knowledge of early child-care and has grown to inspire women to develop their talents and interests to enrich their lives.

In July 1920, on her 50th wedding anniversary, 1,507 women in West Penwith arranged to present Augusta with a gold tray, silver inkstand and a vellum with the names of the contributors. Unfortunately she had fallen downstairs the day before and was unable to attend the ceremony. It says something of Augusta Bolitho that so many women wished to pay her such a warm tribute.

THE SUFFRAGIST MOVEMENT

Augusta was one of the first supporters of the Women's Social and Political Union and the Honorary Secretary of the Penzance branch of the National Union of Women's Societies. She greeted the suffragists on the first leg of their journey from Land's End to Hyde Park, travelling with them to Penzance on the 19th of July 1913 where they received a mixed welcome, arriving as they did on market day!

The Cornishman newspaper gave a fair and sympathetic treatment to the start of the pilgrimage:

Four ladies 'this little band of zealots' comprising Miss Misick (organising secretary), Mrs Ramsay (Plymouth), Miss Raby (Exeter) and Miss Helen Fraser (London) were given a hearty send off by Mrs Robins Bolitho, Honorary Chairman of the Penzance Branch of the NUWS, alongside a number of men who had assembled to raise a cheer. They travelled with a covered wagon with 'National Union of Women's Societies, Non Militant, Non Party – President Mrs Fawcett' painted on its sides. It must be said that her husband supported the movement for women's suffrage.

GOLDEN WEDDING

The Bolithos' golden wedding anniversary was made much of in *The Cornishman* newspaper. On the 17th of July 1920 it reported on:

a garden party and lunch at Trengwainton for 1,000 guests including 100 tenant family members. The sun was shining as the Royal Naval Band from Plymouth played in the afternoon through to the evening dancing accompanied by Penzance Independent Band.

Augusta's contribution to Trengwainton and the community was outstanding in that her investment in community organisations has survived and grown for more than a century, and will flourish in the years to come – as the women of 1920 recognised and appreciated.

GEORGE JAMES

Trengwainton about 1920

Pauline Sheppard, Writer and Project Volunteer

In his later life, George James recorded an account of an extraordinary year he spent at Trengwainton as carriage boy, waiter, boot and shoe cleaner and attendant to Thomas Robins. He greatly admired Augusta Bolitho. He kept a diary which is part of the Bolitho Family estate.

The following is an imagined interpretation of George's words, abstracted from some of the factual information from the diary, which was shared in a talk by Edward Bolitho at Landithy Hall, Madron on 28th October 2017.

Moss

opp
Flower palettes
made in communnity
workshop by Jane
Bailey

My name's George James. When I was fourteen year of age I was paid ten shillun a week an' I had my own room in the servants' quarters up Trengwainton House. The servants' quarters were in the attic. Some smart I was. I was sent to Messrs Rowe, down the terrace in Penzance, where I was fitted for a top hat, an' a great coat an boots. Bein' a carriage boy I used to ride into Penzance on the coach.

I had to make sure Mistress an the Master was tucked up warm an comfy with blankets an' a foot muff an' all; then I could climb aboard myself. I liked my mistress. Augusta. She was a fine lady. She wasen from 'ere, family up Yorkshire way. She'd go off shopping in town while Mr Thomas Robins went Barclays Bank. They have a special 'Bolitho Room' in Barclays Bank.

There was strict rules in the House. Mr Mitchell, he was butler, he supervised all the indoor staff; thirteen there were back then. Each and every one was given their own best butter each week. We had daily prayers in the library. The Mistress, Augusta, she used to play organ. It was a fancy piece, made by one of the greatest organ makers of all time they say, Father Willis.

Years later it was donated to Breage Church. Sunday mornings we'd all walk to Madron Church for Canon Jenkins' service.

Sometimes there was tennis games played up the House in summer; and tuition was give to any guests who didden know the rules. I remember A Christmas Concert up Madron Workhouse.

It was all organised by Augusta. That was the kind of woman she was, I remember singing in the concert after the meal.

One of my reg'lar duties was every day at four o'clock I had to take a satchel up to the postman at the main gate, had to go up by pony an' cart. See the Bolitho family had their own post boy to make deliveries. Roy Matthew's grandfather used to hold the position. Used to like to time his round to finish at Trengwainton in time for tea!

T'was a great treat to serve in the dining room. I saw the artist Alfred Munnings while attendin' in the dining room, charmin' man he was too. And Marconi, some clever he was; an this one time Canon Spooner was there, use to get his words mixed more'n me.

A poem by Elaine Stammers, inspired by the workshop day at Trengwainton.

You both sat there stiffly
in that donkey carriage,
symbols of a lost, forgotten age,
going nowhere.

We carried you away that day
to explore,
let you off the page,
to travel a little, out of left field.

We let the spirit of the place,
the garden,
speak its own story,
and set you free.

Trengwainton Garden / Shallal 23rd September 2016

FRANK KINGDON-WARD

Oliver Tooley, grandson of Frank Kingdon-Ward
www.bluepoppypublishing.co.uk

Francis Kingdon-Ward was born in Manchester in 1885, the son of Harry Marshall Ward, and Selina Mary (neé Kingdon). Selina came from a long line of successful lace-makers in Exeter, while Harry was a lecturer at Owens College in Manchester and would later go on to become a professor of Botany at Cambridge. Francis was always an adventurer, getting into quite a few scrapes, and a great deal of mischief, which would have landed him in very serious trouble if caught. Indeed, he was very nearly 'sent down' from Cambridge on one occasion, but for the intervention of his sister, Winifred, who doted on him.

When his father died, aged just 52, Francis was forced to sit Tripos a year early, for financial reasons. Having attained a 'second' and wanting nothing more than to become an explorer but lacking the connections or resources to do so, he accepted a job teaching in a Shanghai public school so that he would be closer to the field. Sure enough, an offer came to travel up the Yangtze river which he accepted at a moment's notice. From 1909 until his death in 1958 he was almost continually on expeditions, mainly to China, Tibet, Burma, and Assam, interrupted only briefly by two world wars in which, despite his earnest efforts to throw himself at the front lines, he played only supporting roles.

His visits to Britain, and other western nations, were brief and infrequent, long enough to plan the next expedition, attend whichever functions he could, give lectures about his travels, and deal with any business matters such as meeting with publishers.

In 1923, he married Florinda Norman Thompson, who relieved him of much of the business side of things and introduced him to Jonathan Cape, who published all his future books. They had two daughters, Pleione, in 1926 and Martha, in 1928. By then, he had already established himself as one of the most important collectors of his

opp

Frank Kingdon-Ward

Collecting and transporting plants from overseas, C19th

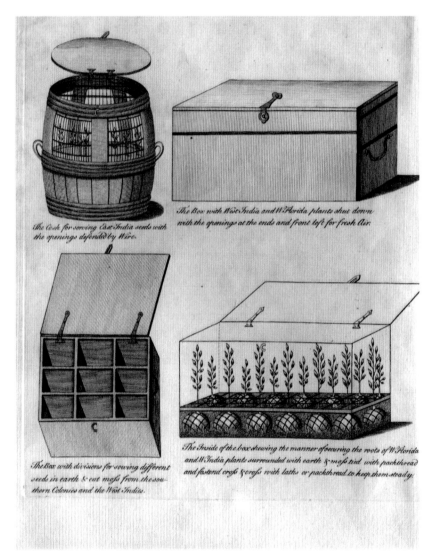

The Cask for sowing East India seeds with the openings defended by Wire.

The Box with West India and W.Florida plants shut down with the openings at the ends and front left for fresh Air.

The Box with divisions for sowing different seeds in earth & cut moss from the southern Colonies and the West Indies.

The Inside of the box shewing the manner of securing the roots of W.Florida and W.India plants surrounded with earth & moss tied with packthread and fastend cross & cross with laths or packthread to keep them steady.

day with the 1924 expedition to seek out the legendary Shangri-La falls on the Tsangpo river and in Tibet. He was now commonly known as 'Frank Kingdon-Ward' after his usual nom-de-plume.

During 1926 – 1928 he went on two related expeditions to Assam and Burma; funded, for the most part, by the Percy Sladen Memorial fund. Funding also came from the government grant committee of the Royal Society, and a consortium of backers described by Frank in his book *Plant Hunting on the Edge of the World*, as '*a syndicate of enthusiastic and famous gardeners*,' headed by Lionel De Rothschild and including Sir Edward Bolitho of Trengwainton. Frank describes his objectives as

(i) to collect seeds of beautiful flowering plants for English gardens. That is my profession.

(ii) To collect dried specimens of interesting plants for study. That is also part of my profession.

(iii) To explore unknown mountain ranges, and find out something about their past history, the distribution of their plants, and any other secrets they are willing to reveal. That is my hobby.

On the second expedition, 1927 – 28, he was joined by Hugh Clutterbuck, an arctic explorer who also contributed some £600 to the costs. Clutterbuck, being mild-mannered, placid, and patient was the perfect companion to Frank who could be moody and introspective, or so driven by work that he would ignore those around him almost entirely. In 1924 Lord Cawdor, who accompanied Frank to Tibet, had written, '*It drives me clean daft to walk behind him… always stopping to gape at weeds!*' Evidently Clutterbuck had no such feelings. Frank gave him the nickname Buttercup and dedicated his book to him:

My dear Buttercup,

Travel books must be dedicated; and to whom could I dedicate this one more aptly than to you, who shared the privations, disappointments, and (dare I say it?) triumphs of the Assam journey? So you find yourself, for better or worse, godfather to a bantling of sorts.

Yours ever, K.W.

Herbarium specimens are numbered alongside the collector's abbreviation, in Frank's case, K.W. He collected some 3,000 specimens on these expeditions, and brought back seed for as many plants as he thought might be hardy, or half hardy, in Britain. It would be impossible to list all the plants collected, and impractical to list even those for which seed was obtained, but one in particular from the 1927-8 expedition was outstanding.

Rhododendron macabeanum was first recorded for western science in 1882 by Sir George Watt, but no seed was collected, and it had not been found again since.

One of Frank's greatest assets was his ability to track down a difficult to locate plant and, more importantly, to recall exactly where it was for future reference. His profession required that he collect herbarium specimens in the spring, to show the flower and foliage to best effect, but then to return to the same spot in late autumn to collect seeds. By then the ground might be covered in snow, the trees bare of leaves, and yet he could unerringly return to plants with great potential. *R. macabeanum* (KW 7724) was one such. Found growing at 8-10,000 feet on Mt Japvo, in the Naga hills Assam, he wrote *'A forest tree with handsome foliage, truss with 12-18 flowers…it goes right to the summit where it forms forests…it should be hardy'*.

He collected the seed on 1st December 1927 and by spring of the following year seeds arrived at Trengwainton. The plant did indeed turn out to be hardy, and with the mild climate of Cornwall, it is able to grow to its full stature, although the process takes a great deal of time. *Rhododendron elliotii* (KW 7725) also first recorded by Watt in 1882, was a blood red variety which can be seen at Trengwainton.

Unlike many other explorers and plant hunters of the 19th and 20th centuries, Frank never settled down, despite more than once being offered well paid and important jobs at places like Kew Gardens.

He also managed to avoid death in the field on an almost 'feline' number of occasions. Then in 1958, in a Kensington pub, while planning another expedition, he had a stroke from which he never recovered. He has been called the 'Last of the Great Plant Hunters' and his epitaph blooms every spring in gardens across Britain, and the rest of the world. The only tribute he would have desired is the pleasure you derive from them.

Greenhouses, 1890

THE OLD ORCHARD

Barbara Santi

The old orchard can be found next to the Dig for Victory plot. It has delicious apples with wonderful names. Some of the windfall apples are for sale outside the Head Gardener's Cottage (now the secondhand bookshop).

The Old Orchard

Mulberry tree

Here are some of the apple tree varieties:

- Arthur Turner Early Cooker
- Ben's Red Early Dessert
- Lane's Prince Albert Late Cooker
- Cornish Aromatic Late Dessert
- Charles Ross Dual Purpose
- Crawlet Beauty Late Cooker

In this area you will also see the most beautiful old mulberry tree, all gnarled and twisted. It's spectacular but often overlooked. Mulberry trees were brought to England by the Romans and over time have had admirers such as Henry VIII, Thomas Gainsborough and William Shakespeare.

We ate windfall apples and knew the sweetest ones had holes in them (holes were made by wasps).

Nancy Carter

157

The scalloped windows

Greenhouses

1890

THE VICTORIAN MESSENGER GREENHOUSE

Nancy Carter

Trengwainton originally had at least seven glasshouses to facilitate the amount of propagation that was being undertaken, probably in the 1870s. Only one of them is still in existence and this glasshouse, designed and manufactured by Messenger & Co. of Loughborough, was erected in 1860. It is not known whether the other glasshouses were also Messenger structures.

Thomas Goode Messenger was a plumber and glazier. His business evolved and by 1871, as a 'Horticultural Builder', he employed 52 men and 12 boys. His products were varied and included glasshouses, vineries and conservatories and all the necessary fittings. As well as designs available from catalogues, he also undertook commissioned work both in Britain and overseas.

Trengwainton's current Head Gardener, Phil Griffiths, has not been able to find the exact design of the remaining three-quarter span glasshouse, in any of the catalogues that he has seen. It would appear, however, that cast-iron fittings could be mixed and matched according to the needs and budget of the purchaser. The structure features glass that has been cut into a scallop shape.

Phil Griffiths explains, "The scalloped glass seems to have been a specialism of Messenger as they did not recommend putting putty on top of the glass, as most would. The glass was scalloped to encourage rain to run more quickly down the centre, drawing more rain water with it. This is evident when you stand there on a rainy day. There were two options when buying a Messenger glasshouse. The glasshouse was delivered 'flat-pack'

from the factory and you could either pay for their team to come and build it for you or have it erected by your own team of estate staff. It is not known which option was taken at Trengwainton." A system was installed to enable the easy opening and closing of air vents by means of a single lever. Phil Griffiths continues, "The lever opens all of the front air vents at once with one pull or push of the lever. I have a catalogue in which it is described as 'a lever tackle of the latest type'. The top vents may have originally had a similar system that was later replaced with sash cord and pulleys."

There is a very similar system employed on the windows of Landithy Hall at Madron. The building was completed in 1909, and paid for by the Bolitho family. In one of the garden archives from the years covering the 1950s and 1960s the glasshouse was being used as a tomato house. It may have always been used for the production of salad crops. Gareth Wearne, Trengwainton gardener, recalls it being used to grow early potatoes when he first started working at the gardens in the late 1980s. The glasshouse underwent a restoration programme over a six-month period between 2007 – 2008.

AUTUMN

Phil Griffiths

- If it's a year when we are working on the stream, autumn is when we would divide herbaceous perennials to stop overcrowding.

- We continue to collect and sow seed from perennials and hardy annuals.

- Plant spring-flowering bulbs.

- Cut back perennials that have died down.

- Clean out cold frames and greenhouses so that they are ready for use in the autumn.

- In the Kitchen Garden cover leafy vegetable crops with bird-proof netting.

- Divide established rhubarb crowns to create new plants.

- Plant out spring cabbages and dig up remaining potatoes before slug damage spoils them.

- Harvest apples, pears and grapes.

- We would start to move tender plants, including ones from the dipping pond, into a greenhouse, and bring in the succulents in the granite troughs to stop them damping off.

- As soon as the garden closes we start renovating worn-out areas of lawn by laying turf or reseeding.

- We cover some of the larger tender plants like *Ensete ventricosum,* the black banana from Ethiopia, and the *Tibouchina urvilleana* or glory bush from Brazil, to protect them from frost.

- We would be keeping an eye on the weather.

- After a good storm we collect seaweed from the beach at Marazion to mulch the Kitchen Garden beds with.

- Throughout autumn and winter we carry out tree surveys on every tree in the garden, checking for decay, infection movement in the roots etc.

- We would try to cut the grass right until it's too wet to put any machines on.

IN THE VEGETABLE GARDEN

Ian Willsdon

SEPTEMBER

In the Cornish climate there is still time to sow crops for winter and early spring in September. One good crop to sow now is 'Giant Winter' spinach. An early September sowing may give you a late October harvest if the weather is kind, but this crop will be more suitable for early spring harvesting.

The plants will not grow much during December and January with low light levels, but will start to grow again in February, providing leaves in March, April and beyond until they start to bolt as the weather warms up.

You can sow direct and thin out the seedlings but it is probably better to sow under glass in modules, making sure to harden off plants before finally planting out.

The plants will grow quite large as the name implies so it is a good idea to space them at least 20cm apart to ensure good air circulation and stop overcrowding. Leaving clear ground around plants also means fewer hiding places for slugs which can be a problem in mild wet winters. Depending on what crop was in the ground before the spinach it is probably a good idea to mulch around

Cercidiphyllum japonicum

Illustration by Dominica Williamson

161

the plants with compost as spinach thrives in fertile soil. This will also help to suppress weeds around the new plants. Spinach likes nitrogen so it can be a good crop to follow nitrogen setting crops like peas or beans.

This will give the plants a good start and help them to bulk up before low light levels slow them down. Once the weather warms up and the plants start to grow in spring it can help to give a feed such as liquid seaweed or pelleted chicken manure to ensure a heavy crop.

OCTOBER

Garlic can be a difficult crop to grow successfully in the Cornish climate as each clove should ideally spend 30 days and nights below 10°c for bulb formation to occur. Garlic also prefers not to be too wet during the colder months. However, it is worth a try and can be planted from late October or early November. If you have a very wet autumn it can be better to start the garlic off in modules under glass and plant out later to decrease the chances of rotting. To increase drainage in the soil you can add plenty of organic matter to the soil such as compost before planting in ridges. Suitable varieties include Early Purple Wight and Bohemian Rose Wight. Elephant garlic also can do well in Cornwall and I have read that Picardy Wight does well in damper soils but I have not tried this variety.

When planting divide the bulbs into individual cloves and make sure that they are planted the correct way up. Plant about 10 cm deep and about 18cm apart. The cloves should produce little green shoots quite quickly and then slow down until the New Year. You can feed in early spring to encourage growth using liquid seaweed or comfrey feed. Garlic is also best kept weed-free and watered in long dry spells until harvested from June on.

NOVEMBER

November is a good time to prune and take hardwood cuttings of soft fruit such as blackcurrants and redcurrants. You need to remember when pruning that blackcurrants fruit on second year growth while redcurrants and white currants fruit on older wood. This means that you have to prune differently for each type of bush. When pruning blackcurrants it is good to take out a proportion of old wood each year making sure not to touch new growth wood (usually it is easy to tell the difference as old wood is darker in colour).

Take out any crossing branches and any branches that are growing in directions you don't want. Try to keep the bushes open so that light can get in to ripen the fruit and it is easier to pick. If you don't prune blackcurrants regularly you will end up with very tall bushes that only produce fruit at the top.

When pruning red or white currants the objectives are slightly different. You prune to try to create a goblet shaped bush with about 10 main branches growing upwards and outwards with an open centre to the bush, shortening the new growth leaders by about half and pruning to an outward facing bud. It is a good idea to mulch well at this time to feed the bush and prevent weed growth.

Never dig around soft fruit bushes as they have shallow roots that are easily damaged. To take hardwood cuttings of black and redcurrants take cuttings of about 25cm from the current year's growth that have plenty of buds. Make a sloping cut just above a bud at the top and a straight cut just below a bud at the base. Push the cuttings into weed-free well-drained soil leaving about two buds showing. The cuttings will take about a year to develop into strong new bushes.

CERCIDIPHYLLUM JAPONICUM
TOFFEE APPLE TREE

Artist's notes

Dominica Williamson

Toffee Apple became autumn for me because Gareth the gardener led me to it, it's one of his favourites and then I fell for it too – it dances horizontally against the sky and its leaves are heart shaped.

They sit opposite each other and appear as if they are floating due to the thin diagonal burgundy brown stems (the colour of toffee apples!) that prop them up.

It's called the Toffee Apple Tree not because of its stems but the luscious smell it gives out in the autumn. In the breeze you can smell candyfloss floating around it. At this time the floating leaves change from a cushioned green colour to a fiery orange, red and yellow burnt colour matching the floating smell! It originates from Japan and China. It's stunning and I would like to paint its tiny spring flowers next.

Toffee Apple Tree

THE OWNERS
COLONEL EDWARD T BOLITHO

From filmed interview, 2018

left
Trengwainton House
c1870 (SE face) lawn,
ha-ha

Col Edward Bolitho

FAMILY HISTORY

"I am Edward Bolitho and I am the sixth generation of my family to live here. My great-great-grandfather bought Trengwainton in 1866/1867, that was Thomas Simon Bolitho and then his son, Thomas Robins

Bolitho, lived here until 1925. He didn't have any children so when he died he left it to my grandfather, Edward Bolitho, who was his eldest nephew. When my grandfather died in 1969, my father took it on and then some time after my father died, we moved down here in 1998.

My grandfather was a great gardener and he obviously did the majority of the work on the garden. In turn my father and mother were both really good gardeners. My father was incredibly knowledgeable and my mother fantastically so because she had worked at Caerhays for my cousin before she married my father.

They both knew all the magnolias, all the rhododendrons and all the camellias which, sadly, I don't. The knowledge has slightly died because I can remember my father saying that my grandfather, with his wonderful Head Gardener, made a lot of plants, especially rhododendrons.

We have books of the rhododendrons that he made but the trouble is, we don't know where they are. It was all quite secretive in the, '20s, '30s, '40s, '50s and a bit competitive to make the first rhododendrons and make good ones. He never told my father where they were which was a bit disappointing and means we've got lots of rhododendrons that my grandfather probably introduced, but we don't know where they are which is a shame.

My father, I'm sure, was brought up to do things in the garden but for my grandfather I am less sure. He was in the army in India before the First World War and he went on quite a few expeditions, for which we've got his letters. He didn't actually mention the plants in them but whether, presumably, he would have seen some of these plants in the wild, making him more interested

or whether it may have been something that just came to him in later life. He was obviously extremely keen and he drummed it into my father's head. My father used to take us around the garden and so it subliminally went into you.

It's an interesting garden because if it was a formal garden that my grandfather had made, you would be able to see it exactly as it was. I suspect if he came back now he would recognise bits of it but not that much of it. I think it's very much changed because of disease, winds and just plants getting old. It does change all the time but I think the basics are still what he would like and there are still lots of plants that he planted. I'm delighted the National Trust are now trying to propagate the ones that were made here and will make sure that there will be continuity going forward.

My grandfather was interested in making plants grow; it was a plant zoo in some ways. I can see that it's very exciting and for him to plant something, when he didn't know what would happen to it, then maybe 15 or 20 years later when it flowered for the first time, it must have been pretty exciting.

My grandfather gave the garden to the National Trust when he was eighty so he only lived another six or seven years after that but he very much thought of it as 'his garden'. My father very much thought of it as 'his garden' too and he was also very much in charge of it, with most of the planning done with Peter Horder who was an excellent Head Gardener who talked to my father a lot and they worked out together what they were going to do. Things have changed since then, partly because if you think when my grandfather gave it over there were, in those first few years, probably about two or three thousand people who visited it. Now we've got sixty-thousand plus as well as a tea room and a shop.

NOTHING STANDS STILL

Noticing how things change, I remember when I was young there was no car parking so all the parking was at the bottom of the drive by the lodge. Three or four times a year, every Easter and bank holidays, there was a bit of a crisis when parked cars would be spread around the lanes but normally that was completely fine. Then in the early '80s we built the car park in a bit of the woodland next door to what is now the Tea Room.

Then after another ten or fifteen years we find we need another car park. That just shows how the visitors have grown and again, if you look at the visitor facilities, I remember when Mr and Mrs Brain lived in the lodge. When visitors turned up they took the money from their sitting room window. You bought your ticket and maybe bought a few postcards. They always used to win the prize for the most number of people persuaded to join the National Trust which was fantastic.

Then we got a garden shed which was put across the road and that lasted a few years. Then the second lodge was built in order to cope with visitors. Now we wonder whether that lodge is big enough in itself, so it gets bigger and bigger and bigger.

Nothing stands still.

EXCELLENCE AND INNOVATION

My favourite plants are the magnolias. The stream which my grandfather opened is a great thing because it's a spring garden essentially and the stream really helps prolong it, so it's the sort of herbaceous border for the rest of the garden which is wonderful.

Going along The Terrace of an evening, looking out towards the Lizard, is wonderful. Going anywhere in the garden, seeing the flowers and experiencing the smells is pretty good.

When my grandfather gave the garden to the National Trust none of the Kitchen Garden was open at all because that was not of interest; what was important was the collection of shrubs. I think when we moved in, the middle bit of the walled garden was open just by the Head Gardener's house which was full of exotics and it's only been in the last fifteen years that more and more of the walled garden was opened up.

I'd love to keep Trengwainton going and improve it. It should be a place of horticultural excellence and innovation; the gardeners are keen that it should be and I am really keen that we should do that. I am also very keen that the family and the National Trust should work together. I think having the family involved does add quite a lot and the Trust recognise that, because people like to see places that are lived in and are not museums, so that's important."

LT COL SIR EDWARD H. W. BOLITHO, KBE CB DSO

At Trengwainton 1925 – 1969

Pauline Hope

TRENGWAINTON GARDEN

In 1925 Edward Hoblyn inherited Trengwainton from his uncle, Thomas Robins Bolitho. This new challenge offered him the opportunity to develop the garden to become one of the finest in Cornwall.

With the advice and encouragement of his cousins, J. C. Williams of Caerhays Castle (whom he followed as Lord Lieutenant), P. D. Williams of Lanarth, and Canon Boscawen of Ludgvan, he began to develop the gardens with choice trees and shrubs. George Johnstone of Trewithen and Lawrence Johnston of Hidcote Manor, Gloucestershire, offered Edward Hoblyn a share in F. Kingdon-Ward's expedition to Burma and Assam in 1927/8. Many of these specimens flowered here for the first time in Britain and are very much in evidence at Trengwainton Garden today.

Mr A. Creek, the Head Gardener at the time, was able to raise plants from seeds, propagate trees and to breed an impressive display of hybrid rhododendrons of various colours. These tasks needed time, skill and patience, so after Mr Creek's retirement in 1934, Mr G. W. Thomas took over the responsibility. In turn, Edward Hoblyn was able to help John Carew Pole with his gardens at Antony, on the bank of the Tamar in Cornwall. The five southern enclosures were developed from about 1925 as ornamental gardens, with many rare and tender trees and shrubs being planted within the walls by Edward Hoblyn.

A gothic-arched doorway in the centre of the north wall leads from the southern ornamental enclosures to the five Kitchen Garden enclosures, the centre one of which retains a central circular dipping pool surrounded by rustic rockwork and ferns.

Trengwainton Garden was opened to the public on the 31st May 1931 for 12 hours from 08:30 in the morning in aid of Madron Nurses' Association. Special features to look out for were a white clematis growing on a fir tree, pink clematis in the area of the house and beautiful red rhododendrons up to 20' high.

To the north was a grove of tree ferns adjacent to the Azalea Garden, planted in 1931. Immediately to the west of the Walled Gardens the Camellia Walk was planted by Edward Hoblyn in 1939. The Head Gardener of the time, G. Hulbert, planted the Stream Garden beside the long drive in the 1950s. The old drive became the Long Walk. It was in this decade that Queen Elizabeth the Queen Mother was invited to a lunch at the house and the Brownies formed a guard of honour outside the front door. In 1953 the garden was registered by English Heritage under the Historic Buildings and Ancient Monuments Act within the Register of Historic Parks and Gardens. In 1961 Edward Hoblyn was awarded the Royal Horticultural Society's Victoria medal.

THE NATIONAL TRUST

In 1961, Edward Hoblyn gifted Trengwainton Garden to the National Trust, with provision for the family to remain in residence at the house. The garden is about 98 acres with a further 2 acres surrounding the house. His hope was that people would enjoy the garden. In 1962 Queen Elizabeth the Queen Mother planted a Bhutan pine in the garden.

Camellia japonica
'Alba Plena'

HENRY LEWIS STEPHENS JP

At Trengwainton 1835 - 1866

Pauline Hope

The Stephens coat of arms was reputedly granted in Henry VIII's reign. It consisted of three eagles and a crest of the lion rampant. During the lifetime of Henry Lewis, the fortunes of the family reached their highest point. Later, John Stephens refused a knighthood from James I, preferring business to politics, so the coat of arms could have been withdrawn.

Henry Lewis Stephens was born in 1810. The son of Samuel Stephens and grandson of John Stephens. Henry Lewis was educated at Oriel College, Oxford and was called to the bar in 1832.[48] He was a barrister, a Justice of the Peace and a partner in Williams, Foster and Company, copper smelters and manufacturers of Swansea which was dissolved on 5 September 1842.[49]

After 20 years of ill health, Henry Lewis died an invalid in London on 17 May 1867. As there were no children to inherit, his estate was left to his eldest brother, John Augustus.[50]

In November 1835, the Royal Statistics Society gave this careful description of Trengwainton:

Trengwainton and other adjoining estates in this parish, the property of the late Sir Rose Price, Bart., were sold to H. L. Stephens, Esq, for £28,500. The total number of statute acres was 773; it therefore averaged only £37 per acre: but 519 of these acres have never been cultivated, being used as a rabbit-warren and for pasturing sheep; and of the remaining 254 there are 71 acres of plantation, leaving only 183 of arable land.

The buildings on the estate were not valued at more than £2,000. The nearest part of the land is not within a mile of the town.[51]

In 1835/6 the house at Trengwainton was sold to Henry Lewis Stephens of Tregenna. The Reverend Charles William Davy MA was the named tenant until 1855. His widow and Henry Lewis's only sister, Sarah Maria Davy, took over the tenancy.

According to records held at Penzance Old Cornwall Society, Henry Lewis built a new croquet ground at Trengwainton. He pulled down a wing of Trengwainton House, using the material for farm buildings at Hendra, Nanceglos House and the first farm buildings that ever stood on the site of Farm Steading. He converted the laundry into a dwelling for the tenant farmer and altered the carriage drive so that it wound to the west of the road from the Heamoor crossroads.

On 15 September 1840 Trengwainton Farm was sold with all its stock by auction. In 1841 estimable tithable lands in acres at Trengwainton were:

- Total 5,940 acres. Value assessed at £1,091.10.

- Arable 1,180 acres. Pasture 2,260 acres. Woodland 60 acres. Common, domestic and croft 2,440 acres. [52]

Henry Lewis was living at Tregenna in 1856.[53] The Post Office directory of Devon and Cornwall 1856 does not list Trengwainton. In November 1866 Henry Lewis sold Trengwainton to Thomas Simon Bolitho.

Henry Lewis's legacy must include the Tregenna Castle and the Castle Inn in St Ives. He enhanced and enlarged Trengwainton for the future and ensured that Penzance had a clean water supply, enabling it too to flourish.

THE PRICE FAMILY OF JAMAICA AND TRENGWAINTON

At Trengwainton 1814 – 1834

Roy Blewett, Project Volunteer

HISTORY OF THE PRICE FAMILY

The Prices first came to recognition in a Lieutenant Francis Price, born in 1635. He was an officer in Oliver Cromwell's army or navy under the command of Admiral John Penn and General Venables that in 1655 captured Jamaica from the Spanish. In the event he stayed in Jamaica and became the sole owner of 175 acres at Guanaboa and partner in a holding of 150 acres in neighbouring St Catherine's.[59]

Francis Price may have come from Barbados where the surname Price is by no means uncommon. He was an astute man, selecting the best land and site for Worthy Park in the Lluidas Valley. Over time he consolidated all the surrounding land patents into his own using the existing local slaves left from the Spanish, and importing more to serve his purposes. Francis married Elizabeth Coxon who may have been a Bermudian. They had three sons and a girl. It is through the third son Charles, born in 1678 and married to a Sarah Edwards (or Edmunds), that the line and connection in Cornwall descends. Francis's only daughter Elizabeth married the Hon. Francis Rose and they had two children but the line ends with them. From then on the Prices incorporated the name Rose into the generations that followed.[60]

THE CORNISH CONNECTION

The two sons of Francis and Elizabeth were sent to England for their health and education. The eldest, another Charles, went to Trinity College, Oxford and this is where the Cornish connection starts. His tutor was the eminent Dr Frank Nicholls of Trereife, Penzance. John, the younger brother, went to Winchester College where he became ill. Charles, being concerned for his brother, consulted Dr Frank Nicholls on the best course of action and was recommended the sea breezes and mild climate of West Cornwall for John.[61] He therefore came to Penzance and stayed with Henry Babcock in Chapel Street who was, for a time, the Collector of Customs.

On recovering his health in February 1736 John married Marjorie Babcock, the daughter of Henry, at Madron Church. She was known as Margaret during her lifetime.[62] By this time John had become half-owner of Worthy Park in Jamaica which was giving him an income of £2,000 a year in the 1740s. Two years later they had a son called John but sadly his father died when he was only one. Margaret with her unmarried sisters brought up the child to be rather spoiled and as a result he was much disliked.[63]

In 1757 John went to Trinity College, Oxford, but did not complete his degree. Instead he went to Jamaica with his mother for the next eight years, staying with his uncle Charles who was now a Colonel and the Speaker of the House of Assembly.[64] Later in August 1764 John married Elizabeth (Williams) Brammer and in 1765 their first child, Charles Godolphin Rose Price, was born.

Two years after John's marriage his mother Margaret died. The family returned to Penzance where Margaret was buried in the family vault at St Mary's Chapel on 23 September 1766. John and Elizabeth moved into a house at the top of Chapel Street and John Price was appointed to the town council in spite of the Vicar of Madron, William Borlase, raising objections.[65] The house was next to the Ship and the Castle Inn where all meetings of importance for the town were held. Only two days after his appointment he was made an Alderman.[66]

In 1768 John's uncle Charles in Jamaica was made a Baronet, becoming Sir Charles Price of Rose Hall. His eldest son Rose Price had already died so his second son, another Charles, and John here in Cornwall became the joint owners of Worthy Park. John then named his second son Rose Price.

That year John Price was made Mayor of Penzance. He quickly requested troops to be returned to combat the vast amount of smuggling occurring at home. He became a J.P. signing warrants for house searches.[67] John was also buying land including Chywoone (where he later built a home) Faugan and Kerris, all originally of the Nicholls' Trereife Estate.[68] John had many interests. The great Cornish artist John Opie painted John Price.

Opie's mentor Dr Wolcot (the very well-known English satirist who wrote under the pseudonym of Peter Pindar) had stayed with the Prices in Jamaica. He was also fascinated by history having a collection of wills, deeds and pedigrees which Davies Gilbert acknowledges in his book *History of Cornwall*.[69] He and his wife established a more cultured life in the town with Elizabeth forming the Ladies' Book Club, and regular fortnightly winter assemblies were begun in 1770.[70]

In 1779 John became the Mayor and had the town clock and the cupola built at a cost of £150. It was considered by his fellow members to be a wild extravagance.

They demanded he should contribute to the expense but to no avail; his standing was such in the town, his pew in St Mary's Church being next to the high altar and before the corporation pews.[71] In 1774 John Price

became the High Sheriff of the Duchy for that year and supported his friend William Lemon as MP in the second contested election against Humphrey Mackworth Praed of Trevethoe. He won but was accused by his opponents of malpractice by holding the elections in Truro and not in Bodmin as was customary.[72] However, all was not well at home as Elizabeth had formed an attachment with the young vicar of Gulval. The Rev. John Penneck was written about locally, as in 'These words are often spoken in jest, a Penneck found within a cuckoo's nest.'[73]

ROSE PRICE

The two Price boys, Charles and Rose, were taught by the Curate of St Mary's Church, the schoolmaster of the Latin School and also a boy called John Vinicombe from Madron. Eight years senior to the Prices he was born in 1760 and was the fourth generation of John Vinicombes in Madron; a fine family that had fallen on hard times. Due to his ability John Price was asked to pay for John Vinicombe to stay longer in the school and in return to assist the teaching of the Price boys.

John Price duly paid for Vinicombe to go to Pembroke College, Oxford where he achieved an MA and where he tutored Rose Price at Magdalen.

John's first son Charles Godolphin Rose Price (b.1765) died aged only 18. Rose Price, the only remaining son, became the heir to John Price, High Sheriff of the Duchy. In 1788 Rose Price, together with John Vinicombe, travelled abroad on the Grand Tour for the next three years. Whilst returning they narrowly escaped capture in the French Revolution. On their return both went to Jamaica to take management of all the Prices' estates. Rose Price threw himself into the complete restructure and modernisation of the plantations, building new roads, increasing the area of sugar cane, even building a brick hospital and training the slaves for artisan work.[74]

Another local man William Pengelly, an experienced mill worker and son of the miller at Treneere Mill, was also engaged by Rose Price. He was brought to Jamaica to modernise the machinery and working practices then being used in the Cornish mines and mills. Rose Price also took Charles Dale, a blacksmith, and other local craftsmen to the island.[75]

After many improvements, putting Worthy Park in a very good financial position, Rose Price and John Vinicombe returned to Cornwall on 3 October 1795, living at that time at Trevaylor. However, he had spent over £48,000 in Jamaica which ruined his father.[76] John Price, died at Chywoone on 3 January 1797 owing £1800, estranged from his wife, and heavily in debt due to his son's spending in Jamaica.[77] John had made a very complicated will creating trusts for 1,000 years and involving half of Cornwall in carrying them through so that Rose Price could live in luxury for the rest of his life.[78]

Rose Price replaced his father, becoming a Magistrate. He then raised two companies of infantry, mostly of miners from the Paul parish, known as the Cornwall Infantry and Engineering Volunteers, as the war with France continued.[79]

ROSE PRICE'S MARRIAGE

Rose Price, then aged 29, married Elizabeth Lambart, aged only 16, on 6 August 1798. They had met at Holkham Hall in Norfolk on one of his regular and extended hunting visits. She was born on 12 April 1782 and was later painted by John Opie. At this time they lived at Trevaylor but Rose Price was looking for a piece of land suitable to build a family mansion and found a place 'Chi-oowne' between Paul Churchtown and Tredavoe from which there was a magnificent view of Mount's Bay. It was however exposed to the east wind and to shelter his proposed house, in about 1801, he planted trees and commenced the erection of an immense mound of earth and stone.

The work, now marked on the OS map as 'Price's Folly', took several years to complete and the walls or mound form two sides of a square. It is 20 feet wide at the top, and is nearly a quarter of a mile long, known locally as the 'Chinese Wall'. His wife Elizabeth did not like it and the story goes that she won a wager with her husband in 1806 by jumping a five bar gate on her horse, she being an excellent horse rider due to her Irish family interests. He, as always, honoured a wager so the family moved to Kenegie where they lived for some ten years and where most of her 14 children were born.[80]

TRENGWAINTON

In 1814 Rose Price bought Trengwainton and was made the High Sheriff of Cornwall. In the December of that year he and Elizabeth had their 12th child. Rose Price was made a Baronet on 30 May 1815 due, it was said, for doing the King a favour.[81] Improvements were made to the house, water was laid on and the most modern WCs installed. The drawing room was built as a dining room with the library opposite. The drawing rooms occupied the whole of the front of the house on the first floor. The present dining room and billiard room was added by the next major owners, the Bolithos. There were 11 bedrooms but by now there were 12 children beside Sir Rose and Lady Price who was expecting again. They moved into the house in about 1817. At great expense a very extensive pile of buildings was built on the summit of a small hill which commanded a fine view of St Michael's Mount and of Mount's Bay. An extensive terrace was formed on one side of the house, and the whole was surrounded by 71 acres of plantations and shrubberies laid out under the direction of Mr George Brown.[182] Many of the exotic plants, trees and shrubs were collected by the famous plant hunters of the day. The lodges were also made ornamental and the main drive to the house was bordered with laurels which quickly became large trees.[183]

Elizabeth had 14 children with the last being born in 1819, too many for Elizabeth's health. In her later years she spent much time away from Trengwainton trying to recover. In 1824 their first-born, Rose Lambart, married a young Irish widow, the Countess of Desart, but sad to relate only survived for a short period and just long enough to see the birth of his only child, a girl, in December 1825. He died in January 1826. This was very sad as he was an intellectual who spoke six languages and would have made, in the writer's opinion, a great man; and it is wished more was known about him. This was a great blow to Rose Price and the last straw for Elizabeth who lingered on until she died. She was returned to be buried on 20 December 1826 in the great Mausoleum in Madron Churchyard. Only four others are buried there, the last in 1927. Rose Price confided his great grief to his friend Sir Christopher Hawkins of Trewinnard.[184] During his time at Trengwainton he planted the Forest Carn and across the road, on the Trengwainton side, he planted additional pines. The barren granite hills of Trengwainton Carn and its neighbourhood were also planted with fir trees.

The family used the walled gardens for food supply and they are said to have been built to the dimensions of

Solomon's Temple. The bricks used were made in brick kilns in Brick Lane which runs down from across the road that passes the entrance gates. Next, the valley to the west of the house was taken in hand and three fine fish ponds were made in which there was good trout fishing. Ducks were also bred in these ponds. Near this area an ice-house was built which was probably the first ever built in the Penzance area. Near Sunny Corner at Madron, he built kennels. These, together with the pack of hounds, carriages, thoroughbred horses and a large number of servants completed the establishment.

Sir Rose Price and his family lived in style for some 17 years, keeping an open house.[185]

Just one month before he died Parliament passed the Anti-Slavery Act. Sir Rose Price died on 26 September 1834 aged 66. Like his wife before him Price was buried in the large granite Mausoleum in Madron Churchyard on the 9th October 1834. This was a great shock due to the loss of such a prominent and influential man to the area. No proper obituary notice was issued for many years.

Due to the still outstanding debts of £30,000 incurred in Jamaica, Trengwainton had to be sold but again a complicated will ensured that the estate was split into several parts to prevent the debts falling on one person. In 1835 Trengwainton was sold to Henry Lewis Stephens Esq. for £28,500. Sir Rose Price's sons George and Thomas, who became President of St Kitts, took over the running of Worthy Park, Jamaica in 1840 and they and the family received an income until 1866 when it was finally sold. Worthy Park still remains a sugar plantation to this day.[186]

From the National Records at Kew we see at least two claims from the executors for the Price Rose estate via the two parts of Worthy Park for compensation for the freed slaves. The first in 1835 was for £1,662.0s.5d for 79 slaves of Spring Garden. St Dorothy and the second in 1836 was for £3,597.3s.2d for 464 slaves of Worthy Park, St John. A total of £5,259.3s.7d valued in today's labour cost at £4,127,000. However, this was a small amount compared to the overall total of some £17bn in today's money that the government of the day paid as compensation to slave owners for the loss of their 'property'. Rose Price was a Justice of the Peace with an excessive zeal in prosecuting those that broke any game laws. He controlled the only right of hunting from Land's End to Hayle for 30 years. He was a benefactor to the town and surrounding area, leaving a legacy in the village of Heamoor of Jamaica Terrace and Jamaica Place built for his workers. He was fair but strict to his tenants and was also a Unitarian, leading him into conflict with the Church of England at one stage. Like his father, John, Rose Price was a complicated man; extremely well read and travelled. He was also a real family man. He established the estate and its famous garden by obtaining rare plants. He left a very important legacy that can be seen today.

John Opie, RA
Elizabeth Lambart,
Mrs Rose Price, later
Lady Price (1782-1826)
Autumn 1798
Oil on canvas

COWLEN, COWLINGE, COWLYN, COWLING

At Trengwainton c1530s – 1668

Pauline Hope

The Cowling family coat of arms consists of an argent and a chevron between three Cornish choughs; Cheqy or and Gu.[54] The name Cowling means 'hazel'. The Cowlyns were in Madron during the reigns of nine monarchs and two Commonwealth leaders. To keep on the right side of politics and religion was a great skill. Henry VIII commissioned Polydore Virgil to carry out a survey of his kingdom. His maps identified four separate counties, England, Wales, Scotland and Cornwall.[55]

COWLINGS AT TRENGWAINTON

The 1549 Records of the Earl of Oxford list: 'William Cowlyn, gained five and a half Cornish acres by knight's service for 1d – Trewanton in Madron.' It is believed that the Cowlings had a house at Trimgwenton from Tudor times as John Norden, official chorographer, places it in the ownership of M. Cowling on the map he drew between 1597 and 1601 and which he presented to King James..[56] He describes Maderne or St Madern as being a:

parish situate under the craggie hill north of Pensance, nere which is Maderne Well, whose fame in former ages was greate.[57]

In 1577 the Cowlings inaugurated the 'Register of Births, Deaths and Marriages' in Madron Church and this wonderful legacy gives us an insight into the prolific

Cowling family's standing in the area until T. G. Cowling sold Trengwainton to Francis Arundel in 1688. [58]

The Cowlings managed Trengwainton in times of tremendous political and religious unrest. Famine, disease and poverty alongside threat of invasion from pirates, the Spanish and Dutch.

As Penzance began to thrive as a port, the differences within the parish would increase gradually and needs would change as the town and countryside become more divided.

For a century and a half the family maintained the stability needed to pass on Trengwainton to the next owners.

Magnolia

176

JOHN OPIE, JOHN WOLCOT AND THE PRICES

Viv Hendra

The Opie portraits at Trengwainton formed an interesting collection. They were painted before the house was built; Opie had died in 1807, by which time he was a nationally known artist. He was born in Trevellas, near St Agnes in Cornwall, son of a carpenter with no great prospects, but by natural genius he went to London where he enjoyed great celebrity.

He rose to become Professor of Painting at the Royal Academy and on his death he was buried next to Sir Joshua Reynolds in St Paul's. Opie was a particular treasure for the Prices because they had played a significant part in his story – they had commissioned paintings from right across the artist's career.

Opie, when only in his teens, was painting portraits around Truro, Helston and Penzance, moving around the region in order to find new commissions. His extraordinary success was the result not just of natural talent but also of the tireless efforts of his tutor and promoter, one Dr John Wolcot, who recognised the potential of the young Opie and taught him everything required to become the fashionable artist. Wolcot was at that time a doctor residing in Truro; but he made the most of all his contacts and acquaintances to promote his young protégé in Cornwall with a plan to launch him in London. He would have had an exceptionally useful link with the Price family – Jamaica.

Wolcot had himself spent about five years at the heart of the political and social world in Jamaica. In 1768 he went out as the doctor accompanying the party of the newly appointed Governor, Sir William Trelawny.

A Cornishman himself, Trelawny included in his party the young Lt William Glanville Boscawen, son of Admiral Boscawen, whose family seat, Tregothnan, was near Truro. Wolcot played a prominent role when Trelawny dispensed hospitality at the King's House, where guests included both visitors to the island and resident landowners such as the Price family.

The Speaker of the Jamaican House of Assembly was none other than Sir Charles Price (2nd Baronet), nephew of John Price, the elder, who had been sent to Penzance for reasons of health. Charles hosted Wolcot and his colleagues at their properties, Decoy Penn and Rose Hall, and their plantation estate, Worthy Park, where Wolcot, always a great raconteur, would have been an entertaining guest. It was while they were enjoying Price's hospitality that a tragedy occurred: young Boscawen drowned while swimming in a pool. It was a devastating event which inspired Wolcot to send a poem to the London press which proved important later.

Life continued in Jamaica – at one stage Wolcot shamelessly had himself ordained into the Church in order to take advantage of the income it would provide, an adventure which was much discussed in Jamaica and England. When Governor Trelawny died, a successor was appointed from London, so in 1773 Wolcot accompanied the widowed Lady Trelawny back to Cornwall.

He also brought back relics of William Boscawen to be buried in the family vault near Truro. Accepting the fact that he could not afford to live in London as he wished, and not interested in pursuing his career as a churchman, he chose to set up as a doctor in Truro where he knew he had various potential contacts – including the influential Boscawens – and the Prices.

promising young boy who was only about fifteen. According to the Trengwainton Memorandum Book their two earliest Opie portraits were Parthesia and Mary Badcock, dating from 1776 – these were among Opie's first works and are now lost. At different times, Opie also produced portraits of John Price and his ten year old son Rose. Price's first cousin John Badcock had portraits of himself and his son John painted by Opie for his own family at that time also. The artist was locally in demand as he was remarkably competent, but at the time he was just an exceptionally talented local boy.

There was a taste for pictures other than family portraits. Opie found a demand for his own self-portraits and he painted several which showed himself as a young man dressed in a rather grand style (Fig. 1). Wolcot had taught him to paint dark backgrounds

When Wolcot spotted the commercial potential of the portraits by the young Opie, he saw an opportunity for them both. He took Opie into his house in Truro and gave him lessons in painting. He persuaded people to have their portraits painted in order to give the boy experience. These early works lacked polish and accomplishment but they were known to catch a 'speaking likeness'.

Wolcot would have made sure of an introduction to the Penzance relatives of the Prices, whom he had so recently seen in Jamaica. He could meet John Price, the younger, and his young son Rose, and the Badcock aunts Parthesia and Mary, who would be keen to talk to him about Jamaica. Wolcot could entertain them with anecdotes about Sir Charles and he could also encourage them to have their portraits done by the

and detailed faces and this led to a popular series of affecting studies of elderly characters – beggars and the like – which were said to display the fine qualities of Rembrandt or Caravaggio. Trengwainton possessed both an early self-portrait and one of the aged beggars.

In 1781, encouraged by those who had acquired his work, Wolcot took Opie and a selection of his best pictures, especially elderly characters, to seek his fortune in London, where he soon became famous as 'the Cornish Wonder'.

The publication in London of Wolcot's poem written on the tragic death of Boscawen in Sir Charles Price's pool led to patronage by Lady Boscawen and an introduction to King George III, who acquired two paintings and ensured Opie's fame. Wolcot later pursued his own career in a literary direction, writing popular satires, while Opie became a successful artist and member of the Royal Academy.

The Prices continued their connection with Opie, as in 1796, there was a portrait of John Price, the younger (Fig. 2) and also in the same year one of Rose Price's former tutors and long-time friend, John Vinicombe (Fig. 3).

By now the portraits were confident, professional and accomplished by London's exacting standards – very different from the early likenesses.

Opie's most significant painting for the Price family came when Rose Price married Elizabeth Lambart in 1798. It was Opie who painted her full-length portrait with a view of St Michael's Mount beyond (Fig. 4). This portrait was altogether more impressive as it was very large and included the landscape rather than the more characteristic plain dark background – a picture to dominate the dining room in a grand house. Thus Trengwainton showed portraits from different stages of the career of a famous local artist who achieved celebrity in London.

There were numerous similar Opie portraits in the houses of neighbouring families, notably the St Aubyns, but the Price collection, being so varied, had a fascinating story. Many years after the dispersal of the Trengwainton contents, attempts were made to create a catalogue of all Opie's known works. Some Opies from the Price collection were located, catalogued and photographed, but others had vanished and were not known at all until the Memorandum Book was recently rediscovered.

A GLIMPSE OF SOME OF THE PICTURES IN TRENGWAINTON

Viv Hendra, Writer

(The paintings and portraits at Trengwainton House transcribed from the Memorandum Book at Cornwall Records Office which was copied in January 1827 from Sir Rose Price's old pocket books).

We can only imagine the appearance of the rooms at Trengwainton in the days when Sir Rose Price, Bt. of Trengwainton, lived there. The many rooms provided ample opportunity to display fine furnishings, paintings and prints. The contents have long been dispersed and we have no photographs – but a Memorandum Book dating from about 1827 has fortunately been preserved, containing a detailed list of the paintings and sculptures displayed in just two rooms – the Drawing Room and the Dining Room. From this list we know that Sir Rose Price decorated Trengwainton with a collection of art which would be very much in the taste of the country house of the period.

THE DRAWING ROOM

There were fourteen paintings in the Drawing Room, mostly continental Old Masters of the sort you might expect to find – religious scenes, landscapes and still lifes, filling the room with colour, sophistication and style. There were important names including Rubens, Durer and Caracci; perhaps some were not by the hand of the artists themselves but this was not so important. Sir Rose noted that the St Jerome was 'said to be by Durer' but the picture of Our Saviour was a 'real sketch by Rubens'. The large flower-piece by Jan Van Huysum was valued not only for its quality but because it was a present from 'old Lord Sherborne'.

Also in this room were some of the important collection of works by John Opie RA, *The Cornish Wonder*. One showed a local beggar dating from 1778, another was an early self-portrait showing the young man wearing a large hat. Neighbouring houses boasted similar paintings of both these subjects by the artist.

An unusual picture showed the *Head Of An Old Man* – it was painted by Catherine St Aubyn, the sister of Sir John St Aubyn of Clowance, Cornwall. This family owned St Michael's Mount which could be seen from Trengwainton. Catherine Molesworth St Aubyn was still alive when Rose Price hung this painting and no doubt she appreciated the compliment. She had been tutored by the famous Opie.

He had cut from a canvas the portrait of an old man who was to be Jephthah in a large biblical scene; he sent the cut-out head to his pupil who copied it. The original remained with other Opies in her family, while her own version hung in distinguished company in the Drawing Room at Trengwainton.

There was an acknowledgment of the distinguished family of Rose Price's wife Elizabeth Lambart in the form of three marble busts. The grandmother and sister Frances Thomasine were accompanied by the latter's prestigious husband, the 2nd Earl Talbot.

The one family picture in this room showed a ten-year old boy in what was described as 'Spanish dress' – which probably involved a hat with a large feather. This was the young John Price, who was later father of Sir Rose Price; it must have dated from about 1748. The artist of this was unknown but the picture must have been shown to John Opie some thirty years later, because he painted the young Rose Price in a similar costume – a portrait which hung in the Dining Room.

THE DINING ROOM

In the Dining Room there were thirteen paintings, all of which were family portraits from four generations. It was not unusual to find the family portraits assembled in the Dining Room of a country house. Displaying the 'faces' here, where the family would sit regularly and guests would be entertained, made a statement about the family's status, providing instruction and conversation as well as historical record. The quality of the portraits varied. Some were by unknown artists, three were by a Mr Clifford, but some were by John Opie.

The Price family was based in Jamaica and from that side there were portraits of Rose Price's father, grandfather, great-uncle and great-grandfather. It was for the good of his health that Rose Price's grandfather John was sent from school at Winchester to Cornwall to grow up in the care of the Badcock family - and he grew fond of them all, marrying Margaret.

Thus Trengwainton had several Badcock portraits, again covering four generations. The oldest was a portrait of *Parthesia Badcock* (1674 – 1764), Rose's maternal great-grandmother; she was a Keigwin, from a notable local family herself. Her husband Henry had moved from Whitstone (Cornwall) to take up the post of the Collector of Customs in Penzance. They had four daughters: Margaret, Parthesia, Joanna and Mary. Margaret married John Price but there was no portrait of her – she died twelve years before John Opie arrived to paint two of her sisters, Parthesia and Mary.

The same sisters were painted again, along with Joanna the married sister, by Mr Clifford 'residing in Truro'. We know little about Clifford except that he could paint in fine detail, so perhaps his portraits were more acceptable than Opie's youthful work.

Rose Price himself was seen in the Opie portrait aged ten and also in a mature Opie portrait at the age of twenty eight, painted at the same time as that of his lifelong friend and tutor, John Vinicombe. The full length portrait of Price's wife Elizabeth would have been the chief focus of attention in this room (Fig. 4).

These Dining Room portraits gave a sweeping view of the history of the Prices and the Badcocks but did not include every person. We only know what was in two rooms of a large house, so there would have been many more which we do not know about.

Over time all the paintings were dispersed. Some were sold, other vanished, one was destroyed in a fire. It is fortunate that the discovery of the Memorandum Book allows us to imagine all those paintings in the Drawing Room and the Dining Room and to begin to have an idea of the appearance of at least some of the paintings that were hanging in Trengwainton in 1827.

PRICE AND RELATED PORTRAITS BY JOHN OPIE, RA AND A PORTRAIT MINIATURE

Viv Hendra and Michael Burrell

Sir Rose Price, Bt of Trengwainton, Cornwall (2nd creation, 1815) (21 November 1768 – 24 September 1834) completed building his country seat Trengwainton, near Penzance, in 1817. The Memorandum Book of 1827, now held at the Cornwall Records Office, lists paintings hanging in the Drawing and Dining Rooms. Of these, eight are portraits by John Opie (16 May 1761-9 April 1807) of members of the Price family and their Badcock relations dated between 1776 and 1798. Another Price portrait and two Badcock portraits by Opie were in related collections, together with a later miniature of

Sir Rose by an unknown miniaturist, which was at Trengwainton.

The earliest portraits by John Opie mentioned in the Memorandum Book are two, now lost, painted in 1776 of *Parthesia Badcock* (1706-80) and *Mary Badcock* (about 1709-87), when elderly. They were the unmarried younger sisters of Margaret Badcock (about 1704-65), wife of John Price, the elder (1712-39). He was the father of John Price, the younger, and the grandfather of Sir Rose. As Opie was only about 15 years old at the time, the portraits may have been relatively naïve. They are not included in Rogers 1878 [87] or Earland 1911. [88] They have not been noted elsewhere.

In 1778 John Opie painted three portraits for John Price, the younger (25 June 1738-3 January 1797): his *Self-portrait*, a portrait of *An Aged Beggar*; and his portrait of *Rose Price when 10 years old*. There was an interesting connection between Dr John Wolcot, who discovered Opie in Cornwall, and John Price, which derived from Jamaica.

Opie continually painted self-portraits to improve his technique. Public Collections hold 13 self-portraits by him (Art UK online). Of these the earliest dated self-portrait is from 1785 in the National Portrait Gallery when he was far more confident, a London celebrity. The *Self-portrait* in a wide brimmed hat (Fig. 1) for John Price was painted about seven years earlier in 1778. It is now owned by Robert B. Simon of Robert Simon Fine Art, New York, a leading Old Master Gallery. He comments: "The extraordinary immediacy and sensitivity conveyed in this self-portrait by the 17 year old painter astonishes today."

Opie's portrait of *Rose Price when 10 years old* 'in a Spanish Costume' (location unknown) may well have been inspired by the portrait of Rose Price's father *John Price, the younger* 'when a boy in a Spanish dress', by an unknown artist (location unknown). This may also have inspired Opie's portrait in about 1781 of John Price's 1st cousin *John Badcock, the elder* 'in Spanish costume, hat with feather'.

In 1796, 18 years after his three portraits painted for John Price, the younger in 1778, John Opie, now an RA, painted the half-length portrait of *John Price* himself (Fig. 2); and that summer the half-length portraits of John's son *Rose Price* and Rose Price's friend and former tutor, *The Revd. John Vinicombe* (Fig. 3).

The portrait of *John Price* is an accomplished portrait which shows Opie at his best. There is a warmth and vitality about the face which confirms Opie's reputation for catching a "speaking likeness". The chair is similar to that seen in other Opie portraits and was probably the one in Opie's studio in Berners Street, London.

Sir Rose Price, Bt, as he became on 30 May 1815, bequeathed Opie's half-length portrait of himself to Charles Chetwynd-Talbot, 2nd Earl Talbot of Ingestre Hall, Staffordshire. He was the husband of Sir Rose's sister-in-law Frances Thomasine Lambart, Countess Talbot, and Sir Rose's Executor. The portrait was burnt in the great fire at Ingestre in 1882. [89]

The half-length portrait of *The Revd. John Vinicombe* (30 January 1760-29 February 1808) was painted for Rose Price. John Vinicombe was his friend and former tutor and was with him on the Grand Tour and in Jamaica. He was the son of John Vinicombe of Madron, near Penzance. He matriculated at Pembroke College, Oxford in 1778, aged 18. He obtained his BA in 1782, his MA in 1785, and his BD in 1799. He was a Scholar of the Ossulstone (Benet) Foundation from 1783 and a

Fellow of the same Foundation from 1785 to 1808, when he died.

After coming back from Jamaica with Rose Price in 1795 Vinicombe returned to Pembroke. Following his death in 1808 Sir Rose Price in his Will bequeathed Opie's portrait of Vinicombe to Pembroke in memory of him.

The portrait is a strong image of Rose Price's tutor and friend. The viewer is looking a little upward to an upstanding man of warm character and sharp intellect. Behind the sitter a red curtain presents a strongly contrasting background. Towards the end of the century, the plain dark backgrounds were increasingly replaced by brighter colours. The curtain was a favourite device: it could be drawn back a little, as here, to allow a few deft brushstrokes to suggest a sylvan landscape beyond. The more colourful portraits would stand out particularly when hanging alongside plain backgrounds. Red was a colour frequently used by Opie.

In the autumn of 1798 John Opie, RA painted the full-length portrait of Rose Price's wife *Elizabeth Lambart, Mrs Rose Price, later Lady Price* (12 April 1782-2 December 1826), aged 16, standing in a very plain cream coloured morning dress with St Michael's Mount in the background (Fig. 4). It was exhibited at the Royal Academy in 1799. It is probably of this portrait that Thomas Holcroft wrote on 1 March 1799: 'Sate to Opie, Northcote there, who warmly praised his whole-length of Mrs Price'.[90] A newspaper commented:

This portrait is a proof that Mr Opie is very much improved in the representation of female beauty – a charm that seemed too light and delicate for his hand, and in which it was thought that he would never be so successful as in portraying strong marked characters. This work, however, plainly shows that, if he

perseveres, his genius will not be confined to one province of his art. The Landscape displays a part of Cornwall, with St Michael's Mount, and is well painted.[91]

The view of St Michael's Mount is as seen from Trevaylor, Gear Hill, near Gulval, about two miles north of Penzance, the first home of Rose and Elizabeth Price.

The portrait of *Lady Price* was painted when Opie was at the heart of the London art establishment. Commissions for large 'whole lengths' were fashionable, costly and prestigious. The usual size for these was about 97 x 60 inches and relatively few houses could accommodate a portrait that was eight feet tall and required a splendid frame. Opie's whole lengths included individuals such as the Earl of Sandwich, the Duke of Gloucester, the Countess of St Germans and, of course, Sir John St Aubyn; some were portraits of mayors and dignitaries intended for public spaces such as Norwich Guildhall. The compositions frequently included a relevant landscape and here St Michael's Mount provided a particularly romantic scene which Opie knew well.

As the Prices would have known the St Aubyns' on the Mount, there was something particularly suitable about this; indeed Opie was painting a landscape of the Mount for Sir John St Aubyn at this time. Such a portrait was guaranteed to attract attention and this one did just that at the Royal Academy and subsequently when it was the focal point of the Dining Room at Trengwainton.

The entry in the Trengwainton Memorandum Book of 1827 states: 'Lady Price full length by Opie done at Ampton in the autumn of 1798 …' The village of Ampton is about five miles north of Bury St Edmunds on a route between London and Norwich. Ampton Hall

Fig. 5

Unknown portrait
miniaturist

*Sir Rose Price, Bt of
Trengwainton*

(2nd creation, 1815)

(1768-1834)

c1815

Watercolour on ivory

3 x 2 ½ in

Gold frame

was the seat of the Fitzroy family, including General Lord Charles Fitzroy (1764-1829), who was MP for Bury St Edmunds between 1787 and 1796, and again from 1802 to 1818. He must have been a friend of Rose Price's or Elizabeth Price's family. The face would have been painted from life at Ampton, but the rest of the picture was perhaps created in Opie's studio using a lay figure as the model for the body. Her left hand rests on a rock, which appears to be the same as one which Opie included in other paintings and which was a studio prop.

Sir Rose Price, Bt bequeathed to his Executor Charles Chetwynd-Talbot, the 2nd Earl Talbot, the husband of his sister-in-law Frances Lambart, Countess Talbot, Opie's portrait of his wife *Lady Price,* exhibited at the Royal Academy in 1799, together with Opie's half-length portrait of himself.

An unknown provincial miniaturist painted a portrait miniature of *Sir Rose Price, Bt of Trengwainton (2nd creation, 1815)* with his cocker spaniel (Fig. 5). Claudia Hill, the miniature expert, dates the miniature to about 1815 from his costume, and the fact that he is wearing his own hair rather than a wig, and sideburns, which were a fashion from about 1800. He was created a Baronet of Trengwainton on 30 May 1815, and began rebuilding Trengwainton, two very special occasions in his life.

Sir Rose was a Founder Member and 1st President of the Morrab Library in Penzance from 1818 to 1824. The Library holds a framed photograph of a similar miniature of Sir Rose with his dog, which is given the date 1820.

The known portraits by Opie are varied and give an interesting view of the development of the artist's career as well as that of the Price family.

Viv Hendra runs the Lander Gallery in Truro. He has a special interest in Cornish art, particularly portraits. He is an authority on the Cornish painter John Opie, a subject on which he gives lectures across the country. His biography *The Cornish Wonder: A Portrait Of John Opie* was published by Truran in 2007.

Michael Burrell is an art historian and a close connection of the Price family.

With thanks to The Assay Office Birmingham, Robert J. Berman, Dr Charlotte Berry, Gillian Broadbent, Paul Cox, Simon Davis-Elwin, Ann Farrant, Pete Hamilton, Claudia Hill, Amanda Ingram, Chris Lacey, Lucy Purvis, Lynn Roberts, Peter Schade, Robert B. Simon, Ben Taylor.

WINTER

Phil Griffiths

- We tend to leaf-blow all year round as birds constantly throw leaves onto the path when looking for insects, but by now hopefully most of the leaves would have dropped from the trees.

- We put bird food throughout the garden all year round, but it's even more important during these lean winter months.

- Check your winter protection is still securely in place.

- Put heaters in the glasshouse for those cold nights, ours are on thermostats so we don't waste energy.

- Harvest leeks, parsnips, winter cabbage, sprouts and remaining root crops.

- Take hardwood cuttings.

- The first weekend in December is our Christmas event so we spend a bit of time prepping and tidying up after that.

- Dig over any vacant plots that have not been dug already.

- Plan your vegetable crop rotations for the coming season.

- Clean glass house on rainy days, this is essential for us to prevent the build-up of any diseases.

- Prune open-grown apples and pears (but not those trained against walls).

- Before we break for Christmas we clean and oil handles on hand tools, give cutting tools a sharpen.

Rhododendron 'Christmas Cheer'

Illustration by Dominica Williamson

- Service machinery, some we do in house, and others we send away.

- As soon as we return from our Christmas break it's time to start getting ready to reopen.

- Start to mulch borders; only if dry enough to stand on to avoid soil compaction.

- If dry enough we would start to mow the grass.

- Top dressing and raking all the paths.

- One final leaf-blow and we are ready to reopen the gates to the public.

IN THE VEGETABLE GARDEN

Ian Willsdon

DECEMBER

December is a good time to plant rhubarb, either buying new plants or dividing existing plants that are at least 3 years old. Rhubarb plants can get congested as they get older and it is a good idea to split them every few years. Dig up the rhubarb and slice the root with a spade to cut off a section that has a dormant bud. Plant with the bud slightly raised above the soil. Rhubarb is a heavy feeder and it is a good idea to mulch all plants with a thick layer of well-rotted manure at this time of year. Rhubarb appreciates being planted in full sun although it will tolerate some shade.

There are many different varieties of rhubarb (our National Trust garden at Clumber Park has the national collection) and good varieties include Timperley Early, Victoria and Champagne. You can also now buy varieties such as Livingstone which will crop right up to late autumn so you can have rhubarb almost the whole year round.

At Trengwainton we have some old terracotta rhubarb forcing pots – not to be confused with the larger seakale blanching pots – and these can be placed over the plants in January or February and stems pulled about 4 to 6 weeks later. You should only force plants every 2 or 3 years to maintain their vigour.

JANUARY

January is usually a wet month in the garden in this part of the world and it is difficult to get on the soil without damaging its structure. However, there's always plenty of planning to be getting on with as well as taking stock of the previous year's successes and failures. It's also a traditional time to make New Year resolutions and here are a few appropriate ones that you could attempt.

Try to use peat-free compost. Peat is primarily sourced from lowland raised bogs – an increasingly rare habitat in the UK and across Europe. We need to conserve this diminishing natural resource as it also supports many rare plants and animals. More good quality peat-free compost is now available.

Reduce chemical use in the garden and learn about their effects on wildlife. Many common items sold in garden centres contain neonicotinoids and other harmful chemicals that have disastrous effects on most pollinators and amphibians and which can also move up the food chain. You should also try to avoid slug pellets as they can also affect animals higher up the food chain such as birds and hedgehogs.

Grow more flowers from seed as many nurseries still buy in or import plants that are treated with neonicotinoids

and fungicides by big wholesalers. This is gradually being addressed but many plants still carry a threat to pollinators. Dr Dave Goulson, from Sussex University stated in a recent report that plants sold as 'pollinator-friendly' are often treated with pesticides during their production.

FEBRUARY

If you have not already done so, February is a good time to sow onions. Many people grow onions from sets but if you grow from seed you have a wider choice of varieties. If you only need a couple of rows of onions one packet of seeds will provide all you need and more. You can sow direct into modules or if you don't have enough room in your greenhouse you can sow the whole packet in one seed tray.

As the onions grow you can begin to harden them off and they are ready for planting out when they are about 10cm high. You can start planting out by mid April if it is not too cold as onions can bolt if planted out in a cold spell. You should plant out about 10-15cm apart. The more space you give the onions the bigger they will grow. Onions like reasonably fertile soil so it is good to have added compost to your onion bed well before planting out. The ground should be trodden firm and then raked to a good tilth.

It is important to keep onions as weed-free as possible, particularly in the early stages of growth as they don't like much competition. You also need to keep onions well watered as they are liable to bolt in hot dry spells. Onions should be ready to harvest after about 20-24 weeks from sowing. If you want to store the onions for any length of time you need to dry them on a rack or similar or indoors if the conditions are wet.

RHODODENDRON 'CHRISTMAS CHEER'

Artist's notes

Dominica Williamson

Rhododendron 'Christmas Cheer' flowers from November to February but sometimes in March. It's a great one for painting as you can study it over a period of time; watching what bud blooms first and where plants are positioned in relationship to the light and height of the garden; and indeed in other gardens – I grew it to study it!

I got hooked on this as it was part of three plants positioned near each other along Trengwainton drive: *Rhododendron* 'Polar Bear', *Magnolia campbellii* and *Rhododendron* 'Christmas Cheer'. Gareth the gardener led me to this location and I started studying this location to understand some of the differences between rhodies and magnolias including their histories.

I photographed the location and watched the changes take place – running to the drive on different Fridays. 'Polar Bear' was on my mind as like the Toffee Apple it had a sweet scent. Gareth made me think about scent as well as colour and of course seasons: "There's a rhody for every season." Autumn is 'Polar Bear', Christmas is 'Christmas Cheer'. When I saw 'Christmas Cheer' flowering,

I realised this had to be winter. Along with Marina's writing on snowdrops, the white and pink of these plants dressed the green and brown of the garden, and it must be noted they are accompanied by pink camellias. 'Christmas Cheer' is like raffia – its bud is this cushiony luxurious pink but when it opens, the flowers are white. It's like magic and as I did the study sheets for the plant, everyone who watched me make them commented on this. It's got this old world feel to it but it's also so fresh. It's a celebration of what's to come; after Christmas we start dreaming of spring and this bud is very dreamy.

Rhododendron 'Christmas Cheer'

189

TRENGWAINTON NEWS ROUND-UP

Linda Collins

A trawl of newspapers in the online British Newspaper Archive, over the past two centuries, gives the clear picture that Trengwainton and its resident families have been at the centre of the social and civic life of the parish of Madron, which included the town of Penzance, playing a major role in bringing together people and organisations. The earliest newspapers record the births, marriages and deaths of Sir Rose Price and family members, property and stock transactions and the occasional legal battle the baronet was engaged in. Sir Rose Price's main interest was in his horses and hunting, and it was sadly reported in 1829 that during a thunderstorm one of his horses was 'struck dead by the electric fluid and another was deprived of sight.'

After the death of Sir Rose Price in 1834, the house and farm had a number of owners and tenants over the next 30+ years, and the newspapers have many advertisements for the letting of the house and/or parts of the estate. *The Cornish Telegraph* (12.10.1853) has the details of an Auction of Household Effects, to be held in Penzance the following week, with a room by room list of contents to be sold, including a harp, a grand piano, paintings, a large amount of furniture and soft furnishings, but interestingly no books in the library.

Thomas Simon Bolitho acquired the estate in 1867 and set about its renovation and extension over the period of his ownership, together with developing and extending the already established garden, which was opened to the public on many occasions. One important improvement was reported in *the Cornish Telegraph* (1.10.1886) when the house, outbuildings and dairy had electric lighting installed, replacing the old gas lamps. Over 350 lamps were connected, and another 50 outside, including the stable clock. It must have been quite a sight at night.

The Cornishman (23.6.1887), reported on a great celebration which took place in Trengwainton grounds – the Queen Victoria Jubilee Fête – over a thousand parishioners and 800 children attended. They were served refreshments, played games and entertainments were provided, including maypole and display dancing, music, sporting events, swings and roundabouts, and a large procession with flags and banners. The newspaper told of one of Madron's old men who remembered the Jubilee of George III in 1809!

T.S. Bolitho continued the hunting tradition of Sir Rose Price, with the Western Hounds meeting at Trengwainton for their day's hunting. *The Cornish Telegraph* (3.12.1878) gives a description of the people and the places visited, including the blood-thirsty kill. Definitely only for those with a strong stomach. Twenty years later *The Cornishman* of 1.12.1898 reports the day's hunting and states that 500 pedestrians and 300 schoolboys viewed the hunt! Both occasions were probably the official Meet on Madron Feast Day, a day when children had the day off school to join village celebrations.

In 1887 the house and estate passed to Thomas Robins Bolitho, the nephew of T.S. Bolitho, who took a great interest in the garden, and laid out the broad driveway as the new approach to the house. The garden became a focus for many and varied causes over the following years: the village fete, fundraising for charity, political rallies and military meetings, and celebrations. Large numbers of local people attended these events which mostly took the format of speeches, processions, games, including friendly cricket matches, tea served on the lawn, and entertainments, sometimes with music and dancing. A typical example may be the celebrations for Empire Day in 1907 which was attended by about 900 people, including 150 militia. The children participated in games and sports while the militia played a friendly cricket match against Madron village, while the band played. *The Cornishman* (10.7.1907) reported that tea was served to all, and the militia members received a gift of a pipe and tobacco. Afterwards there was a tug of war competition and a Punch and Judy show.

In September 1913 Gustav Hamel, the early aviator, brought his plane to Trengwainton for demonstration purposes, only five years after the first plane flew in Britain. The townsfolk were invited to come and view, and poured into the grounds; no doubt the occasion would be remembered for the rest of their lives.

This was only the second time an aeroplane had visited West Cornwall, the first being when aviator Graham White flew over the assembled Naval fleet in Mount's Bay in 1910.

Disasters and accidents too were recorded in the columns of the newspapers. Fire was always a hazard on a farm, and in 1904 Charles Dale, an employee, discovered a fire in a hayrick of 6 or 7 tons, and immediately sent for the Penzance Fire Brigade. In 14.1.1904 *The Cornishman* reported that a servants' ball was underway, but was immediately broken up so they could all assist with fire-fighting.

The Cornishman (11.9.1913) reported that a 40 ton hayrick caught fire, but was safely put out with the help of the Penzance Fire Brigade and the Boy Scouts.

The outbreak of the Great War in 1914 brought many changes to society and Trengwainton was no exception. A speaker at a garden party in 1915 gave a speech about the part women could play in the war, through the work of the Women's Emergency Corps, which was set up to feed Belgian political refugees and destitute people in London. It eventually became the National Food Fund and their work was also supporting canteens and hospitals on the continent, and the troops in East Africa (*The Cornishman*, 15.7.1915).

In the spring of 1915 Mr Creek, the Head Gardener, appealed on the letters page of *The Cornishman* (6.5.1915) for local farmers and market gardeners to donate their surplus vegetables and fruit for the Fleet as part of the war effort. Trengwainton played a major role by acting as the collection and forwarding point for the donated fruit and vegetables from West Penwith.

The aviator Gustav Hamel with members of the Bolitho family at Trengwainton near Penzance. He advertised flying lessons here in September 1913 in his Bleriot XI monoplane

It was about this time that the Board of Agriculture started the Women's Land Army to recruit women to work on farms while the men were away fighting, their job being to maintain the food supply.

The Cornishman of 18.4.1918 reported that efficiency tests for women land workers were held at Trengwainton, with 16 entrants. The girls were praised for the high standards of their work, and Trengwainton offered to train 4 girls.

On Feast Day 1918 a new War Memorial for the village was dedicated at the church service. This was the gift of T.R. Bolitho, and has 50 names of people of the parish who died in the war (*The Cornishman*, 11.12.1918).

Madron WI Fête was held in the grounds of Trengwainton in June 1919, according to *The Cornishman* of 2.7.1919. This was a grand occasion with entertainment by the Penzance Independent Band, the Girls County School, dancing on the lawn, a cricket match and special presentations including an ambulance reassigned after war work to the Penzance St John Ambulance Brigade.

Mr Bolitho also made presentations of gifts to a Mrs Stephens of Madron who had knitted 287 pairs of socks and 17 scarves, and Mrs Ellis of Heamoor who had made 203 pairs of socks during the war.

In 1925 the Trengwainton estate passed to E.H.W Bolitho who maintained the long traditions associated with the property. Over the following years Trengwainton was honoured with many prizes at horticultural shows countrywide, leading in 1962 to Sir Edward being awarded the Royal Horticultural Society Victorian Medal in recognition of his creation of the garden (*Birmingham Post*, 1.3.1962).

The Western Hunt continued its activities, with regular reports of hunting, gymkhanas, hunter trials, and puppy walks appearing in the local papers. One such occasion was held in September 1932 when some unusual horseback games were played, for example, the cup and jam pot race where the object was to fill a vessel with water from horseback, a potato race and a wheelbarrow race! (*The Cornishman*, 1.9.1932).

Garden parties and fêtes continued to be held with ever increasing popularity, supported by the organisations with long ties with Trengwainton, such as the Scouts, Guides, the Women's Institute, the British Legion, the YWCA, the Unionists, to name but a few. A typical event had a guest speaker to address and inspire the crowds, a parade, games like tennis, croquet and clock golf, music provided by a local band, competitions, entertainment and tea – lots of it!

The British Legion County Rally in 1934 was a notable event with a large parade of 1134 supporters representing 31 branches in Cornwall, together with four bands. The invited speaker was the daughter of General Haig, Lady Alexandra Haig, who inspected the troops and said she was very proud of the fact that the county of Cornwall was the first to build Haig Homes, with the generosity of Col Bolitho who had donated the land in Heamoor. She also spoke of the dangerous times we were living in, a reference to the rise of Hitler in Germany (*The Cornishman*, 2.8.1934). Haig Homes was established in 1928 to provide housing for ex-servicemen.

Trengwainton was honoured with a visit from the Royal Institution in the summer of 1935, the significance of which brought Col and Mrs Bolitho back from their visit to London. The annual excursion took members to various sites around West Cornwall looking at antiquities. At Trengwainton the party examined a granite mould, thought to be very old and used in the process of tin smelting (*The Cornishman*, 27.6.1935).

In July 1936 a large camp for 3000 Territorials from the 130th Devon and Cornwall Infantry Brigade came to Trengwainton to participate in training exercises. The paper wryly commented that the Brigade's visit is 'keenly anticipated by the tradespeople – 3000 extra customers are more than welcome.' (*The Cornishman*, 20.2.1936).

More evidence of war threatening came in June 1939 when the Annual Summer Outing of the WI saw a thousand women from all parts of the county descend on Trengwainton (*The Cornishman*, 29.6.1939).

The opening speeches included an appeal on behalf of the Women's Land Army, asking members to encourage young women to join up for 'a jolly good time,' even if they could only manage to work a couple of hours morning and evening.

In October of the same year the *West Briton and Cornwall Advertiser* (19.10.1939) had an article expressing farmers' concerns about the scale of payment to the Land Army Girls. After training the girls would earn 28 shillings a week compared with wages of 5d. (old pence) per hour under the Agricultural Wages Act, a large discrepancy between the rates favouring the Land Army Girls, and farmers felt there would have to be an adjustment as the rate had been fixed too high. The article reports that the seven Land Girls, trained at Trengwainton, the first in West Cornwall, came through their passing-out tests with flying colours.

Two years later the *Western Morning News* (6.11.1941), reported on the Land Army competitions – an

assessment of skills learned through working. Classes included Horse and Field Work, Cabbage Planting, Hoeing and Horse Hoeing, Hedge Paring, Manure Spreading, Clean Milking, and Tractor Ploughing.

Sad news reached Trengwainton in June 1942 when Airman Sgt Gene Barr, the son of Mr and Mrs Barr of West Lodge, was reported missing after a raid over Bremmen. Their second son had been a prisoner of war since Dunkirk (*The Cornishman*, 2.7.1942).

After the war ended, life at Trengwainton settled back into old routines. In October 1950 the Women's Land Army held a Farewell Parade in London, at which Annie Love from Trengwainton attended. The girls took a bowl of Cornish cream as a gift for the Queen (*The Cornishman*, 19.19.1950).

No doubt a cause for celebration was the remarriage of recently widowed Col Bolitho to Sheila Bourne, the manager of Home Farm for some years (*Western Morning News*, 14.9.1950).

1957 saw a visit to Cornwall by the Duke of Edinburgh, who lunched privately with the Col Bolitho, the Lord Lieutenant of the county, at Trengwainton (*Lancashire Evening Post*, 14.11.1957).

Col Bolitho gifted Trengwainton with 98 acres to the National Trust in 1961, with the provision that the family could continue to live in the house. The National Trust staff have continued to care for the property to this day, continuing the tradition of welcoming the public with a full programme of delightful annual events aimed at families. Their programme includes popular seasonal events such as an Easter Egg hunt and a Carving Pumpkin Fun Day followed by Spooky Storytelling, and a Christmas Lantern Walk.

TIMELINE OF EVENTS

1668	Thomas Cowling	Sold Trengwainton to Francis Arundell of Mendarva whose family owned it for several generations (Trimguenton shown as belonging to Arundell's in 1597 – 1601 map of the royal surveyor, John Norden)
1692	Francis Arundell	Rebuilt Trengwainton house
1758	William Arundell	Inherited Trengwainton
1761	Praed of Trevethow	Bought Trengwainton and let it out as a farm
1798	Rose Price	Married at Holkam, Norfolk, Elizabeth Lambart, aged 16, of County Meath
1812	Daniel Esq and Mr Thomas	Residents of Trengwainton House
1814	Sir Rose Price	Bought Trengwainton. Son of a wealthy West Indian sugar planter originated from Penzance and lived at Kenegie, Gulval
1814	William Praed	Sold Trengwainton to Sir Rose Price
1817	Sir Rose Price	House rebuilt
1820	Sir Rose Price	Walled gardens built to dimensions of Noah's Ark
1833		Abolition of slavery
1834	Sir Rose Price	Died
1835	Executors	Sales particulars of Trengwainton
1835	Henry Lewis Stephens	Bought Trengwainton for £28,500
1840		Trengwainton sold by Rose Price's heirs to mortgagees
1855	William Davy	William Davy MA was the named tenant until 1855
1864	Mrs Davy	Recorded as living at Trengwainton
1866/67	Thomas Simon Bolitho	Bought Trengwainton for £33,000, 852 acres
1882	Louise Nugent	Burial of daughter of Sir Rose Price at Madron
1887	Thomas Robins Bolitho	Thomas Simon Bolitho's son, Thomas Robins Bolitho, inherits Trengwainton
1895	Thomas Robins Bolitho	Laid out the broad driveway
1898	Ernest Povey	Appointed as Head Gardener
1906	Ernest Povey	Finished as Head Gardener
1906	Alfred Creek	Appointed as Head Gardener. Very skilled gardener, propagating and raising seedlings of particular specimens from Frank Kingdon-Ward expedition
1924	Lt Col Edward H.W. Bolitho	Inherits Trengwainton. Planting started in earnest
1927/8	Frank Kingdon-Ward	Expedition to Burma Himalayas for plant/seed collection
1934	Alfred Creek	Retired
1934	George Wilfred Thomas	Appointed as Head Gardener. RHS Show, Trengwainton very successful. Very good at propagating rhododendrons

1948	George Hulbert	Became Head Gardener. Planted up stream garden
1961	Lt Col Edward H.W. Bolitho (became Sir Edward Bolitho)	Gave Trengwainton to the National Trust plus 98 acres with provision for family to continue to live there
1961	Sir Edward Bolitho	Honoured by the Royal Horticultural Society the Victorian Medal of Honour for Horticulture
1961	George Hulbert	Retired as Head Gardener
1962	Mr D.G. Austin	Appointed Head Gardener, came from Abbey Gardens, Tresco
1962	National Trust	Opens Trengwainton to public, 3 days per week
1962	HM Queen Mother	Planted a Bhutan pine at Trengwainton
1969	Major Simon Bolitho	Inherits Trengwainton
1970	Peter Horder	Appointed as Head Gardener
1972	HM Princess Anne	Planted a Mexican pine
1977		A new area of the garden opened in honour of the Queen's Silver Jubilee
1985	Peter Horder	The A.J. Waley Medal awarded to Peter Horder for a working gardener who has helped in the cultivation of rhododendrons
1989		Storms devastated over 200 trees at Trengwainton
1991	Col Edward Bolitho	Inherits Trengwainton
1994	National Trust	New £80,000 visitor reception lodge built
1995	Peter Horder	Awarded the National Trust's silver medal for 25 years service
1989	Gareth Wearne	Started as gardener at Trengwainton. 2019 is his 30 year anniversary
2000	Peter Horder	Leaves Trengwainton after 30 years to take up a post in the church
2000	Ian Wright	Appointed as Head Gardener by National Trust
2001		Restoration of walled gardens planned
2002		Severe storms brought down 7 large trees, including an ornamental maple planted by Princess Anne in the 1970s
2003	Joe Hemming (artist)/Bolithos	Toposcope pointing to region's landmarks installed
2007	Ian Wright	Trengwainton leads National Trust count of plants in bloom on Valentine's day with 426 out of total 2317
2008	Ian Wright	Secondment as Gardens Advisor
2010 - current	Phil Griffiths	Appointed as Head Gardener by National Trust

MAP

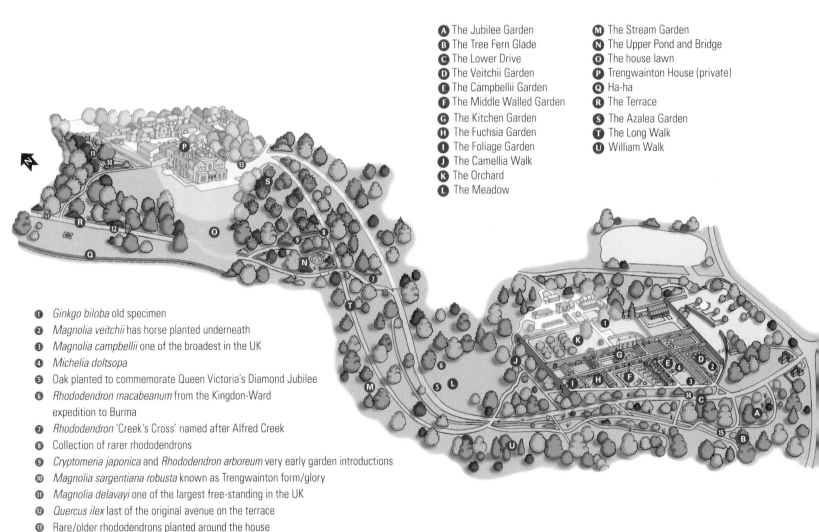

A The Jubilee Garden
B The Tree Fern Glade
C The Lower Drive
D The Veitchii Garden
E The Campbellii Garden
F The Middle Walled Garden
G The Kitchen Garden
H The Fuchsia Garden
I The Foliage Garden
J The Camellia Walk
K The Orchard
L The Meadow

M The Stream Garden
N The Upper Pond and Bridge
O The house lawn
P Trengwainton House (private)
Q Ha-ha
R The Terrace
S The Azalea Garden
T The Long Walk
U William Walk

1 *Ginkgo biloba* old specimen
2 *Magnolia veitchii* has horse planted underneath
3 *Magnolia campbellii* one of the broadest in the UK
4 *Michelia doltsopa*
5 Oak planted to commemorate Queen Victoria's Diamond Jubilee
6 *Rhododendron macabeanum* from the Kingdon-Ward
   expedition to Burma
7 *Rhododendron* 'Creek's Cross' named after Alfred Creek
8 Collection of rarer rhododendrons
9 *Cryptomeria japonica* and *Rhododendron arboreum* very early garden introductions
10 *Magnolia sargentiana robusta* known as Trengwainton form/glory
11 *Magnolia delavayi* one of the largest free-standing in the UK
12 *Quercus ilex* last of the original avenue on the terrace
13 Rare/older rhododendrons planted around the house
14 *Pieris forrestii* old plant possibly early introduction
15 Tree ferns planted circa 1936, came over as ballast in ships

NOTES

[1] 'Trengwainton House given to National Trust', *Western Morning News*, March 1st 1962.

[2] P. King and K. Lambert, eds, 'The Good Gardens Guide', *Daily Telegraph*, 2004, p.66.

[3] Craig Weatherhill, *The Place-Names of the Land's End Peninsula* (Hayle: Penwith Press, 2017), p.31.

[4] Please note: Trengwainton House is not open to the public.

[5] Cornwall Archæological Unit, 'Trengwainton Carn, Madron, Cornwall Archæological watching brief and recording document' (2014), p.18.

[6] A farmyard

[7] National Trust Trengwainton Study (Nicholas Pearson Partnership (2015), https://www.cornwall.gov.uk/media/19379377/m4hs13-73-national-trust-issue-4_additionalstatement_appendix-2-report.pdf p.33.

[8] Katherine Lambert, *National Trust Trengwainton Garden Guidebook* (National Trust, 2017).

[9] Anna Lawson-Jones, 'Trengwainton Carn, Madron, Cornwall Archæological Watching Brief and Recording', Cornwall Council (2014).

[10] 'National Trust Trengwainton Study' (Nicholas Pearson Partnership LLP, 2015), https://www.cornwall.gov.uk/media/19379377/m4hs13-73-national-trust-issue-4_additionalstatement_appendix-2-report.pdf p.33.

[11] 'National Trust Trengwainton Study' (Nicholas Pearson Partnership LLP, 2015), https://www.cornwall.gov.uk/media/19379377/m4hs13-73-national-trust-issue-4_additionalstatement_appendix-2-report.pdf p.34.

[12] 'Gardener's Chronicle', *National Trust Journal*, vol. 151 (March 10 1962), p.169.

[13] Diana Baskervyle-Glegg, 'Garden History', vol. 4 No. 2 (Summer, 1976), pp.5-7.

[14] Katherine Lambert, *Trengwainton Garden Guide Book*, ed. by Anna Groves (Swindon: National Trust, 2016).

[15] *Trewithen Garden* (2018) https://trewithengardens.co.uk/head-gardeners-blog/plant-of-the-month-for-april-3/

[16] G.C. Boase, *Reminiscences of Penzance* (1976). Reprinted from *The Cornishman*, Penzance, 1883-4.

[17] http://www.dendrology.org/site/images/web4events/pdf/Tree%20info%20ids_05_pp7_p28_TreeoftheYear.pdf, p.14
https://www.plantexplorers.com/explorers/biographies/forrest/george-forrest.htm
https://www.revolvy.com/main/index.php?s=1905%20Tibetan%20Rebellion

[18] http://earthguide.ucsd.edu/eoc/teachers/t_tectonics/p_pangaea2.html

[19] http://www.fossilmuseum.net/Paleobiology/Paleozoic_paleobiology.htm

[20] http://blogs.cornell.edu/naturalistoutreach/files/2013/09/Fern-Guide-27sra8m.pdf

[21] https://www.rhs.org.uk/advice/profile?pid=936

[22] http://bodenorchids.co.uk/Phalaenopsis%20Culture%20in%20the%20Uk.htm

[23] http://www.orchids-world.com/potting/osmunda.html
http://pza.sanbi.org/osmunda-regalis

[24] http://powo.science.kew.org/taxon/urn:lsid:ipni.org:names:430593-1
https://fotaframeyardblog.wordpress.com/2017/03/06/from-chinato-fota-the-handkerchief-tree/
http://www.ntsouthwest.co.uk/2017/05/rare-handkerchief-tree-in-bloom-at-national-trusts-dunster-castle/
http://khkeeler.blogspot.co.uk/2014/06/plant-story-handkerchief-tree-davidia.html
http://www.telegraph.co.uk/gardening/plants/8811383/In-praise-of-plant-hunter-Augustine-Henry.html

'It seemed as though the branches had been draped in thousands of ghostly, white handkerchiefs.' Henry's diary, relayed through *In the Footsteps of Augustine Henry* by Seamus O'Brien.

[25] Treasures of the New York Public Library, http://exhibitions.nypl.org/treasures/items/show/49

[26] British Library, https://www.bl.uk/catalogues/photographyinbooks/record.asp?Recordid=3048

[27] Public Domain Review, https://publicdomainreview.org/collections/cyanotypes-of-british-algae-by-anna-atkins-1843/

[28] youngster

[29] A beehive made of wicker or straw.

[30] Rab. Rabb. Ram. Hard gravelly ground. Stone used for road-making www.cornishculture.uk

[31] Nancealverne was owned by Scobell Armstrong. Each summer Madron Church Fete was held there. The family vault is in Madron Churchyard.

[32] Alternative spellings – croust or crowst.

[33] Tomlins farm we believe became Winchester Growers.

[34] When Alfred Creek retired he moved to a cottage next to Landithy Hall, within the village at Madron.

[35] Parliamentary Papers (1835) XXIII

[36] Cornwall Records Office QS/PDW/9/1,2,3

[37] Colin C. Short, *Inspite of Dr Borlase* (Madron, United Kingdom: Madron Methodist Church, 2002).

[38] 'Presentation to Mr Reg. Dale', *The Cornishman* (11 May 1921), p.6.

[39] 'Horse's Kick Fractures a Jaw', *The Cornishman* (4 June 1903), p.2.

[40] 'Mr Robins Bolitho's Will', *The Cornishman* (30 December 1925), p.2.

[41] W. Le Grice, *The Story of Our School* (Madron, United Kingdom: Madron Women's Institute, 1978).

[42] Alfred Munnings, *The Second Burst. The Autobiography of Sir Alfred Munnings* (London, United Kingdom: Museum Press, 1951).

[43] 'Mr Charles Dale – Impending Retirement', *The Cornishman* (22 October 1942), p.2.

[44] 'One Career Opens — Another Closes', *The Cornishman* (19 November 1942), p.7.

[45] 'Wedding of Lord-Lieutenant's Daughter', *The Western Morning News* (16 November 1942), p.2.

[46] References/sources:
www.cornwall-opc-database.org
www.britishnewspaperarchive.co.uk
www.ancestry.com
www.familysearch.org
Special thanks to James Dale's granddaughter, Nancy Fenton, Michigan USA and also to Walter Howard Dale's granddaughter Kathleen Rice, Massachusetts, USA for supplying photographs and information.

[47] The stream garden was created in the years that George Hulbert was Trengwainton's Head Gardener.

[48] Penzance Gazette 11.02.1832.

[49] London Gazette.

[50] Penzance Gazette.

[51] Richard Edmonds , 'Wiley-Blackwell A Statistical Account of the Parish of Madron, Containing the Borough of Penzance, in Cornwall', *Journal of the Statistical Society of London*, Vol. 2 .No. 4 (1839) p.208.

[52] W. Lake, *A Complete Parochial History of the County of Cornwall*, Vol III edn (Truro: William Lake, 1870), p. 208.

[53] West Penwith Resources, *Post Office Directory of Cornwall* (St Clement's, Strand: Kelly's & Co, 1856) p.63.

[54] John Lambrick Vivian, *The Visitations of Cornwall* (Cornwall: W. Pollard, 1887).

[55] Phillip Payton, *The Making of Modern Cornwall* (Redruth: Dyllansow Truran, 1992), p.57.

[56] John Norden's Manuscript Maps of Cornwall and Its Nine Hundreds (University of Exeter, 1972

[57] John Norden, *A Topographical Historical Description of Cornwall 1584* (Newcastle-on-Tyne: Frank Graham,1966), p.189.

[58] John Lambrick Vivian, *The Visitations of Cornwall* (Cornwall: W. Pollard, 1887), p.119.

[59] Michael Craton & James Walvin, *A Jamaican Plantation: The History of Worthy Park 1670-1970* (Toronto: University of Toronto Press, 1970).

[60] Michael Craton & James Walvin, *A Jamaican Plantation: The History of Worthy Park 1670-1970* (Toronto: University of Toronto Press, 1970).

[61] Elizabeth Sparrow, *The Prices of Penzance 1734-1834* (Penzance: The Penzance Library, 1985).

[62] Madron Parish Register

[63] Davis Giddy Diaries Cornwall Records Office Truro

[64] Michael Craton & James Walvin, *A Jamaican Plantation: The History of Worthy Park 1670-1970* (Toronto: University of Toronto Press, 1970).

[65] P.A.S. Pool, M.A, F.S.A., *The History of Penzance* (Penzance: M.S Collection, Walter Borlase, Penzance Morrab Library, 1974).

[66] Penzance Borough records Cornwall Records Office Truro

[67] CUST 68/15 Public Records Office Kew.

[68] Tithe Map 1841 Cornwall Records Office Truro.

[69] J.B Nicholls and Son 1838, https://archive.org/details/parochialhistory03gilb

[70] MS Collection. Penzance Library.

[71] George Brown Millett M.R.C.S, *Penzance Past and Present* (Penzance, 1876).

[72] Cornwall Records Office Truro D.D. R.D. 77.

[73] Davis Giddy Diaries Cornwall Records Office Truro.

[74] George Clement Boase and W.P. Courtney, Boase Collection Cornubiensis, Bibliotheca Cornubiensis (London: Longmans, Green, Reader and Dyer,1878)

[75] Michael Craton & James Walvin, *A Jamaican Plantation: The History of Worthy Park 1670-1970* (Toronto: University of Toronto Press, 1970).

[76] Davis Giddy Diaries Cornwall Records Office Truro.

[77] St Mary's Penzance Register of Burials.

[78] Public Records Office Kew.

[79] Prof. Charles Thomas, Militia in the 18th & 19th Centuries

[80] Elizabeth Sparrow, *The Prices of Penzance 1734-1834* (Penzance: The Penzance Library, 1985).

[81] The Peerage

[82] Historic England, https://historicengland.org.uk/listing/thelist/list-entry/1000657

[83] Deposited document No b1 at Cornwall Records Office.

[84] Hawkins Papers Royal Institute of Cornwall at Truro Museum.

[85] Elizabeth Sparrow, *The Prices of Penzance 1734-1834* (Penzance: The Penzance Library, 1985).

[86] Sue Appleby, Research completed for her forthcoming book *The Cornish in the Caribbean.*

[87] John J Rogers, *Opie and his Works* (London: Paul and Dominic Colnaghi and Co., 1878).

[88] Ada Earland, *John Opie and his Circle* (London: Hutchinson & Co., 1911).

[89] Anne Andrews, *A Short History of Ingestre* (Ingestre, Stafford), 2013, pp. 17-19.

[90] John J Rogers, *Opie and his Works* (London: Paul and Dominic Colnaghi and Co., 1878), p. 148.

[91] Ada Earland, *John Opie and his Circle* (London: Hutchinson & Co., 1911), p.134.

ADDITIONAL BIBLIOGRAPHY

Andrews Anne, *A Short History of Ingestre*
(Stafford: Ingestre, 2013).

Bence-Jones, Mark, *A Guide to Irish Country Houses*, 2nd revised
edn (London: Constable, 1990).

Boase, George Clement, *Reminiscences of Penzance* (Penzance:
Penzance Old Cornwall Society, 1976).

Bolitho, Edward, 'Trengwainton, Past, Present and Future',
Cornwall Gardens Trust Journal (2001).

British Newspaper Archive online,
www.britishnewspaperarchive.co.uk/

Carew, Richard, *Survey of Cornwall 1580* (John Jaggard, 1602).

Catalogue of Paintings: Ingestre Hall Residential Arts Centre
(Stafford: Ingestre, 2013).

Craton, Michael and Walvin, James, *A Jamaican Plantation: The
History of Worthy Park 1670-1970* (London and
New York: W H Allen, 1970).

Crispin, Gill, *Great Cornish Families: A History of the People and
Their Houses* (Wellington: Halsgrove, 1995).

Desond, S. C., 'The Walled Garden at Trengwainton – A Survey
Report' (April 2002).

Domesday Book, http://www.domesdaybook.co.uk/

Earland, Ada, *John Opie and his Circle*
(London: Hutchinson & Co, 1911).

Farrant, Ann, *Amelia Opie: The Quaker Celebrity* (Hindringham,
Norfolk: JJG Publishing, 2014).

Gilbert, C.S., *A Historical Survey of the County of Cornwall*
(Plymouth-Dock: J. Condgon, 1817-1820).

Girtin, Tom, *Doctor with Two Aunts, A biography of Peter Pindar*
(London: Hutchinson, 1959).

Gorden, Roberts, 'Trengwainton, Place of the Spring', *The Cornish
Garden No. 21* (March 1978).

Harris, Derek and Russell, Tony, *Cornwall Great Gardens* (Spalding:
Woodland and Garden Publishing Co, 1998),
pp. 134 – 136.

Hendra, Viv, *The Cornish Wonder: A Portrait of John Opie*
(Truro: Truran, 2007).

Hinton Ampner, Hampshire (Swindon: The National Trust, 1988).

Hitchens, Fortescue and Drew, Samuel, *The History of Cornwall,
From the Earliest Records and Traditions, to the Present Time*
(Helston: W. Penaluna, 1824).

Kingdon-Ward, Frank, *Expedition 1928 list.*

Lawson-Jones, Anna, 'Trengwainton Carn, Madron, Cornwall,
Archæological Watching Brief and Recording.'
(Cornwall Archæology Unit, 2009-2014).

Lear, Micheal, 'Trengwainton Garden Woody Plant Catalogue
Report' (1984).

'Lodge Park, Gloucestershire.' (The National Trust: Swindon,
2002). *Memorandum Book at Cornwall Records Office copied in
January 1827 from Sir Rose Price's old pocket books.*

Mitchell, Paul and Roberts, Lynn, *A History of European Picture
Frames* (London: Paul Mitchell Ltd, in Association with Merrell
Holberton, 1996).

Norden, John, *Speculi Britanniæ (1728, surveyed c 1597).*

Paton, Jean, A., *Magnolias in Cornish Gardens* (Alexander
Associates, 2001).

Pett, Douglas Ellory, *The Parks and Gardens of Cornwall:
A Companion Guide* (St. Day: Alison Hodge, 1998).

Polsue, J, *Lake's Parochial History of the County of Cornwall Vol. 3* (Cornwall County Library,1870).

Poole, PAS, *The History of Penzance* (Penzance: Penzance Old Cornwall Society, 1970).

Price, Cyril, *Trengwainton*. Reminiscences of visits in the early 20th century. In the collection of Price family paper at Morrab Library, Penzance.

Pring, Sue, *Glorious Gardens of Cornwall* (Cornwall Gardens Trust, 1996).

Roberts, Gordon, 'Trengwainton: Place of the Spring'*, The Journal of the Cornwall Garden Society - The Cornish Garden No 21* (1978).

Rogers, John J, *Opie and his Works* (London: Paul and Dominic Colnaghi and Co., 1878).

Royal Cornwall Gazette (23.01.1884).

Roscoe, Ingrid and others, *A Biographical Dictionary of Sculptors in Britain 1660-1851* (New Haven and London: Yale University Press, 2009).

Sale Particulars for Trengwainton (Truro: Cornwall Records Office, 1866).

Simon, Jacob, *The Art of the Picture Frame: Artists, Patrons and the Framing of Portraits in Britain* (London: National Portrait Gallery, 1996).

Simon, Robin, *John Opie, Oxford Dictionary of National Biography* (online, 2016).

Sir Rose Price Will (Truro: Cornwall Records Office).

Smelt, Maurice, *101 Cornish Lives* (St. Day: Alison Hodge, 2006).

Synge, Patrick M, 'Rhododendrons at Trengwainton'. *Rhododendron and Camellia Yearbook* (Royal Horticultural Society Group,1957) pp. 29 – 35.

Taylor, Thomas, *The Victorian County History of Cornwall* (unpublished draft in the Courtney Library of the Royal Institute of Cornwall, Truro, 1908).

The Cornish Lands of the Arundells of Lanherne, fourteenth to sixteenth centuries, ed. by H.S.A. Fox and O.J. Padel (Exeter: Devon and Cornwall Record Society, 2000).

The Gardener's Chronicle (London, 1874 and 1894).

The London Chronicle (October 17-19 1758).

Trengwainton Garden Guidebook (Swindon: The National Trust, 1999, 2016 and 2017).

'Trengwainton House Given to the National Trust', *Western Morning News* (March 1st 1962).

Trinick, Michael, *The National Trust's Cornish Gardens* (Swindon: National Trust, 1981).

Webster, Mary, *Johan Zoffany 1733-1810* (New Haven and London: Yale University Press, 2011).

Wikipedia, *John Opie* (online, 2017).

Wilson, John, *Opie, John* (Oxford Art Online,2017).

Wright, Ian, *Trengwainton Garden NT Conservation Plan* (2002).

W.T., 'Trengwainton, Cornwall', *The Gardener's Chronicle,* (December 15, 1894).

Maps

1908 Ordnance Survey. Cornish Study Library, Redruth.

1877 Ordnance Survey. Cornish Study Library, Redruth.

1840 Tithe Map of the Parish of Madron with apportionment. Cornwall Records Office.

IMAGES

ABOUT THE PRODUCER

Barbara Santi

Barbara is a documentary filmmaker and co-director of Cornwall-based awen productions CIC with over 19 years of professional media experience and rural community participation. At the heart of Barbara's work is the raising of under-represented people's voices through film. Her practice has developed and evolved to push the boundaries of collaboration and authorship. Barbara develops participatory/collaborative projects with communities to explore the film medium, concepts of place and identity and new storytelling models. www.barbarasanti.co.uk

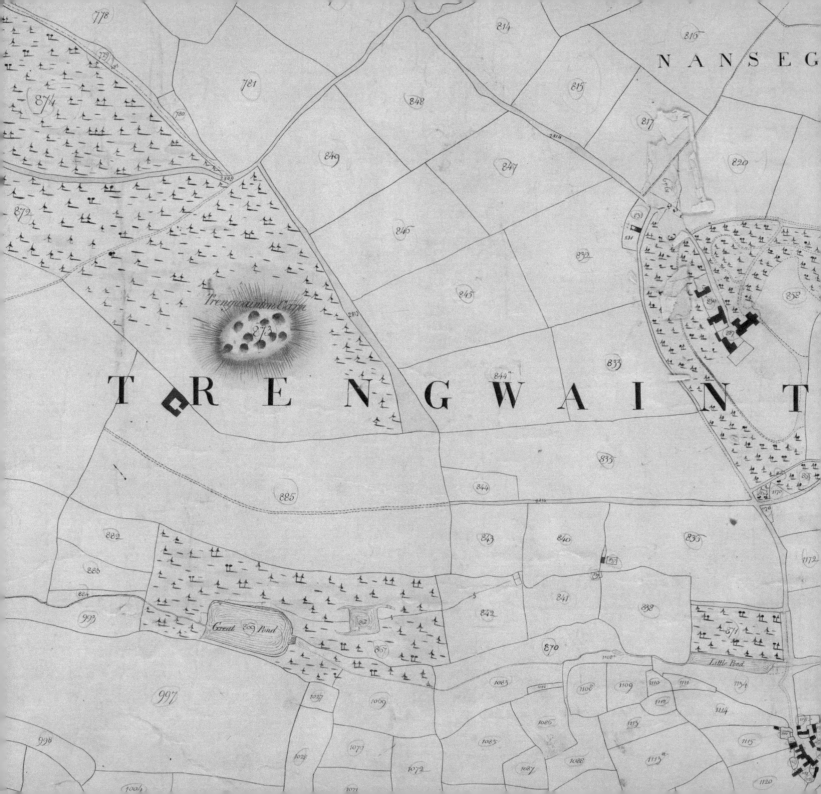